The Promise of Scriptural Re<del>asoning</del>

The Promise of Scriptural Reasoning

Edited by
David F. Ford and C. C. Pecknold

Blackwell
Publishing

BLACKWELL PUBLISHING
350 Main Street, Malden, MA 02148-5020, USA
9600 Garsington Road, Oxford OX4 2DQ, UK
550 Swanston Street, Carlton, Victoria 3053, Australia

First published 2006 by Blackwell Publishing Ltd

Library of Congress Cataloging-in-Publication Data has been applied for

ISBN-10: 1-4051-4630-3
ISBN-13: 978-1-4051-4630-2

A catalogue record for this title is available from the British Library.

Set in 10 on 12 pt Palatino
by SNP Best-set Typesetter Ltd., Hong Kong
Printed and bound in Great Britain by
Marston Book Services Limited, Oxford

The publisher's policy is to use permanent paper from mills that operate a sustainable forestry policy, and which has been manufactured from pulp processed using acid-free and elementary chlorine-free practices. Furthermore, the publisher ensures that the text paper and cover board used have met acceptable environmental accreditation standards.

For further information on
Blackwell Publishing, visit our website:
www.blackwellpublishing.com

CONTENTS

EDITORIAL PREFACE: THE PROMISE OF SCRIPTURAL REASONING

Scriptural Reasoning is a risky practice. It resists dominant modes of neutral public reasoning. And it embraces inherited, embodied traditions of faith and judgment, particularly those traditions generated by the story of Abraham's God. It is a practice which is local and provisional and yet risks a long-term commitment to patient dialogical contestations and conversations on a scriptural plane. The risks involved in making long-term commitments between Jews, Christians, and Muslims are real, but are worth taking, now more than ever.

Like other postliberal projects, Scriptural Reasoning places a strong emphasis upon "traditions". But it also resists isolationist, monological and hermetic modes of engagement. Unlike pluralist political rhetoric, Scriptural Reasoning does not conceal its conflicts or tensions, but makes public the depths of our disagreements non-violently. It renews the possibilities that were latent in medieval culture amongst the three Abrahamic religions, not to repristinate the past but in order to generate new possibilities for our future. In David Ford's words, it is a practice for "twenty-first century citizenship", and it is a model for high-quality public debate in late-modern liberal democracies.

Rather than monological traditionalism, Scriptural Reasoning is concerned with "generating the right kinds of tension" (MacIntyre, *After Virtue*, p. 160) between and within traditions, and seeks to render our contestations more constructive through an innovative practice. In Ben Quash's words, the task is to improve "the quality of our disagreements" rather than to increase tolerance and secure consensus (whenever tolerance names the logic of indifference and consensus enforces a false homogeneity). This is "tension-dwelling" traditionalism which is morally, politically and theologically demanding, adventurous and educative, not only for each tradition (or "house") but in the spaces "in-between" them and for the diverse publics which are being addressed.

This special issue of *Modern Theology* invites twelve scholars who are practiced in this art of Scriptural Reasoning. David Ford frames the issue with his essay on inter-faith wisdom, providing a framework for understanding the genealogy of this practice, its shape, its relation to each of the traditions, the academy, and civil society. Ford's essay also frames what follows in three separate sections: "describing", "reading", and "reasoning". These categories are intended to help the reader discern how each writer is reflecting on the *practice* of Scriptural Reasoning. That is, the essays do not themselves perform "Scriptural Reasoning", they perceive, they judge, they reason through their cultivated practice in the art itself.

The descriptions offered by Steven Kepnes, Nicholas Adams and Ben Quash are each very different from one another. Kepnes provides a description of what he takes to be the "emergent rules" of the practice, Adams provides a largely philosophical description of what it means for Scriptural Reasoning (SR) to "make deep reasonings public", and Ben Quash offers a literary "account of SR's traditioned, critically imaginative character". Steven Kepnes provides twelve rules which describe Scriptural Reasoning, its discursive practices, its monotheist character and temporality, and its eschatological contestations. These rules are then explicated as richer descriptions which complicate the nature of the rules themselves. Kepnes ends his essay with practical advice for performing the art of Scriptural Reasoning.

Nicholas Adams is concerned to describe how Scriptural Reasoning "makes deep reasonings public". The first of his six claims is that SR does not try to "ground its own possibility". That does not mean that SR is disinterested in metaphysics, only that it "approaches metaphysics as an account of what is taken to be true" rather than as a "means to demonstrate necessary truths". That is an important philosophical description of Scriptural Reasoning and gives weight to his claims that SR relies on luck, language learning, friendship and the making public of deep reasonings as a reparative activity in our traditions, in the academy and in society.

Examining key virtues of the practice, Ben Quash turns to literary-critical approaches to texts and their interpretation in order to enrich what he describes as the four "marks" of SR: particularity, provisionality, sociality and readiness for surprise. Quash shows SR's aversion to abstract, tradition-free universal reason, and SR's preference for the concrete and the particular. "Scriptural Reasoners" must speak from a particular place, from their own distinctive viewpoint, from the specificity of their traditions and with a heightened pitch of attention to their particular texts in relation to others. This particularity enables attentiveness to texts, time, contingency, and the provisionality of the practice, as well as the sociality it enables when particularity is so valued. Quash's essay itself is a testimony to SR's readiness for surprise, illuminating the practice of Scriptural Reasoning through critical engagements with Hans Urs Von Balthasar, Mikhail Bakhtin and John Beer.

Susannah Ticciati, Oliver Davies and Timothy Winter are situated under the heading of "reading" not because they provide readings of scriptural texts—though they do—but because they are reasoning about the reading of scripture itself, and the complexities of reading one another's scriptures together in the world. Ticciati's essay is especially concerned with providing a Christian rationale for the practice of Scriptural Reasoning by exploring how it might "constitute a locus for the formation of Christian identity". She argues for a transformative understanding of the universality of the Christian biblical story. And through careful semiotic analysis of the Burning Bush narrative, she displays how Scripture's "resistance to interpretation" corresponds to the embodied resistances offered to Christians by Jews and Muslims—and she reads these resistances as theologically generative in the formation of Christian identity.

A different reading of the Burning Bush narrative is offered by Oliver Davies, who makes it central in "the evolution and development of Christian metaphysics". Rather than "resistances" discovered in the scriptures, Davies finds that attention to the dynamics of the scriptural universe enables the reader to give greater "attentiveness to the sensible real of the empirical world". Here it is interesting to see tensions within the Christian tradition by comparing Davies' metaphysical reading with that offered by Ticciati, and compared yet again with the description of metaphysics offered by Nicholas Adams in the first section.

Timothy Winter opens his essay with an illuminating account of the multiple senses involved in Muslim interpretations of the Qur'an, and reflects on how such traditional readings relate to Qur'anic study in the modern academy. He also offers readers a compelling account of "the rapidly-increasing Muslim participation in the Scriptural Reasoning project", and helpfully contextualizes this increase in relation to recent shifts in hermeneutics. Winter displays the liveliness and need for a "discrepant voice" that can challenge postmodern and postliberal assumptions uncritically implicit in our reasoning. Here it is interesting to compare Islamic universalism to the universalism of the Christian story that Ticciati refers to in this section, and also, as Winter especially commends, to consider the teleological difference that both Jewish and Muslim readings offer, in contrast to Christian views of (messianic) time.

All the writers offer tradition-constituted reasons in these pages, but we have gathered four essays in particular under the heading of "reasoning". These are the essays that offer specifically reparative engagements with their philosophical disciplines. Peter Ochs writes on the philosophical warrants of SR, Basit Koshul on social scientific reasoning, Gavin Flood on phenomenological reasoning, and Robert Gibbs writes on learning within different modes of philosophical reasoning. One of the promises of Scriptural Reasoning is that its ethos of engagement, its mode of hospitality and its habits of reasoning together will bring fresh resources to bear on difficult problems in a variety of academic disciplines, and these essays display a particular attentiveness to the "reparative reasoning" implicit in the practice.

This reparative reasoning is first identified by Peter Ochs as a strategy to distinguish "the logic of suffering" (in the binary terms of propositional logic) from "the logic of repair" which is logically triadic and non-reducible to binary, propositional terms. This essay converses in important ways with David Ford's theology of the "cry", and is also employed by Basit Koshul in his Qur'anic repair of social scientific reasoning. Koshul's essay provides valuable insight into the way in which Scriptural Reasoning can and does relate to non-religious traditions of rationality in the "secular" academy. His essay aims at creating mutual ground between the "religious" and "secular" from a Muslim perspective. Gavin Flood raises his questions "within a hermeneutical phenomenology" that is non-teleological. This essay raises interesting questions about "mediations" between traditions, displaying tensions between teleological and non-teleological textual engagements in SR, and shedding light on the "semiotics of Scripture" that Flood believes is implicit in the practice.

Daniel Hardy responds to all of the essays in a constructive critical essay on "The Promise of Scriptural Reasoning". Hardy re-describes all of the essays, providing his own synthesis and evaluation, and creatively juxtaposing themes that emerge throughout. His response to the essays is not only descriptive, but also helpfully provides his own reasons for "pushing forward". Hardy questions, for example, certain reductive tendencies that he sees in those who write with phenomenological, semiotic or pragmatic philosophical tools of mediation. In doing so, he aims to raise important questions about the "inner dynamics of truth" in the practice of Scriptural Reasoning (which might find one Christian response in a strong pneumatology). In the Ochsian terms of the need for the "third" to heal binaries, Hardy asks "where does this 'third' come from?" He concludes the issue by asking those committed to the practice of Scriptural Reasoning to keep the question of God at the center of their descriptions, readings, and reasonings.

Like other special issues, this one is best read whole. Each of these contributors engage in risky border-crossings, and each are committed to generating new possibilities for their traditions, their disciplines, and their world. The essays offer descriptions, readings, and reasons which are born from patient practice in the communal art of Scriptural Reasoning. Perhaps most crucially, these essays pay attention to how our judgments are formed as philosophers and theologians.

Being generous and critically receptive, even vulnerable, to one another's judgments has been a key part of the ethos of engagement in SR. This is not a matter of being nice to one another. This ethos matters because it enables each of us to make our texts and our traditions, indeed our God, strange to us again. This ethos enables each participant to discern the genuine otherness of their tradition. As many of the contributors to this issue will attest, it is a communal practice which demands that participants dwell more deeply within their own complex traditions and houses of worship while at the same time engage in high-quality public debates with those who read the story of Abraham's God differently. This ethos of scriptural engagement with one another involves a theological recognition that each tradition-constituted, tension-dwelling identity remains open to, and hopes to be formed by, God's judgment. The scriptures that witness to Abraham's God are the scriptures that form, and reform, the children of Abraham. This is the timely promise of Scriptural Reasoning, and the essays of this special issue renew a very old conversation about the future of our world.

C. C. Pecknold
Faculty of Divinity
University of Cambridge
West Road
Cambridge, CB3 9BS
UK

1

AN INTERFAITH WISDOM: SCRIPTURAL REASONING BETWEEN JEWS, CHRISTIANS AND MUSLIMS

DAVID F. FORD

Scriptural reasoning can be approached from many angles, as other essays in this issue demonstrate. This essay considers it as a wisdom-seeking engagement with Jewish, Christian and Muslim scriptures. Its origins, practices, understandings and social settings are described and discussed, with some concluding remarks on its possible contribution to the public sphere in the twenty-first century.

1. Core Identities in Conversation

There are many convergent reasons why it makes sense for interfaith engagement among Jews, Christians and Muslims to make their scriptures a primary focus. Each tradition's scripture is at the heart of its identity. This is so in rather different ways, but recognizing those differences can be a source of illumination to each. Scriptures are formative for understanding of God and God's purposes; for prayer, worship and liturgy; for normative teaching; for imagination and ethos; and so on. All religions meet new situations and are challenged to change over time, and if a new development is at all important it is inevitable that debate about it will appeal to scripture. Many of the bitterest disputes within and between all three faiths centre on appeals to scripture. So an attempt to deal with the core identity of any of the three will inevitably involve its scripture.

This is sometimes taken as a reason for avoiding scriptures in dialogue situations. The Tanakh, the Bible and the Qur'an are the main platforms of those within each tradition who stand against dialogue and in favour of self-protective or aggressive confrontation. Each of these scriptures has

David F. Ford
Faculty of Divinity, University of Cambridge, West Road, Cambridge, CB3 9BS, UK

texts that can be used to legitimate violence, claims to superiority, blanket condemnations, cruel punishments, suspicions, oppressive morality, and hostility to those who are not believers in God as identified by one's own tradition. Their scriptures are where the particularity of each is evident "warts and all", and have been widely used in polemics between them as well as in attacks on each by secular critics. Even for many of those who do believe it right to engage in dialogue and collaboration the scriptures are where they find what is most distinctive, most difficult and least negotiable. So to study together anything other than very carefully selected passages might seem a recipe for increasing tensions and meeting many impasses.

Yet, despite the problems, the attractiveness of this approach is considerable. If it were to succeed it could not only bring core identities into conversation; it could also sustain them there. Within each tradition, scriptures are a focus of endless study, conversation and dispute, and around them have grown up enduring forms of collegiality. One of the critical things lacking in relations between Jews, Christians and Muslims is such centres of long term collegiality where ways of study, understanding and application can be worked at and passed on across generations. The study of their scriptures has been overwhelmingly intra-traditional, supplemented in varying degrees by academic study in uncommitted environments. Yet, given the fundamental nature of the issues between them (with roots going back many centuries), given the necessity of engaging with scriptures if those issues are to be satisfactorily dealt with, and given the richness and complexity of each scripture and its associated traditions, then the only appropriate way is that which each faith has followed itself: the creation of groups, traditions, networks and institutions able to form readers dedicated to study and discussion.

These are matters which require more than one person and more than one lifetime. They have to be handled by communities who can learn together how to go about this novel and urgent task. There are almost no places in the world at present where collegial conversations are sustained jointly around these three scriptures and traditions of interpretation. In a few universities the scriptures of each tradition are studied alongside each other, but that has very rarely led to deep interplay between all three. Yet there are some initiatives in this direction, and I will devote the rest of this essay to discussing one in which I have been privileged to take part.

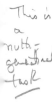

2. Scriptural Reasoning: An Introductory Description

This initial description of scriptural reasoning (and, even more, the discussion in later sections) is offered as only one portrayal of something that has already evoked many other descriptions and is constantly producing more.[1] Because scriptural reasoning by definition draws people of very different commitments and disciplines into engagement with each other it is a phenomenon which is bound to be described differently even (perhaps especially) by those who know it best: part of its own approach is to resist "authoritative overviews" of the three scriptures and traditions of interpretation that are being brought into conversation, and so its own character likewise calls for diverse descriptions. What follows in this and the following sections portrays and interprets it from the standpoint of a Christian academic participant whose main academic areas are biblical interpretation and contemporary critical and constructive thought, and whose chief interest in this article is in the wisdom it might yield for interfaith engagement today.

Scriptural reasoning had its immediate origins in "textual reasoning" among a group of academic Jewish text scholars (mostly of Tanakh and Talmud), on the one hand, and philosophers and theologians, on the other hand, who were concerned that there was little fruitful engagement between their sets of disciplines.[2] They began to meet together to study texts from scripture and Talmud in dialogue with Western philosophy, in particular those Jewish philosophers who had themselves tried to cross this divide, such as Hermann Cohen, Franz Rosenzweig (perhaps the most embracing influence), Martin Buber, Emmanuel Levinas, and Eugene Borowitz. The text scholars were trained in both traditional Jewish interpretation and the methods of the modern Western academy, and the philosophers and theologians were likewise students of Jewish thought as well as of Western thought from classical Greece up to the present. The name they gave to what they did, "textual reasoning", simply referred to the two sides that were brought together: the interpretation of traditional texts and the practices of philosophical and theological reasoning. A core question they shared was about Judaism after the Shoah, leading them to interrogate both the Western modernity within which the Shoah had been possible and also the resources—premodern, modern and postmodern[3] or contemporary—for responding to it within Judaism.

One perhaps surprising conclusion[4] that many of them came to was that post-Shoah Judaism needed both to appropriate afresh its scriptures and traditions of interpretation and at the same time to engage more deeply with others who are wrestling with the meaning of their faith today, especially Christians and Muslims. This latter conclusion had not been arrived at abstractly. It was rooted in some of the group already having found congenial Christian thinking going on, especially in Yale around Hans Frei and George Lindbeck.[5] Their Christian postcritical, "postliberal" hermeneutics, which had learnt much from Karl Barth, had many resonances with the Rosenzweig approach to Judaism.[6] In addition, at Drew University in the late 1980s and early 1990s there was a scriptural interpretation group[7] around the Jewish thinker Peter Ochs (who had previously been at Yale and knew Frei and Lindbeck) that included Christians and later Muslims. So when the textual reasoning group, whose first co-chairs were Ochs and the philosopher David Novak, began in 1991 there were already within it the seeds of later Abrahamic developments.

These began to be cultivated when some Christian academics (including Daniel Hardy and myself) began to attend the lively, learned and argumentative textual reasoning sessions at the annual meetings of the American Academy of Religion in the early 1990s. This led into "scriptural reasoning", which was first Jewish-Christian[8] and then in the late 1990s became Jewish-Christian-Muslim. There were large questions to be tackled if this was to work. They were wrestled with in two settings, a summer meeting of a small group for a few days of intensive scripture study, with discussion of the various dimensions of scriptural reasoning (cf. the sections to follow below); and a larger group that eventually met twice a year, in Cambridge and wherever the American Academy of Religion was meeting.[9]

The four key strands that were brought together in these ways were: Jewish textual reasoning as already described; Christian postliberal text interpretation (whose main theological reference point was Karl Barth, in particular as interpreted by Frei at Yale); a range of less text-centred Christian philosophies and theologies, both Protestant and Catholic; and Muslim concern simultaneously for the Qur'an and for Islam in relation to Western modernity (especially understood through the natural and human sciences and technology).

In what follows I will think through this young movement from various angles—its collegiality, its institutional relations, its ways of coping with the meaning of scriptures, and its significance for public education and debate.

3. An Abrahamic Collegiality: Not Consensus but Friendship

At the centre of the collegiality of scriptural reasoning is reading and interpreting selected texts from the Tanakh, Old Testament/New Testament and Qur'an in small groups, whose inspiration is the Jewish practice of *chevruta* study,[10] and also (when there is more than one group) in plenary sessions, which often have the purpose of pursuing more theoretical, philosophical, theological and "public issue" questions related to the text study and of discussing matters relating to the group's process, governance and future development.

In scriptural reasoning done between academic Jews, Christians and Muslims[11] the priority of small group study means that each one is first of all bringing to the table his or her own scripture, a much-studied and much-loved book. They also bring what Aref Nayed has named their "internal libraries":[12] all they have learnt not only through tradition-specific activity in study, prayer, worship and experience but also what they have learnt through whatever academic disciplines they have studied—and also, of course, elements from a range of cultures, arts, economic, political and social contexts.

A recurring image used to describe the social dynamics of this encounter is that of hospitality—and the resources of each scripture on hospitality have often been a focus for study. Yet this is three-way mutual hospitality: each is host to the others and guest to the others as each welcomes the other two to their "home" scripture and its traditions of interpretation. As in any form of hospitality, joint study is helped by observing certain customs and guidelines which have been developed through experience over time. These are the prudential wisdom of the practice of scriptural reasoning and, like most such customs, are best learnt by apprenticeship that sees them being performed and imitates them or improvises upon them. Put in the form of maxims, a selection of those most important for collegiality would include:

- Acknowledge *the sacredness* of the others' scriptures to them (without having to acknowledge its authority for oneself)—each believes in different ways (which can be discussed) that their scripture is in some sense from God and that the group is interpreting it before God, in God's presence.[13]
- The "native speakers" hosting a scripture and its tradition need to acknowledge that they do not exclusively own their scriptures—they are *not experts on its final meaning*: guests need to acknowledge that hosts are to be questioned and listened to attentively as the *court of first (but not last) appeal*.
- The aim is *not consensus*—that may happen, but it is more likely that the conclusion will be a recognition of deep differences.
- Do not be afraid of *argument*, as one intellectually honest way of responding to differences—part of mutual hospitality is learning to argue in courtesy and truth, and each tradition as well as each academic discipline embraces complex practices of discussion and dispute.
- Draw on *shared academic resources* to build understanding—members of different faith communities may be trained in the same field or share a philosophy (pragmatism, critical realism, phenomenology, idealism).
- *Allow time* to read and re-read, to entertain many questions and possibilities, to let the texts unfold within their own traditions of interpretation and in (often unprecedented) engagement with each other, to stick with a text without premature resolution of its difficulties, and to sound the depths.
- Read and interpret with a view to the fulfilment of *God's purpose of peace* between all—this shared hope (however differently specified) can sustain endurance through inevitable differences, misunderstandings, confrontations and resentments.

- Be open to *mutual hospitality turning into friendship*—each tradition values friendship, and for it to happen now might be seen as the most tangible anticipation of future peace.

Many of those maxims are embraced in the following account by Nicholas Adams:

> Scriptural reasoning is a practice of "publicizing" deep reasonings, so that others may learn to understand them and discover why particular trains of reasoning, and not just particular assumptions, are attractive or problematic. *Scriptural reasoning makes deep reasonings public.* It sees them not as particularistic obstacles to debate, but as conditions for conversation, friendship and mutual understanding. Without deep reasonings, there are no religious traditions to speak of. Depth is not obscurity, however: the acknowledgement of depth is a recognition that it takes time to plumb. Scriptural reasoning models the discovery that making deep reasoning public is not only risky—because one makes oneself vulnerable when revealing what one loves—but time-consuming. It is a non-hasty practice, and is thus a kind of beacon in our time-poor world . . . Each of the three Abrahamic traditions has its own rules for interpreting scripture (and internal disagreement about these rules), and, even if there is overlap between them, it is not the overlap that makes scriptural reasoning possible. The significant point of contact is a shared acknowledgement that scriptural texts are sacred, together with a shared desire to do scriptural reasoning. The most striking thing about the context of scriptural reasoning is not consensus but friendship. To use the word *chevruta* [related to "friendship"] to describe the meeting of Muslims, Jews and Christians is itself surprising, and the actual friendships that are formed through such study do not lessen the surprise. Consensus can be measured and managed, and that to an extent is an appropriate object of a theory like Habermas'. Friendship is altogether more confusing, and even the most sophisticated philosophical accounts of it somehow repeat the absurdity of the hopeless lover who tries to persuade the other to love him by using arguments. Abstract description of friendship is nearly as pointless as thirstily trying to make sense of water. Friendship is nonetheless the true ground of scriptural reasoning, and who can give a good overview of that? The traditions have different understandings of friendship with God, friendship with members of one's own family, one's own tradition and with strangers. Somehow, the recognition that each worships the one true God moves scriptural reasoning beyond an interaction determined by conventions for showing strangers hospitality. Showing strangers hospitality is a significant enough miracle. Yet scriptural reasoning does not quite reproduce this context: when members of three traditions meet together to study shared scripture, who is the

guest and who is the host? In a way that is difficult to be clear about, the participants in scriptural reasoning all find themselves invited, not by each other, but by an agency that is not theirs to command or shape. There is an "other" to the three traditions, and that seems in an obscure way to make friendships possible.[14]

The picture of a collegiality of intensive study and conversation that emerges from such description might be seen as a boundary-crossing liturgy. This gathers in hospitality and friendship members of academic institutions whose primary communities are synagogue, church and mosque. Its quasi-liturgical character is appropriate, since it is likely that study of scripture which acknowledges the presence of God (variously identified) comes as close to worshipping together as faithful members of these three traditions can come with integrity.

A further question arising from this is about the institutional location of this collegiality of scriptural reasoning.

4. House, Campus and Tent

In the sort of scriptural reasoning I have been discussing,[15] the participants are simultaneously members of a synagogue, church or mosque ("houses"), of a university ("campus"), and of a scriptural reasoning group ("tent"). What is the relation of the tent to the house and campus? They are clearly very different types of location.

4.1. House

The houses are the main homes of the three scriptures and their traditions of interpretation. Synagogues, churches and mosques are of course themselves diverse, not least in how their scriptures are understood and acted upon. Scriptural reasoning has in fact drawn participants from various strands of Islam, Judaism and Christianity, and the setting of interfaith interpretation can open the way for fresh dialogue within each community. Yet it is not part of any of the traditions to engage in joint study of their scriptures with the others. So scriptural reasoning is a complex combination of what is at the core of each tradition with what is novel for each. As with any innovation it needs to be discussed and tested, not least with reference to scripture.

Is there a valid justification for scriptural reasoning from within Judaism, Islam and Christianity? I have heard many, some of them incompatible even within one faith tradition. But the practice of scriptural reasoning can proceed without agreement on its rationale. There are of course some within each tradition who would dispute its validity, but so long as faithful members of each tradition in fact practise it and justify it in tradition-specific ways the presumption must be that it can have a place in relation to each house.

The matter goes deeper than justification of its validity and its permissibility. There is also a case to be made for the positive enhancement of each house. The origins of scriptural reasoning, as recounted above, included a specifically Jewish group of "textual reasoning". This intra-traditional dynamic has been repeated within the other two traditions. There are Muslim quranic reasoning groups and Christian biblical reasoning groups which were begun by those already participating in scriptural reasoning. It is as if the intensity of study and conversation around the three scriptures increases the need of participants for a comparable "in-house" intensity. *Far from interfaith engagement being in competition with involvement in one's own tradition, the depths of one evoke the depths of the other.* So part of the promise of scriptural reasoning is to be a stimulus to "house" members to study and interpret their own scriptures and traditions of interpretation with new energy.

Such renewal need not happen only among those who also take part in scriptural reasoning—for many reasons interfaith study is more restricted in numbers than in-house study and likely to remain so. Scriptural reasoning might be seen as one niche in a house's ecosystem that is more likely to flourish if within other niches there is lively, faithful and thoughtful study of the house's own scripture. "Thoughtful" indicates the presence in each house of traditions of reasoning and argument in relation to their scriptures, and of institutions where there is transgenerational collegiality dedicated to sustaining and developing these. It is especially important that such places are seeking wisdom both within and across their own boundaries.

For those who take part in scriptural reasoning an issue raised by its non-competitive dynamic is about the balance of interfaith and intra-faith study. One way of approaching this is in terms of time. Scriptural reasoning ideally requires a long time at any one session, but that does not mean it has to happen very frequently. This is a matter for discernment within each community. Judging from experience so far, the ideal periodicity of the practice of scriptural reasoning is not that of one's daily in-house scripture-saturated prayer, scripture study/recitation, meditation, and such-like; nor that of one's weekly (or more frequent) gathering for community worship, instruction, and such-like; rather its optimal rhythm seems to be of less frequent meetings, perhaps monthly or quarterly. During its development its main participants met twice or three times a year. Yet, however frequent the meetings, as in most groups the value is proportionate to regularity, which is all the more important if gatherings are seldom.

The other essential feature of a group that meets relatively seldom is the quality of communication between meetings, both within itself and more widely. Here electronic communication has greatly helped. Scriptural reasoning has a website and an electronic journal so that those in the wider community of the houses and campuses can listen in and respond to what is going on; and e-mail ensures that there can also be regular communication among direct participants. The combination of face to face meetings with electronic interaction produces a new dimension of collegiality uniting "richness" with "reach".[16] As the "houses" too become better networked and alert to such possibilities a practice such as scriptural reasoning has the potential to help those who seek to develop rich scripture study within and across the boundaries of their own house.

4.2. Campus

Just as the "traditional and untraditional" nature of scriptural reasoning tests the character of any mosque, synagogue or church and provokes various responses, so its "scriptural and reasoning" nature is a sensitive matter in universities. If the ideal "house" for scriptural reasoning is one that acknowledges a strong internal justification for this new practice and then uses it to go deeper simultaneously into its own scripture and the scriptures of others, the ideal university in the present state of our complexly "religious and secular" world might be described as "interfaith and secular", a campus where there is shared ground among those of many faiths and none.

I will summarise briefly the rationale for such a university that I have discussed at greater length elsewhere.[17] The model for the modern research university, the University of Berlin founded in 1810, was a renewal and reform of the Medieval university pattern, with a new thrust towards innovation in research, uniting this with teaching in a context of academic freedom. A further and less remarked aspect of Berlin was its "religious and secular" character. There was academic freedom without church control, the state founded, financed and controlled it, and the philosophy faculty with its ideal of *Wissenschaft* was the overarching integrator: all of which justifies its description as secular. It also included theology as an academic discipline not simply subsumable under *Wissenschaft*, it educated clergy for the state church, and it had a good deal of continuity with the religiously-rooted values of the Medieval university, so that it also had a religious character—very different from the militantly secular higher education institutions generated by the French Revolution. The Berlin model of a research university uniting *wissenschaftlich* teaching and research across a wide range of disciplines generally won out over the French in the later development of universities in most countries, but its religious and secular character had a more mixed history.

On the one hand, German academic theology and philological and historical research in the field of religion led the world in rigorous thought and *wissenschaftlich* scholarship, and German-speaking universities were the arena for many formative debates about the nature of religion, faith and reason, faith and history, religion and modernity, and so on. On the other hand, the university as a whole tended to become more secularised, and its religious character continued to be limited to Protestant and Catholic strands of Christianity. So, whereas Berlin in 1810 could be seen as genuinely religious and secular and also responsive to the actual religious character of its society, most of its successors in Germany and around the world (and especially the world-class universities with a global horizon) have failed to sustain either feature: they are predominantly secularist in an ideological sense; and in a multifaith and secular world, where the vast majority of people are directly related to a religious tradition, and where each major religious tradition is in complex relationships with other religions and with secular forces and worldviews, the largely secularised universities are unable to respond academically. They do not on the whole educate people able to engage intelligently in this multifaith and secular world, nor do they foster the high-quality religion-related study and debate across disciplines necessary to make thoughtful critical and constructive contributions to the public sphere or its various dimensions (political, economic, cultural, technological, religious).

Perhaps it is time for a new Berlin-like surprise, enabling the twenty-first century, globally-oriented university to be reformed both in relation to key elements that shape it as an academic institution (interdisciplinarity, the integration of teaching and research, all-round educational formation, collegiality, polity and control, and contribution to society) and also in relation to its hospitality to the religious and the secular together. In this way a plurality of wisdom traditions could contribute to its conversations, deliberations and decisions in the interests of education and research that have a fundamental concern for the long-term flourishing of humanity and its environment.

Yet even without such an ideal comprehensive surprise, there are some universities where the religious and secular dimensions are both taken seriously. They provide conditions where questions raised by the religions, between the religions and about the religions can be pursued through a range of academic disciplines in both critical and constructive ways.[18] Those conditions include above all the creation of an institutional space that might be described as "shared ground" or "mutual ground". It is to be contrasted with both "neutral ground" and "contested ground". Neutral ground is what a secular society or institution often claims to provide in matters of religion. A problem is that the conditions for entering it are usually secular in the sense of requiring particular religious identities to be left behind: norms, concepts and methods have to be justifiable in non-religious terms.[19] Contested ground is where there is no agreement about how to constitute it. Historically, neutral ground is a solution to otherwise irresolvable conflict, especially over religious matters. But the high cost of this has been illustrated above by the ill match between secular universities and our religious and secular world. Neutral ground is best seen as a necessary, temporary but in the long term unsatisfactory solution to the need for places of peaceful engagement that respect the integrity of all participants and encourage them to contribute from the riches of their traditions.

Mutual or shared ground[20] is the preferable solution. It is to be found in various forms in a range of universities, especially in Britain and North America. It is the most congenial space for scriptural reasoning, since it might be seen as a wider version of scriptural reasoning's practice of mutual hospitality. Scriptural reasoning can both benefit from an environment of shared ground and also in its own small way try to enrich it. Its ability to gather Jewish, Muslim and Christian academics from many disciplines into a form of collegiality that is productive in academic as well as other ways can be a sign to secularised universities that academic integrity is not in tension with all forms of religious conviction. Yet it can also easily act as a provocation to those in the university who are still rightly sensitive to the dangers of religious domination, dogmatism and divisiveness. The practice of scriptural reasoning in university settings, even those that offer shared ground, must meet strong challenges from several sides. Can it practice relevant disciplines (which can range through a great many faculties) to the highest standards of the various international "guilds" of academic peers? Can it relate across these disciplines? Can scriptural reasoning be taught well in universities according to appropriate norms and standards? Can it give plausible theoretical accounts of a hermeneutics that critically and constructively draws together the three scriptures and their premodern, modern and late modern traditions of interpretation? Above all, what about its "reasoning"? How does it relate to the *Wissenschaft* that was so important in the founding of the University of Berlin? This ideal has since pluralized in various directions in different fields, though without losing a family resemblance that generally still exerts a strong pressure towards academic accountability in rational terms?

In the course of trying to meet such challenges there are inevitable counter-challenges which the university must meet—it is the character of shared ground that the questioning is mutual. This is sometimes a matter of confronting common academic prejudices and *idées fixes*, such as a modern parochialism that cannot take the premodern seriously in matters of truth, or an incapacity to appreciate intellectual achievement in the area of religious thought, or a failure to respect the large numbers of religious academics who are at least as intelligent, well-educated, sophisticated and critically alert as their secular colleagues, or an insistence on religious and theological positions meeting standards of rationality that are by no means accepted throughout the university, or a blindness to the complexly religious and secular character of our world. It also has potential implications for how disciplines are conceived, researched and taught, especially those that have to do with the religions. And it brings into the seminar room ways of approaching substantive matters, such as God, revelation, the nature of scripture, faith, tradition, ethics, politics, and so on, that can differ greatly from usual approaches.

Overall, scriptural reasoning is a small sign of something more widespread but still contested in the academic world: the emergence of new "religious and secular" settlements that provide mutual ground for exchanges across many boundaries. Whether such ground expands is likely to be the major factor in its university future.[21] But it is important that, for all its flourishing in some university environments, it is not simply assimilable to any university setting or model. It has its own character which will now be described.

4.3. Tent

Academic scriptural reasoning sessions have been carried on in hotels, conference centres, universities, seminaries and private homes. "Tent" is an image for the space of study and conversation wherever they actually happen. It has scriptural resonances of hospitality (cf. Genesis 18) and divine presence (cf. Exodus 40), and with the whole Middle Eastern culture of nomads and desert travel in which the Abrahamic scriptures are rooted. It suggests the fragility of a network of Jews, Muslims and Christians who are part of the well-established structures of houses and campuses but who also gather in this lightly structured setting. It is of a different order to a house or campus, suggesting (at least in our culture) a place that is not one's permanent home, and not in competition with the others as religious or academic institutions.

A tent is also connected with travel between places. This "in-betweenness" is a significant metaphor in various ways for scriptural reasoning. It is concerned with what happens in the interpretative space between the three scriptures; in the social space between mosque, church and synagogue; in the intellectual space between "houses" and "campuses", and between disciplines on the campuses; in the religious and secular space between the houses and the various spheres and institutions of society; and in the spiritual space between interpreters of scripture and God. These are spaces inviting movement in different directions and discouraging permanent resting places, and are suited to the tent's lightness, mobility and even vulnerability. Yet in addition there is resilience and durability in a good tent, and it can be used at short notice and in conditions and locations that are unsuited to large buildings. It also allows for an intimacy of encounter that may be harder to achieve in more institutionalised settings.

A further resonance is with leisure activity. This may seem odd for something that is taken seriously and is the focus for a good deal of work. But it is in line with the appropriately peripheral character of scriptural reasoning within both house and academy. Within the house, as discussed above, studying scriptures with those of other houses can never have the focal importance of studying one's own scriptures. Within the academy, too, scriptural reasoning is non-focal with regard to any particular academic's field (at least at present).[22] Scriptural reasoning does not encourage anyone to become an "expert" in scriptural reasoning, as if it were possible to know all three scriptures and their traditions of interpretation in a specialist mode. It is an advantage to try to learn each other's languages, both literally (especially Hebrew, Greek and Arabic) and metaphorically (customs, history, traditions of thought and practice, and so on), and it is helpful if some members of one house have made a special study of another house; but none of this is essential for scripture reasoning. The usual pattern is for each to be especially proficient in their own tradition and to be able to "host" discussion of their scripture. But at least one of the other traditions is generally outside one's academic specialty, and so study of that, together with study of all three together, is more like a leisure activity, something peripheral to whatever one writes most of one's books about. This does not mean that books cannot be written about it, but they are likely to be jointly authored or else, like the present article, acutely aware of the limitations of one perspective on something that intrinsically requires at least three perspectives.

Scriptural reasoning's tent can be pitched within the grounds of a house or a campus, but it has to be wary of becoming too much at home there, for different reasons in each case. Within a specific "house"—under the auspices of a church, mosque or synagogue—the obvious danger is of the host inhibiting full mutuality between the three as hosts and guests, since the ground is "owned" by one party. Within a campus there is more possibility of fully mutual ground, though it is probable that for historical reasons any particular university will be weighted towards one or two of the three. There are other possible problems with universities: policy, curricula, appointments and funding are not necessarily in the hands of those who appreciate a practice such as scriptural reasoning; university and even departmental politics can swing in different directions; and universities are not always unselfish enough to share in something that is at home in many places, including some of which they might not completely approve.

For these and other reasons scriptural reasoning has tended not to become too dependent on any particular house or campus, however good the camping there; but it is very young, and, if it continues, new institutional forms more integrated with houses or with campuses or other settings may be generated by it in time.[23]

5. Coping with Superabundant Meaning

When the three scriptures and the traditions of interpretation that they have inspired are put alongside one another one is faced with three unfathomable oceans, three universes of meaning.

Not only that, but beyond the traditions there is a further universe of academic study dedicated to these three scriptures and their histories of interpretation, drawing on philology, literary theory and criticism, history, theology, philosophy, psychology, psychoanalysis, social anthropology, sociology, political theory and ideology, postcolonial theory, art history, media studies, cultural studies, music, and liturgy.

Not only that, but each of the universes is expanding daily as unprecedented numbers of people in all three traditions (billions worldwide) and beyond them continue to search for meaning in these scriptures and in the responses to them.

Now in addition imagine the possibilities of the three in interaction with each other, and the further infinity of interconnections that open up.

Finally, imagine the three, in interaction with each other, exploring issues in contemporary life, seeking wisdom for each tradition, for the three in their relations with each other, and for the flourishing of our world.

That overwhelming superabundance of meaning is clearly beyond any individual human comprehension, any encyclopaedic mind, or any series of volumes, or computer database. This is not just because of the problem of sheer quantity. Much of the meaning—the interconnecting that is only possible for a well-trained memory and mind, the making of judgements that have taken into account an appropriate range of factors, the discernment that grows out of years of prayer and meditation, the capacity for self-awareness and self-critique that require spiritual as well as intellectual maturity, the immersion in community life that shapes a sense of what rings true, the education in a discipline that has accumulated and tested learning over centuries—is embodied in people who have been formed over long periods, and whose way of understanding is inseparable from who they are. Even such people can only begin to cope with the abundance if they are in sustained collegial relationships with each other. Further, the essential responsibility towards the future is only possible if the collegiality includes apprenticeships across generations. So a necessary condition for coping is groups and networks of people of different generations who embody vital dimensions of the seeking and finding of meaning. The most vital of all these dimensions is that of living, wise embodiment of the core identities of Islam, Judaism and Christianity. This is the most obvious and simple reason for the impossibility of overviews or comprehensive expertise: no one can live and think bearing more than one of these core identities at the same time.

Within this collegiality, how is the abundance coped with? The basic way is through each coming with their scriptures and "internal libraries" and engaging in reading, listening and interpretation in conversation with the others. Within that I would identify in particular three fundamental and coinherent elements.

5.1. Plain Sense with Midrash
The first task of an interpreter of scripture is to try to do justice to its plain sense. There is of course much discussion about what the plain sense is, but

the sorts of things that need to be taken into consideration are the manuscript evidence; the lexical meanings of words in their semantic fields; the significance of syntax, figures of speech, genres, contexts, and resonances with other texts; sequences and habits of thought and expression; the relation of sense to reference; implicit presuppositions; and (most complex of all) different ways of construing and relating those things in different strands of the tradition and in the various schools and disciplines of interpretation today.

The latter points to the insufficiency of the plain sense in certain crucial respects. Its polyvalence, surplus of meaning and openness to multiple interpretations frequently generate an abundance of possibilities. This laying out of many interpretations may be sufficient if one's interest is phenomenological, surveying these fascinating possibilities without concern for any current relevance or application. But, if one believes that these texts can be retrieved as sources for understanding and living today (and scriptural reasoning includes at least three sets of people who do believe that about their own scriptures), and that that involves the search for their contemporary meaning and the risk of application, then more is required. One Jewish way of naming this "more" that has been the topic of much discussion in scriptural reasoning is "midrash", and Christian and Muslim traditions have their equivalents of this.[24] Midrash is the discovery of a sense for the time and place of the interpreter.

Midrash can seem idiosyncratic, an improvisation on the text that may seem to maintain only a tenuous relation to its plain sense. But in any scriptural tradition it is unavoidable if the meaning of the text is to be "performed" today. Its combination of recognition of the plain sense with discernment of an applied sense is at the heart of what I call a wisdom interpretation of scripture.[25] This is the central way in which scriptural reasoning copes with the abundance of meaning: by trying to take as much as possible of it into account, by always giving priority (as Judaism, Christianity and Islam traditionally do) to the plain sense, and by risking a contemporary extended, midrashic sense that has emerged out of wisdom-seeking conversation across traditions and disciplines. This contemporary sense is a performance of interpretation for now. It does not seek to be normative knowledge or to be the only valid interpretation or to be demonstrable and invulnerable; rather it seeks to be wise. It is not so much about mapping the ocean (though maps help) as about diving in search of the pearl of a deep sense that rings true now.

5.2. Theory

Midrash copes with the abundance of meaning through first-order interpretation, seeking to improvise wise contemporary senses of specific texts. A complementary, second-order strategy is the development of theory. Indeed one might say that as midrash has been the characteristic outcome of the small *chevruta*-style text-study scriptural reasoning groups, so theory has been the typical product of plenary sessions. The larger setting is less suited to close study of texts, but better at trying to distil into concepts and theories a second-order description of what has gone on in a number of smaller groups and discussing their wider connections and implications.

Theory, often closely connected with particular philosophies, theologies, social sciences or natural sciences, is also prominent in published writings on scriptural reasoning. The second-order "moment" of concepts interconnected in theory is suited to written presentation—such as most of the essays in the present issue. On the other hand, it is extremely hard to do justice in print to the complex oral exchanges of small groups studying three scriptures at once, and even harder for one person to do so. An early draft of the present article attempted to give an example of scriptural reasoning focussed on texts from Tanakh, Bible and Quran that had been discussed during a five-day conference. It faced some problems that in combination I judged to be insuperable. The chief one was the impossibility of condensing hours of discussion (often apparently fragmented or centrifugal) around these texts into anything that would fit in an article. A second problem was that the oral character of the exchanges, together with their context in the biographies of the members, in the history of the group and in all the other things that were going on in the conference (including a good deal of theoretical and political discussion) repeatedly made specific interpretations, if reproduced in writing, seem not only bare but even misleading. They cried out for "thick" description, for substantial annotation, for explanation, and for sensitive characterisation of each "voice" if justice were to be done to what had actually gone on. It is not surprising that there has been considerable discussion among those taking part in scriptural reasoning about the importance of developing forms of rich, multidimensional description and the use of social (or cultural) anthropology to assist in this. A third problem was that I became acutely aware that my account of the discussion around these texts was that of a certain Christian interpreter and needed to be complemented by accounts from the other participants—this would be possible, but not in the space available here.

So I decided not to try to give an example of actual text interpretation, and to remain content for now with introducing scriptural reasoning from various angles. The practical conclusion is not that it is impossible to be more descriptive but that it is not possible now in the genre of an article; therefore as scriptural reasoning continues there needs to be more work on appropriate forms of description. But even so, as regards actually learning scriptural reasoning, one should not have too high expectations of such work. It is in the nature of an intensive, dialogical social practice that it is best learnt by initiation into the group followed by apprenticeship.

What might be an appropriate fixed form for presenting conversation around these three sets of texts? The printed page is especially limited—it is stretched to its limits in presenting the rabbinic debates around scripture in the Talmud, which are probably the nearest traditional equivalent to scriptural reasoning—and they are only coping with one scriptural "ocean of meaning". It may be that an interactive electronic medium with the possibility of pursuing several different lines of thought from the one word or verse (as through hypertext) and of holding on screen several text boxes, any of which can be searched with reference to the other (and variant translations called up at will), would do better, not least because it might be able to draw users into the creative process rather than just reproducing one past instance of it. But, like Talmud, any attempt to reproduce the results of face to face interplay is likely to be difficult, underdetermined, and in need of long apprenticeship in order to follow the allusions, moves and leaps. One is reminded of Plato on the dangers and disadvantages of writing over against live conversation: a writing cannot respond to questions and cannot adapt to particular audiences, and so is inferior to oral διαλεγεσθαι (*dialegesthai*—conversation, dialogue or dialectic).[26] But it can present sets of interconnected ideas well.

Theory's second-order discourse is also relatively well suited to the individual authorship that is the norm in specialist academic publishing in theology, philosophy and other arts and humanities subjects. Again, Plato is instructive. His earlier works were fully dialogical, trying to catch the dynamics of Socrates in conversation. After the *Phaedrus* the dialogue form is minimal, the readers for whom his works are written seem to be philosophers or trainee philosophers and the theoretical sophistication of the works increases. For Plato, philosophy was learned and developed through face to face conversation in the context of a whole way of life, and his later writings are aids to that process rather than attempts to produce a literary imitation of it in dialogue form.[27] In the centuries that followed, the living heart of his philosophical tradition was the conversational teaching of the Academy in Athens.

With regard to scriptural reasoning, this underlines the emphasis above on its collegiality; and, while it reduces any expectation that it will be done justice by theoretical accounts, it also makes theory modestly complementary to discussion of scripture. The unreproducible density and dynamics of conversation in small groups gathered around scriptural texts may be central to its practice and to the quality of its collegial scriptural wisdom, but that quality also needs the contribution of theory to sustain intellectual rigour and creativity.

At the beginning the most influential theoretical contribution was Peter Ochs' use of C. S. Peirce's semiotics and relational logic, and that has continued to be a fruitful resource.[28] It has Christian counterparts in Oliver Davies[29] and Chad Pecknold[30] and a Muslim appropriation is seen in Basit Koshul, who also draws on the social theory of Max Weber and the philosophy of Mohammed Iqbal.[31] Nicholas Adams has engaged in critical discussion with Jürgen Habermas in dialogue with German Idealist philosophy from Kant to Schelling and Hegel,[32] while Randi Rashkover has given theoretical consideration to the original Jewish-Christian dimension to scriptural reasoning.[33] Other important theoretical contributions have been made by Gavin Flood, Timothy Winter, Ben Quash, Robert Gibbs and Daniel Hardy.[34]

Such variety shows the capacity of scriptural interpretation to stimulate conceptual thinking in dialogue with pragmatism, idealism, phenomenology, social theory, legal theory, scientific theory, ethical theory, philosophy of language, philosophy of history, systems thinking, feminist theory, and hermeneutical philosophy. The very diversity also resists any theoretical overview—there can be no overall master theory where so many conceptual descriptions and analyses engage with each other. The intersection of such theoretical accounts also intensifies the conversation around scriptural texts and their implications.

So the effort to "make deep reasoning public" (Adams, above) simultaneously leads deep into scriptures and deep into theories, interweaving premodern and modern discourses.

5.2. Analogous Wisdoms

A further dimension of coping with the superabundance of meaning is the relating of these mutually informing discourses of theory and scriptural interpretation (plain sense and midrash) to their practical implications in various spheres of life—which is, of course, a leading concern of the rabbinic sages in their midrash and of comparable strands in Christianity and Islam. The condition for wise Abrahamic practicality is that each tradition allows itself to have its own wisdom questioned and transformed in engagement with the others. This means recognising them as analogous wisdoms with the potential of worthwhile interplay.

Collegial wisdom-seeking by Jews, Christians and Muslims can go on in other ways than through conversation around their scriptures, but considering each scripture is essential to any wisdom that might claim to be in line with each tradition. Above all, attention to the scriptures helps ensure that emergent wisdom is related to God and God's purposes in history and for the future. Within scriptural reasoning perhaps nothing has been theologically more fundamental than the threefold sense that study and interpretation are happening in the presence of God and for the sake of God, in the midst of the contingencies and complexities of a purposeful history, and in openness to God's future and for the sake of God's purposes. Yet precisely in the understanding of God, history and eschatology lie some of the most profound and stubborn differences—the Christian description of which is in terms of God as Trinity, and an account of creation, history and the future in which Jesus Christ is both central and ultimate.

How might this situation of radical differences with regard to analogous categories be coped with wisely? Christian participants in Scriptural reasoning have not found it helpful to concentrate on arriving at doctrinal agreement with Jews and Muslims on the Trinity, christology and eschatology (or at agreement on analogously distinctive Jewish or Muslim beliefs and practices). That is not only virtually inconceivable but may in most contexts be an unwise path, leading deep into the marshes created by centuries of misunderstandings and polemics. A well-worn path into interfaith cul de sacs is to focus on "secure disagreements" which complacently reinforce the identity of each with minimal mutual exploration, learning or challenge. Rather, what has been found fruitful is continual engagement with the scriptures that have contributed both to such doctrines and to the shaping of a whole way of life (with worship, ethics, institutions and so on). This can lead to conversation and understanding that do not ignore the disagreements but also do not get stuck in them. Ways of handling fundamental disputes can be worked out, essential to which is each tradition trying to discern and share its own wisdom of dispute. And intrinsic to that discernment is the wise interpretation of scripture. That is an urgent quest within each tradition and one that can benefit from both of the others.

6. Scriptural Reasoning in the Public Sphere

Finally, a brief word about the possibilities of scriptural reasoning in the public sphere. The main point is an extension of what was said about scriptural reasoning in universities—which might indeed be considered part of the public sphere. Once it is recognised that we are in a multi-faith and secular world and that secular worldviews and principles have no right to monopolise the public sphere in the name of neutrality, then we need ways of forming the sort of "mutual ground" that allows each tradition to contribute from their core belief, understanding and practice. That requires many bilateral and multilateral engagements, and among those is trilateral dialogue between Jews, Christians and Muslims. Earlier sections have described scriptural reasoning as allowing rich and deep encounter that both does justice to differences and also forms strong relationships across them. It is a new collegiality that might have an impact on the public world in several ways: by being a sign of reconciliation; by being a site where Jews, Christians and Muslims can work out in dialogue the considerable ethical and political implications of their scriptures; and by encouraging analogous practices among Jews, Christians and Muslims in positions of public responsibility.

Secularised societies have generally failed to mobilise religious resources for public wisdom and for peace. Religions have often reacted against them, faced with a choice between assimilation or confrontation. But there

is another possibility: mutually critical engagement among all the participants aimed at transforming the public sphere for the better.[35] For Jews,
Christians and Muslims committed to this the best way forward is through
simultaneously going deeper into their own scriptures and traditions,
deeper into wisdom-seeking conversation with each other and with all who
have a stake in the public good, and deeper into activity dedicated to the
common good. So one promise of scriptural reasoning is the formation of
people through collegial study, wise interpretation and friendship who
might be exemplary citizens of the twenty-first century, seeking the public
good for the sake of God and God's peaceful purposes.

NOTES

1   Nicholas Adams, "Scriptural Difference and Scriptural Reasoning"—chapter 11 in the
    forthcoming *Habermas and Theology* (Cambridge: Cambridge University Press, 2006),
    available   on-line   at   http://etext.lib.virginia.edu/journals/jsrforum/writings/
    AdaHabe.html; Peter Ochs, "Reading Scripture Together in Sight of Our Open Doors",
    The Princeton Seminary Bulletin Vol. XXVI, no. 1, new series (2005), pp. 36–47; Aref Ali
    Nayed, "Reading Scripture Together: Towards a Sacred Hermeneutics of Togetherness",
    The Princeton Seminary Bulletin Vol. XXVI, no. 1, new series (2005), pp. 48–53; Basit Bilal
    Koshul, "Affirming the self through accepting the Other" in *Scriptures in Dialogue:
    Christians and Muslims Studying the Bible and the Qur'an Together*, edited by Michael Ipgrave
    (London: Church House Publishing, 2004), pp. 111–118; Randi Rashkover, "Cultivating
    Theology: Overcoming America's Skepticism about Religious Rationality", *Cross Currents*
    Vol. 55, No. 2 (June 2005), pp. 241–251; C. C. Pecknold, *Transforming Postliberal Theology:
    George Lindbeck, Pragmatism, and Scripture* (New York and London: T. & T. Clark/
    Continuum, 2005); Ben Quash, "Holy Seeds: The Trisagion and the Liturgical Untilling of
    Time" in *Liturgy, Time, and the Politics of Redemption*, edited by C. C. Pecknold and Randi
    Rashkover (Grand Rapids, MI: Wm. B. Eerdmans Publishing Company, 2006). For further
    resources, see also the web-site of the *Journal of Scriptural Reasoning* Forum at http://
    etext.lib.virginia.edu/journals/jsrforum/.
2   For the best account of textual reasoning by participants and commentators, see *Textual
    Reasonings*, edited by Peter Ochs and Nancy Levene (London: SCM Press, 2002).
3   In the early years they used "postmodern" in self-description, but as that term has
    become overused and ceased to have much specific meaning they have tended to drop
    it. My own preferred term for the modernity that has been traumatised by the Shoah and
    other twentieth century horrors and disasters is "late modernity", with "chastened
    modernity" for those aspects of it that have tried best to learn from the twentieth century.
4   Cf. Peter Ochs, "Reading Scripture Together in Sight of Our Open Doors".
5   For a good gathering of the types of thinking that fed into this pre-history of scriptural
    reasoning see *The Return to Scripture in Judaism and Christianity: Essays in Postcritical
    Scriptural Interpretation*, edited by Peter Ochs (Mahwah, NJ: Paulist Press, 1993).
6   Randi Rashkover, *Revelation and Theopolitics*.
7   This grew out of a course on "Kant and Scripture".
8   For a Jewish account of Christian theological engagement with Judaism that includes
    discussion of various strands that have fed into scriptural reasoning see Peter Ochs,
    "Judaism and Christian Theology" in *The Modern Theologians. An Introduction to Christian
    Theology since 1918*, edited by David F. Ford with Rachel Muers, third edition, (Oxford:
    Blackwell, 2005), pp. 645–662.
9   Out of these have grown a variety of elements, including: a unit in the programme of the
    annual meeting of the AAR, groups in various parts of the world, a grassroots body called
    the Children of Abraham Institute (CHAI), the online *Journal of Scriptural Reasoning*, a
    research group based at the Center of Theological Inquiry in Princeton focussing on

medieval scriptural interpretation in Judaism, Islam and Christianity, a scriptural reasoning programme at St. Ethelburga's Centre for Peace and Reconciliation in London, postgraduate programmes in the University of Virginia, contributions to interfaith gatherings in Qatar, South Africa, Karachi, London, Durham, Berlin, Georgetown, and much else—cf. the article introducing Scriptural Reasoning in *Christian Century* by Jeffrey W. Bailey, forthcoming 2006.

10 *Chevruta* (fellowship) study is an ancient rabbinic method of studying Jewish texts that continues into the present. By engaging with a text in very small group settings, students learn through interaction both with the text and with each other. The method not only facilitates and deepens their education, but can also forge and strengthen relationships among students. The traditional setting for *chevruta* study was the *yeshivah*, a Jewish institution for the advanced study of religious texts. In scriptural reasoning the usual group size is between six and nine, allowing for two to three members of each faith tradition.

11 The other main types so far have been among Jews, Christians and Muslims from congregations (who may or may not have academic training) and among academics who include Jews, Christians, Muslims and others (usually specialists in one of the scriptures or traditions).

12 In plenary discussion at a scriptural reasoning conference in Cambridge, June 2003. Cf. Aref Ali Nayed, "Reading Scripture Together: Towards a Sacred Hermeneutics of Togetherness".

13 In a situation, such as the second one described in the previous note, in which some participants are not in any sense members of one of the three faith communities, scriptural reasoning is only likely to work well if those in this fourth category, together with those who are Jewish, Muslim or Christian, conform to certain norms, such as imaginative understanding and respect for how the others take their scriptures, willingness to be as vulnerable as the others in exposing their basic convictions to argument, and unwillingness to claim either an overview or a neutral vantage point.

14 Nicholas Adams, from chapter 11 of *Habermas and Theology*.

15 Cf. note 11 above on other types.

16 The Jewish textual reasoning group has drawn on Jewish traditional resources to think about the significance of their intensive electronic interaction with each other, seeing it as a form of "oral Torah".

17 Cf. David F. Ford, "Faith and Universities in a Religious and Secular World (1)", *Svensk Teologisk Kvartalskrift* Vol. 81, no. 2 (2005), pp. 83–91 and "Faith and Universities in a Religious and Secular World (2)", *Svensk Teologisk Kvartalskrift* Vol. 81, no. 3 (2005), pp. 97–106.

18 For a brief account of the field of theology and religious studies in such a setting see David F. Ford, *Theology: A Very Short Introduction* (Oxford: Oxford University Press, 1999, 2000), especially Chapters 1 and 2; for a discussion of the field with reference to several countries and types of institution, see *Fields of Faith. Theology and Religious Studies in the Twenty-first Century*, edited by David F. Ford, Ben Quash and Janet Martin Soskice (Cambridge: Cambridge University Press, 2005).

19 Cf. *Fields of Faith*, Part 1 "The End of the Enlightenment's Neutral Ground"; also Jeffrey Stout, *Democracy and Tradition* (Princeton, NJ: Princeton University Press, 2003) for a secular critique of the neutral public sphere in the United States.

20 See *Fields of Faith*, Part II "Meetings on Mutual Ground" and the perceptive discussion by Nicholas Adams, Oliver Davies and Ben Quash in *ibid*. Chapter 13 "Fields of faith: an experiment in the study of theology and the religions".

21 For the sake of brevity I have not covered a range of other institutional settings where scriptural reasoning can be practised, such as seminaries (some of which are closely related to or even integrated with universities), or institutions with Muslim, Jewish and Christian chaplaincy but no academic study of religion or theology. Each raises issues which require discussion with reference to their specific conditions.

22 It is of course possible to imagine it as an academic specialty in which one person might fill an academic post devoted to it. This would require a careful job description to avoid the impossible demand for threefold expertise, and the ideal would be a team of at least three.

23 Historical parallels would suggest that a driver of new forms is likely to be divisions among scriptural reasoners leading to different schools of thought and varying relationships with religious communities, universities and other settings.

24 For a Jewish understanding of midrash in relation to scriptural reasoning see Ochs, "Reading Scripture Together in Sight of Our Open Doors". On Muslim interpretation see Aref Ali Nayed, "Reading Scripture Together: Towards a Sacred Hermeneutics of Togetherness".

25 Cf. David F. Ford, "Reading Scripture with Intensity: Academic, Ecclesial, Interfaith, and Divine", *The Princeton Seminary Bulletin* Vol. XXVI no. 1, new series (2005), pp. 22–35.

26 Cf. Plato, *Phaedrus* 275C, 257D, 275E, 276C, 277D.

27 Cf. Charles H. Kahn, *Plato and the Socratic Dialogue. The philosophical use of a literary form* (Cambridge: Cambridge University Press, 1996), pp. 376–392.

28 See Peter Ochs, *Peirce, Pragmatism and the Logic of Scripture* (Cambridge: Cambridge University Press, 1998), and "Scriptural Logic: Diagrams for a Postcritical Metaphysics", *Modern Theology* Vol. 11, no. 1 (January, 1995), pp. 65–92.

29 Oliver Davies, "The Sign Redeemed: A Study in Christian Fundamental Semiotics", *Modern Theology* Vol. 19, no. 2 (April, 2003), pp. 219–241; *The Creativity of God: World, Eucharist, Reason* (Cambridge: Cambridge University Press, 2004), especially chapters 2, 4, 5, 6; for reference to scriptural reasoning see e.g. p. 121.

30 C. C. Pecknold, *Transforming Postliberal Theology.*

31 Basit Bilal Koshul, "Studying the Western Other, Understanding the Islamic Self: A Qur'anically Reasoned Perspective", *Iqbal Review* Vol. 46, no. 2/4 (April & October, 2005), special issue, pp. 149–174.

32 Nicholas Adams, *Habermas and Theology.*

33 Randi Rashkover, *Revelation and Theopolitics.*

34 Cf. the following essays in this special issue *The Promise of Scriptural Reasoning*: Flood, "The Phenomenology of Scripture"; Timothy Winter, "Quranic Reasoning as an Academic Practice"; Quash, "Heavenly Semantics: Some literary-critical approaches to scriptural reasoning"; Robert Gibbs, "Reading with Others: Levinas' Ethic and Scriptural Reasoning"; and Daniel Hardy, "The Promise of Scriptural Reasoning", on the way these can be understood together.

35 Potential contributions to a Stout-like public space might be found in such works as: Peter Ochs, "Abrahamic Theo-politics: A Jewish View" in the *Blackwell Companion to Political Theology*, edited by William Cavanaugh and Peter Scott (Oxford: Blackwell, 2003); Adams, "Scriptural Difference and Scriptural Reasoning"; C. C. Pecknold, "Democracy and the Politics of the Word: Stout and Hauerwas on Democracy and Scripture", *Scottish Journal of Theology* Vol. 59, no. 2 (2006), pp. 1–12; Robert Gibbs, "The Rules of Scriptural Reasoning", *The Journal of Scriptural Reasoning* Vol. 2, no. 1 (May, 2002), available on-line at http://etext.virginia.edu/journals/ssr/issues/volume2/number1/ssr02-01-gr01.html, and Robert Gibbs, *Why Ethics?: Signs of Responsibilities* (Princeton, NJ: Princeton University Press, 2000); Mike Higton, *Christ, Providence and History: Hans W. Frei's Public Theology* (New York and London: T. & T. Clark/Continuum, 2004); Randi Rashkover, *Revelation and Theopolitics*; and cf. the article introducing Scriptural Reasoning in *Christian Century* by Jeffrey W. Bailey, forthcoming 2006.

2

A HANDBOOK FOR SCRIPTURAL REASONING

STEVEN KEPNES

In what follows the reader will find twelve "rules" that I have set forth to define the nature and goals of the practice of Scriptural Reasoning (SR). The rules are authored by one person who cannot be seen to represent the diverse views of the many people who participate in SR activities. However, given these limitations, this Handbook is written for heuristic and pedagogic purposes to introduce Scriptural Reasoning to those who have little experience in and knowledge of the practice of SR. These rules were presented to the SR Theory Group at Cambridge University in May of 2004 where I received extensive comments. I use the notion of a "rule" rather than a "principle" or "statement" because SR is first a practice and then a set of ideas and a theory. The rules emerged from my observations of SR practice and taken together the rules are meant to be a guide or "handbook" for future SR practice.

After presenting the twelve rules in list form, I return to each rule to explicate it in more detail. I then conclude with a brief description of how SR is done. The description focuses more on necessary conditions and attitudes than rigid steps and instructions.

A. Twelve Rules of Scriptural Reasoning (SR)

What is Scriptural Reasoning?
1. SR is a practice of group reading of the scriptures of Judaism, Christianity, and Islam that builds sociality among its practitioners and releases sources of reason, compassion, and divine spirit for healing our separate communities and for repair of the world. Thus, SR theory aims at a scripturally reasoned triadic response to the problems of the world that is motivated and sustained by the healing and divine spirit of scripture.

Steven Kepnes
Department of Philosophy and Religion, Colgate University, Hamilton, NY 13346, USA

2. Participants in SR practice come to it as both representatives of academic institutions and particular "houses" (churches, mosques, synagogues) of worship. SR meets, however, outside of these institutions and houses in special times and in separate spaces that are likened to Biblical "tents of meeting". Practitioners come together in these tents of meeting to read and reason with scriptures. They then return to their academic and religious institutions and to the world with renewed energy and wisdom for these institutions and the world.

3. SR begins with the scriptural sense that the human world is broken, in exile, off the straight path, filled with corruption, sickness, war and genocide. SR practitioners come together out of a sense of impoverishment, suffering, and conflict to seek resources for healing.

4. SR is neither about the roots of Christianity in Judaism nor the roots of Islam in Jewish and Christian traditions. SR is also not about academic Jewish-Christian-Islamic understanding. SR acknowledges Abraham (and Adam before him) as a source figure for the three monotheistic religions, but SR does not seek to reduce or dissolve these religions into some universal Abrahamic faith. Rather, SR is about serious conversation between three religious traditions that preserves difference as it establishes relations.

The Reason of Scriptural Reasoning
5. SR is the thinking that occurs when scripture is taken up and discussed by a group of interpreters. It therefore works through both the reasoning that is implicit in scripture and the reasoning that practitioners, as interpreters, bring to scripture. But, most importantly, scriptural reasoning is the reasoning that is "disclosed" as members engage in dialogue about scripture.

6. SR functions with a triadic semiotic that assumes that meaning arises out of the relationship between the sign, referent and community of interpreters (in Peirce's terms, the "interpretant") that reads the text. This type of semiotic transfers hermeneutic power to scriptural reasoners who bring their knowledge of scripture and its traditional interpretations and the academic disciples of history, sociology, and philosophy, with them when they meet to read together.

7. SR includes moments of reflection on group practices of reading that collect, summarize, and organize the insights that are generated. These acts of reflection will take the form of commentary and rules rather than systematic philosophies or theological treatises. Further "second order" reflections on the summaries of SR sessions by individual scholars contribute to the ongoing development of SR theory. The triadic form of its practice means that SR theory developed by a scholar of one monotheistic tradition will necessarily address the other two traditions.

8. The final stage of scriptural reasoning is the application of SR to the problems and issues that inspired SR practice in the first place. This final stage of SR involves bringing SR into the world to heal it. This is scriptural reasoning in action. It is scriptural reasoning as peace-making.

Why Monotheisms?
9. SR begins with the scriptures of the Monotheistic religions because the initial members of the SR community came from the traditions of Judaism, Christianity and Islam. SR also begins with Monotheisms because some of the most grave problems that plague today's world are generated by tensions between Jews and Muslims and Christians. SR members believe that there are overlooked resources within the religious traditions that can have an ameliorative effect on these tensions.

10. In including Islam and the Qur'an as an equal partner in SR discussions, SR intends to move beyond the popular "clash of civilizations" thesis that pits a "Western Judeo-Christian civilization" against a "Non-Western and Anti-Modern Islamic civilization". SR attempts to move beyond this clash of civilization thesis by focusing on the mutual respect for scripture in the three Monotheistic traditions and by recapturing the human values, traditions of learning, and devotion to God that these scriptures each espouse and give rise to.

Our Time and the End Time
11. SR seeks a "third space" between anti-modern religious fundamentalism and modern liberalism. SR shares some of the epistemological moves of philosophical postmodernism that is critical of the modern reliance on the rational subject and the attempt to discover universal principles that could substitute for particular traditions of knowing and living. Yet SR is wary of the nihilistic ideologies that emerge from some deconstructivist forms of postmodernism. SR members sometimes refer to themselves as "postliberal", in that they seek to retain liberal democratic values and the liberal dedication to the alleviation of suffering throughout the world, while recapturing a positive public role for the particular traditions of thought and living that are present in the Monotheistic scriptures.

12. SR is liturgical and eschatological in that it anticipates an end time in which all the children of Abraham will live together in peace. Yet SR members believe that Jews , Christians, and Muslims can participate in something of that end time by entering into "tents of meeting" in which members of the three traditions read their scriptures together in an atmosphere of respectful dialogue and friendship.

B. *An Explication of the Rules*

What is SR?

1. *SR is a practice of group reading of the scriptures of Judaism, Christianity, and Islam that builds sociality among its practitioners and releases sources of reason, compassion, and divine spirit for healing our separate communities and for repair of the world. Thus, SR theory aims at a scripturally reasoned triadic response to the problems of the world that is motivated and sustained by the healing and divine spirit of scripture.*

SR is a practice before it is a theory. It properly can only be known in its performance. The performative dimension gives SR a time-bound and context-specific characteristic. This means that every SR event is dependent upon the specific time and place and the particular group of individuals that assemble to practice SR. The primary texts of SR sessions are the Hebrew Bible, the New Testament, and the Qur'an. These texts are primary because they constitute the originative and contemporary sources of the separate religious communities. SR regards these books not only as texts but as scripture and this means that they are regarded as living sources of divine interaction with humanity. SR members believe that the religious traditions of Judaism, Christianity, and Islam remain central vehicles through which the presence of God is known and experienced.

Although religions and Western religions, in particular, contain more than scriptures—e.g. symbols, doctrines, and saints—we begin with scriptures. We do this, most simply, because Jews, Christians and Muslims share common narratives and they share a common respect for scripture as fundamental documents of revelation and religious foundation.

Beginning with scriptures, which are by definition closed canons, imposes a helpful limit which yields a set body of initial texts that can easily be worked with. However, we readily turn to secondary scriptures from the Midrash and Talmud, the works of the Church Fathers, the Hadith and Tafsir, and a host of exegetical texts from all three traditions.

Participants in SR have found that reading scriptures together builds sociality between members. SR members come to seek and expect sociality and friendship to deepen with successive SR sessions. The friendships and sociality that develop around SR sessions should not be confused with a conflict-free sphere full of easy agreements and consensus. But SR does hope to engender respectful conversation across differences and it has shown itself to be able to forge hospitality and friendship not in spite of, but because of difference.

2. *Participants in SR practice come to it as both representatives of academic institutions and particular "houses" (churches, mosques, synagogues) of worship. SR meets, however, outside of these institutions and houses in special times and in separate spaces that are likened to Biblical "tents of meeting". Practitioners come together in these tents of meeting to read and reason with scriptures. They*

then return to their academic and religious institutions and to the world with
renewed energy and wisdom for these institutions and the world.

Participants in SR come to it being trained, formed by, and often teaching
in two dominant institutions of learning: the University and the Religious
Seminary. The double training and double allegiance to both the University
and the Seminary with their distinct and overlapping canons of truth,
methods of study, and traditions of learning, is part of what makes SR
unique. This dual allegiance means that no science, no philosophical
system of truth, no form of artistry, no spiritual discipline, is, from the
outset, ruled out or rendered "foreign" to SR. This dual allegiance of SR
means that it can hope to take advantage of the best of the traditions of
liberal learning and move between and across the destructive contemporary divisions: secular and sacred, modern and traditional, material and
spiritual.

Given that SR members are specialists in their academic fields and
worshippers in religious communities, most SR members have an allegiance not only to a religious tradition in general, e.g. Islam and a field in
the academy, e.g. philosophy, but to a particular form of religious tradition,
e.g. Anglicanism and a particular movement (or, as Nicholas Adams refers
to it, as a "seminar") in their academic discipline, e.g. phenomenology.
Furthermore, members of the same religious tradition may be formed by
vastly different academic methods. And members of different religious
traditions may share the same allegiance to a particular academic method.
This leads to creative cross-cutting relations among scriptural reasoners and
interesting "temporary alliances" where members of different religious
traditions may find themselves closer to each other on the basis of an
allegiance to a shared academic method of study than they are to members
of their own religious traditions.

There is, however, a crucial distinction between religious traditions and
an academic methodology. Where an academic methodology can be shared
across the religions (i.e. a Jew, a Christian and a Muslim may all share the
methodology of phenomenology), the scriptures of Judaism, Christianity,
and Islam remain tied to their traditions and their traditional interpretations cannot be "shared" among Jews, Christians, and Muslims in the same
way. For example, Jews, Christians, and Muslims can all read the Qur'an,
but the assumption of SR is that the Qur'an cannot be pulled out of the
matrix of tradition, family, community, worship, learning, and belief that
the Muslim stands in. In this sense, the Muslim holds an authority over the
text as its lover and teacher that the Jew or Christian does not possess. And
the same situation holds with the Jew in relation to the Torah and the
Christian in relation to the New Testament.

Whatever the religious and academic affiliation of SR members, SR
meetings take place in spaces and times that are set apart from the formal
confines of individual religious and academic institutions. Members of the

Society for Scriptural Reasoning like to refer to these spaces, figuratively, as "tents of meeting" to convey the sense of a marginal and transitional sacred space where institutional restraints are temporarily relaxed and experimental forms of scriptural interpretation and reasoning can be developed.

3. *SR begins with the scriptural sense that the human world is broken, in exile, off the straight path, filled with corruption, sickness, war and genocide. SR practitioners come together out of a sense of impoverishment, suffering, and conflict to seek resources for healing.*

More than anything, SR is motivated by a global awareness of the predominance of human suffering. Although this is an assessment of the contemporary world, we see parallels in our scriptural traditions which also grew out of a sense of the moral, spiritual, and material collapse of the world as described in Genesis, in the Gospels, and in the Qur'an. We do not take these scriptural assessments as prophesies of our contemporary predicament or simple portraits of our contemporary world, but as signs that our scriptures are fundamentally concerned with the worldly realities of human suffering and centrally focused on addressing that suffering.

SR members join together out a desire, as people of faith and knowledge, to address human suffering in all of its variations. For Robert Gibbs and Laurie Zoloth, this means that SR is primarily a form of ethics. Human suffering and its alleviation establishes the ultimate criterion of the truth of SR. This is a pragmatic criterion that means that the truth of SR will be shown in its ability to help heal the suffering in the world.

4. *SR is neither about the roots of Christianity in Judaism nor the roots of Islam in Jewish and Christian traditions. SR is also not about academic Jewish-Christian-Islamic understanding. SR acknowledges Abraham (and Adam before him) as a source figure for the three monotheistic religions, but SR does not seek to reduce or dissolve these religions into some universal Abrahamic faith. Rather, SR is about serious conversation between three religious traditions that preserves difference as it establishes relations.*

SR is not a purely historical exercise in tracing the later Monotheistic traditions back to earlier forms. It also does not seek to find "underlying conceptual unities", "overarching principles" or "universal essences" into which the scriptures and traditions can be dissolved. It is not about developing and applying objective methods and models for understanding "the nature and thought" of the religions of Judaism, Christianity, and Islam. In attempting to move beyond these objectives, SR seeks to move beyond much modern scholarship in the study of religion and much liberal interfaith dialogue.

SR attempts to articulate and preserve the separate identities of each of the three religions as it builds a dialogue that is tuned to the pressing ethical issues of the contemporary world. SR assumes that the individual traditions constitute, in George Lindbeck's terms, unique "cultural-linguistic" religious systems that maintain internal principles and mechanisms of coherence. This means, at a minimum, that when a word is used in a religious tradition it can best be defined by a series of words and terms from the religion in which it sits. Thus, even though the same term appears in one or two or three religions, it will necessarily carry a unique 'semantic aura', a set of cognates and uses, that is specific to its use in a particular religious "language-game".

Beginning with scriptures and following scriptural forms of reasoning, gives SR a way of preserving forms of religious expression that are unique to each of the three traditions. SR does not avoid historical, philological and documentary analysis of scripture; indeed, it recognizes these forms of scholarship as crucial to the task of establishing the historical context, semantic horizon and rhetorical forms that scriptures employ. But SR only begins with these forms of scholarship and then seeks to move beyond them to engage both the traditions of religious exegesis and the current practitioners of SR that take up the scriptures in their group readings.

Beginning with scriptural forms of reasoning is also intended to move inter-faith discussion away from conceptual and doctrinal categories of analysis. These categories often force the complex religious traditions into artificial and abstract theological concepts and dilute the complexity and specificity of the cultural-linguistic religions systems. Given the highly developed tradition of theology in the Christian tradition, inter-faith dialogue based on conceptual analysis tends to favor Christianity and to force the other traditions to speak in its terms. Scriptural reasoning is not against theology or philosophy, but it endeavors to use scripture to find a new/old philosophical idiom that is better attuned to religious particularity. It offers a more supple tool to lead to a richer, more complex and sensitive inter-faith dialogue.

The Reason of Scriptural Reasoning

5. *SR is the thinking that occurs when scripture is taken up and discussed by a group of interpreters. It therefore works through both the reasoning that is implicit in scripture and the reasoning that practitioners, as interpreters, bring to scripture. But, most importantly, scriptural reasoning is the reasoning that is "disclosed" as members engage in dialogue about scripture.*

SR recognizes that reason is a central tool of human liberation. Yet at the same time its practitioners believe that they need to reason better, more wisely, more thoroughly. SR practitioners believe that they need to find a form of reason that is neither abstract nor purely utilitarian, but is a reasoning of the heart. They need to find a form of reason that is simultaneously a practical moral reasoning that, in the words of David Ford, might be best expressed simply as "wisdom".

For this wise form of reasoning we look to scripture. In scripture we find a form of reasoning that is the beginning of wisdom. The reasoning of scripture is built out of the language—the grammar, the semantics, the rhetorics and poetics, the narrative and law—of scripture itself. In Jewish terms, this is the *"pshat"* or plain sense meaning of scripture. Reason in scripture is not only embedded in the language of scripture, but it is embedded in human persons, communities, peoples, geography, and history. This suggests that scriptural reasoning itself is embodied reasoning. And it is precisely because scriptural reasoning is embodied that is it such a transparent medium to relate human suffering. But scripture does not only relate human suffering. The plain sense meaning of scripture is also theological. As Daniel Hardy emphatically puts this, scripture is about God and about God's healing interactions with humans; and thus scriptural reasoning is a form of theology. SR is about faith, providence, hope, creation, judgment, mercy, salvation and redemption. And it is about these theological notions as they are taken up in scripture.

Scriptural reasoning about God is not traditional theology. Since SR follows the *pshat* of scripture, its theology is necessarily tied to a language, narrative, and law that is not self-evident. Scripture is full of ambiguities, gaps and lacunae. And, as we see in the literary devices of parables and allegory, scriptures appear to even be purposefully vague. As purposefully vague texts, scriptures then require interpretation. Given this, scripture requires us as readers to add our human reasoning to the divine reasoning of scripture.

I have used the notion of adding human reason and creativity to the divine reason of scripture. But this is a somewhat artificial way of talking about the process of scriptural interpretation. In the actual practice of scriptural reasoning it is not clear what is human and what divine. In the spontaneous moment of insight into and across scriptures, participants are overtaken by the movement of the spirit that many recognize as a disclosure of truth.

6. *SR functions with a triadic semiotic that assumes that meaning arises out of the relationship between the sign, referent and community of interpreters (in Peirce's terms, the "interpretant") that reads the text. This type of semiotic transfers hermeneutic power to scriptural reasoners who bring their knowledge of scripture and its traditional interpretations and the academic disciples of history, sociology, and philosophy, with them when they meet to read together.*

Peter Ochs has argued that much of contemporary biblical scholarship utilizes a dyadic sign/referent model for assigning meaning to scripture. This means that each semiotic sign refers to one object or concept. Interpretation is then a matter of determining the one meaning through historical scholarship, philology, or a variety of literary methodologies. Most critical biblical scholarship prioritizes the original audience of the historical period in which the text was written and thereby historicizes textual meaning. This process locks the meaning away into its ancient historical period. Looking at scripture as a historical document also assures that the theological element in scripture is either ignored or severely truncated. Indeed, as R. R. Reno has suggested, one can look at much modern biblical scholarship as an attempt to wall off scripture from theology.

The triadic semiotic model includes the figure of the interpreter in the semantic equation. This recognizes the primary function of a sign as medium of communication. In this view, scripture is not a dead memorial to the past, but a living message, a call, that sounds through the ages up until today. On the triadic semiotic model, the meaning of scripture is only known as it is heard and used by a contemporary reader and a contemporary community of interpreters.

Aref Nayed has suggested that when SR practitioners read scripture they each bring their own "internal library" with them. This library starts with knowledge of Arabic, Hebrew, Aramaic and Greek and includes historical information, theology, modern and postmodern philosophy and science. It also includes previous readings of the texts and hearings of it in ritual and liturgical contexts and, finally, understandings of God, the present historical moment, and the reasoner's own personal life.

In bringing their libraries and awareness of the contemporary world to the act of interpreting scripture, SR practitioners necessarily bring new questions and problems to the ancient texts. Where the ancient scriptures are written in societies that assumed the institutions of patriarchy, slavery, and monarchy, SR members bring contemporary feminist and democratic sensibilities to the texts that challenge and radically question them. This initiates a process of dialogue between the traditional texts and modern values. However, the experience of participants in SR sessions has been that these new questions breathe new life into the ancient scriptures. In addition, participants find that their questions are illumined in startling clarity and contemporary problems are addressed by the wisdom and guidance of the scriptures aroused and renewed. Although SR will challenge the presuppositions of patriarchy, slavery, and monarchy in the traditional text, it finds that the overarching scriptural values of freedom, redemption, salvation, and divine mercy can serve as powerful engines of hermeneutic creativity for the re-interpretation of scripture. Scriptures present powerful narratives and parables of societal transformation that work, analogically, to both critique and confirm the contemporary attempt to initiate human liberation and healing.

7. *SR includes moments of reflection on group practices of reading that collect, summarize, and organize the insights that are generated. These acts of reflection will take the form of commentary and rules rather than systematic philosophies or theological treatises. Further "second order" reflections on the summaries of SR sessions by individual scholars contribute to the ongoing development of SR theory. The triadic form of its practice means that SR theory developed by a scholar of one monotheistic tradition will necessarily address the other two traditions.*

After a creative session of scriptural interpretation in which the spirit moves as it wills, the process of SR moves into a purposely reflective moment in which the interpretations that have been brought, discovered, and created are collected together and organized. The reflective moment in scriptural reasoning is necessarily an analytic, comparative, synthetic enterprise. Here, practitioners of SR come together, after the interpretive event, to structure the various interpretations which group text study has engendered. The act of collecting and analyzing interpretations is not aimed at producing a single meaning for the texts read, but will issue in a multiplicity of different often conflicting interpretations that generate a number of "hypothetical" and provisional meanings. Scriptural reasoners often assemble the readings along a series of continuums that stretch from one kind of interpretation to the other. Since they are dealing with at least three scriptural texts, creative triadic schemata might be employed or a web of interactive meanings may need to be constructed. Beyond this, scriptural reasoners often seek to place interpretations in the wider contexts of Jewish, Christian, Islamic and various academic hermeneutical traditions.

Further reflections on SR reading sessions conducted by individual scholars produce more traditional forms of religious, philosophical, and theological research and scholarship. These will lead to articles and books on a vast array of subjects related to SR from individual studies of scripture that seek to display the forms of reasoning implicit in them, to studies of the forms of reasoning of ancient and medieval interpreters, to studies of scriptural economics and politics, to practical applications of SR to social issues. Taken together, this can be considered the work of SR theory. The uniqueness of this theory is that it emerges from collective practices of reading that attempt to use scriptural reasoning to address matters of urgent ethical concern. Beyond this, SR theory is distinguished by commitment from members of each religious tradition to do their scholarship in the context of and in relation to the other two traditions. Thus, the triadic structure of SR is carried into SR scholarship. This means that SR theorists believe that all constructive religious thought in the monotheistic traditions today must reflect the complex interactions of the traditions through history and especially in the present and into the future.

8. *The final stage of scriptural reasoning is the application of SR to the problems and issues that inspired SR practice in the first place. This final stage of SR involves bringing SR into the world to heal it. This is scriptural reasoning in action. It is scriptural reasoning as peace-making.*

Because scripture requires human reasoning to be added to it to yield its meaning, scripture places a burden upon its readers. This is the moral burden of carrying forward God's reasoning, God's word, into our lives and into the world. But as texts of communities that were given in public acts of revelation, the burden of carrying the word of God is a collective one, one that is to be borne by a community of interpretation. We are accustomed to bearing God's word in our own individual communities. However, one of the unique aspects of SR is that scriptural reasoning is carried to a mixed community of Jewish, Christians, and Muslims scholars with training both in academic and traditional discourses of interpretation. Here, the reason implicit in scripture is refracted in multiple ways and here a highly creative and mixed community of inquiry joins to receive and carry forward the reasoning of scripture to new forms of ethical action in the world.

Given their expertise as word-smiths, teachers, philosophers, and theologians, SR practitioners view themselves as second-order technicians of systems of knowledge and spirit. Peter Ochs speaks of first-order religious and secular systems as orders of formation and maintenance of the human world. Priests, doctors, social workers, politicians and economists, run the world and "fix" its problems on the basis of the given systems of knowledge and spirit that they have been trained in. These first-order practitioners make sure that the systems of health, economics, law, government, education, and moral guidance work effectively. Yet there are times when the first-order systems no longer work well. There are times when we face problems that our given systems of knowledge and order cannot adequately address. At such times, more thorough application and better understanding of the given systems will not serve to fix the world's problems. At these times, second-order technicians must be called in to repair the first-order systems upon which the human world stands and is maintained.

SR members recognize that they are not only living in a time of upheaval and transformation but, more importantly, that, as philosophers and theologians, they are called to assume the role of second-order technicians of knowledge and spirit. To distinguish themselves from philosophers and theologians who function as teachers of the given systems of human order, and to highlight the extent to which they see scriptures as guiding their work, many SR members like to refer to themselves as scriptural reasoners who read scriptures together in order to repair given systems of repair. What this formulation of their relation to the world suggests is that they do not always intervene *directly* in the world like doctors, social workers, politicians, and pastors do. Yet they believe that they can play a crucial role, precisely as readers, thinkers and writers, in helping to repair the world.

A fundamental conclusion of this way in which the SR relation to the world is conceived is that SR is not here to overthrow the given systems of knowledge and the sacred but to "repair" and thus reform them. This follows, at least in part, from a sense that the "new" systems of world order—e.g. nationalism, humanism, socialism—that were innovated in modernity, failed, at least partially, because they sought to overthrow the "old traditions" instead of continuing and reforming them. Each of the revolutions of modernity were followed by a reign of terror in which a totalitarian system was established to oversee the institution of a new and supposedly liberating order. The model of repair and healing attempts to preserve continuity with our cultural treasures of truth-seeking and spirit as we move forward to adapt our traditions to the human needs of the contemporary moment.

Why Monotheisms?

9. *SR begins with the scriptures of the Monotheistic religions because the initial members of the SR community came from the traditions of Judaism, Christianity and Islam. SR also begins with Monotheisms because some of the most grave problems that plague today's world are generated by tensions between Jews and Muslims and Christians. SR members believe that there are overlooked resources within the religious traditions that can have an ameliorative effect on these tensions.*

Monotheisms are the traditions that SR members know best and these are the traditions that give them life and energy and knowledge to want to repair the world. That is a simple answer to the question, "Why Monotheisms"? But beyond this, SR takes from these monotheisms the sense of a moral mission to the world. The moral meaning of the One God is that all humans are in his image are therefore of infinite worth. The moral meaning of monotheism is that the God of the universe cares for the entire world and that, as people of God, humans have responsibilities for the healing of the world. The comprehensive obligation to the entire world brings Jews, Christians and Muslims together in a shared task.

SR does not claim that the non-monotheistic religions are false or incapable of serving the goals that they have set. Indeed, as members of the great universities of the world, with experts in all of the world's religions and cultures, SR practitioners recognize that pejorative and stereotypical characterizations of the "other" religions as "pagan", or "primitive", or "atheistic" are both unfair and inaccurate. These formulations force the complex religions of the world into monotheistic categories, which necessarily distort them. Since SR is intrinsically scriptural, it necessarily is less appreciative of non-literate religious forms. Nevertheless, as one SR member, Oliver Davies, has stressed, there is a distinctive power of oral expression to scripture and the practice of SR is precisely the attempt to move the written word into the oral in the moment of dialogue and interpretation. Furthermore, most religions do include scriptural forms and SR members have and will continue to move beyond the borders of monotheistic scriptures by reading Buddhist, Hindu and other scriptures with representatives of these traditions.

10. *In including Islam and the Qur'an as an equal partner in SR discussions, SR intends to move beyond the popular "clash of civilizations" thesis that pits a "Western Judeo-Christian civilization" against a "Non-Western and Anti-Modern Islamic civilization". SR attempts to move beyond this clash of civilization thesis by focusing on the mutual respect for scripture in the three Monotheistic traditions* *and by recapturing the human values, traditions of learning, and devotion to God that these scriptures each espouse and give rise to.*

After the Holocaust and the Second World War and with the establishment of the State of Israel, Christians and Jews have drawn closer together. Especially in the United States, one hears of a common "Judeo-Christian tradition". Since 9/11, a formulation that has significantly shaped academic and popular discourse on the relationship between contemporary Islam and the West is that "Islam" and the "West" are two entities that are completely and fundamentally alien to each other. This, in turn, means that perpetual conflict between the two entities is not only inevitable but also natural. This line of reasoning is most coherently and systematically developed in the "clash of civilizations" thesis.

In contrast to the reasoning underpinning the "clash of civilizations" thesis, SR endeavors to demonstrate that there is an intimate philosophical, cultural, and religious affinity between "Islam" and the Judeo-Christian "West". One way of illustrating this affinity is to demonstrate the shared commitment to scripture and its study in the three traditions. Contemporary "Islam" and the contemporary "West" can best appreciate their own contemporary predicament by critically but empathetically studying the primal religious scriptures of the other. Both contemporary "Islam" and the "West" are facing daunting challenges brought on by global capitalism, consumerism, environmental disasters and increasing ethnic and religious tensions. It is rather simplistic to characterize the challenges that modernity or "postmodernity" presents to both the West and East through the clash of civilization thesis. But the reality is that the West is also plagued by the conflict of fundamentalisms and secularization and the West harbors within it all the horrors that is chooses to project into the Islamic world. In other words, as Basit Koshul has argued, there is a "clash of civilizations" that is occurring in the West itself. By engaging Islam in SR as an equal partner, SR members attempt to address the large issues of religion, secularism and war that together are plaguing the planet.

Our Time and the End Time
11. *SR seeks a "third space" between anti-modern religious fundamentalism and modern liberalism. SR shares some of the epistemological moves of philosophical postmodernism that is critical of the modern reliance on the rational subject and the attempt to discover universal principles that could substitute for particular traditions of knowing and living. Yet SR is wary of the nihilistic ideologies that emerge from some deconstructivist forms of postmodernism. SR members sometimes refer to themselves as "postliberal", in that they seek to retain liberal democratic values and the liberal dedication to the alleviation of suffering throughout the world, while recapturing a positive public role for the particular traditions of thought and living that are present in the Monotheistic scriptures.*

The hermeneutical openness of SR to a multiplicity of meanings for scripture separates it from a fundamentalist or literalist hermeneutics. SR opposes fundamentalist attempts to isolate particular religious traditions from other religions in the contemporary world to reinforce triumphalist claims of superiority. SR cherishes the modern liberal victories for religious tolerance and human rights, but it assails the wholesale attacks on religious traditions that are also associated with secularism. SR seeks a "third" position between fundamentalism and secularism that some of its members have referred to as "post-liberal". Postliberalism follows certain post-enlightenment epistemological moves that have attempted to open up narrow notions of rationality as syllogistic logic. This includes an appreciation for the philosophical import of language, texts, symbols, and art as well as an appreciation for alternative systems of logic suggested both by older religious traditions and contemporary philosophies of science with its uncertainty principle, quantum physics, and multiple-factor computer modeling.

SR appreciates the sociological description of our contemporary world as entering a stage of "postmodernity" in which the philosophical, political, and social institutions of modernity have been surpassed. Although Postliberalism shares some of the epistemological moves and sociological descriptions of postmodernism, it should not be confused with "postmodernism" as an ideology. Postliberalism shares the sociological description of the contemporary world as after or "post" modern. This description holds that the Western world is beyond the great modern metanarratives of Marxism, Free-Market Capitalism, Individualism, Colonialism and Ineluctable Progress. Postliberalism favors postfoundational epistemologies and there are some affinities between these epistemologies and those favored by postmodern thinkers. Yet many postmodern thinkers have taken their critiques to the edge of radical doubt where all absolutes and all notions of rationality, selfhood, humanism, and religion are undermined. Postmodernism thus easily creates a vacuum into which either anti-modern fundamentalism or crass secularism and consumerism can rush in. Postmodernism as an ideology represents something that SR resists; as a sociological description, postmodernity represents the contemporary situation to which SR attempts to respond.

Although the term "postliberalism" is congenial to SR, the movement could equally be called "post-conservative". This means that as SR endeavors to return to scripture and its traditions of interpretation and wisdom it does not seek to restate traditional religious authority and deadly conflicts between different religious traditions. Instead, SR endeavors to carry forward the traditions of truth and the word of God into the contemporary situation to repair and heal it. SR attempts to preserve the liberal values of modernity as its carries these values forward into a postmodern world.

12. *SR is liturgical and eschatological in that it anticipates an end time in which all the children of Abraham will live together in peace. Yet SR members believe that Jews, Christians, and Muslims can participate in something of that end time by entering into "tents of meeting" in which members of the three traditions read their scriptures together in an atmosphere of respectful dialogue and friendship.*

The eschatological dimension of SR practice recognizes that while in the SR "tent of meeting" people whose communities are otherwise at war with each other are sitting down in peaceful conversation. The generosity, friendship, and sense of divine spirit that are released recall to SR members messianic images of the universal recognition of the kingdom of God. This brings us to the liturgical aspect of SR. The word "liturgy" must be used with caution, since SR is clear that it does not seek to create some new syncretism of monotheistic religions and some new amalgams of Jewish, Christians, and Muslim liturgies. Yet there is a ritual and liturgical aspect to SR in the sense that SR practitioners adhere to a reverential attitude toward the scriptures they study and the persons they engage with in study. Also, SR practice follows a series of ideological and practical rules and SR sessions are often started and ended with a formal reading of scripture. SR members often take meals in common before and following SR sessions. Finally, the liturgical aspect of SR can be seen in the belief that many SR members have that an ideal future time, a time of inter-religious peace, is anticipated, "glimpsed" and even "participated in" through SR practice.

Imagining SR practice as a glimpse of the end time is extremely powerful because, as with all eschatological thinking, it necessarily has implications for the present. The new eschatology of SR calls into question some of the exclusivist and triumphantalist aspects of the traditional eschatologies of Judaism, Christianity, and Islam in which one religion triumphs over the other two. One practical result of face-to-face SR readings of eschatological texts of the three monotheistic traditions is that it becomes harder to maintain eschatologies that expect to overcome the religious particularities of each tradition. This allows for the re-imagining of a new type of end-time in which universal peace is won through preserving the particularity of the other instead of obliterating it. Here, the end-time can function as the ideal that pulls the traditions along with it to a future time of human fulfillment, a reign of justice and peace and communion with God. Reading scriptures together as a form of eschatological thinking also recalls past times of rich interaction between Jews, Christians, and Muslims and a beginning time of creation in which the world and the human was created as very good.

C. How Scriptural Reasoning is Done

Given the rules, how is scriptural reasoning actually performed? First of all the conditions for the possibility of scriptural reasoning must be present. This requires participants who are at once dedicated to their religious traditions, knowledgeable in both the discourses of traditional interpretation and contemporary social and human sciences, and willing to read their scripture with others outside their traditions. Before SR sessions begin, thought must be given to the scriptures that will be read. SR practice has been to choose texts from the three traditions that focus on a common figure, e.g. Abraham, or a theme or issue, such as hospitality, or creation, or sacrifice or usury. Scriptures of the Hebrew Bible, New Testament, and Qur'an are the primary texts, but materials from secondary sacred literature are also employed. In SR sessions members are not heavy-handed about "themes", as they find that quickly new themes and issues arise and they want to be free to follow these wherever they lead.

After texts are chosen, attention must be given to where the sessions will be held, what kind of room/space will be used, and how the tables and chairs are to be set up. Scriptural reasoning requires space for small intimate groups of about six to study together as well as a room to bring the small groups together for plenary sessions. Each small group should have representatives of each of the three traditions and it is best to have each tradition represented by more than one person. It is preferable to find a "neutral site" that is not associated directly with one religious tradition, but SR sessions have taken place in Christian, Islamic, and Jewish institutions with good results. However, if these settings are used, it is important that the home tradition not attempt to take special prerogatives in setting or limiting the agenda of the meetings.

It is important to set aside adequate time for both the development of scriptural interpretation and building human relations between interpreters. Multiple two hour sessions work well and small sessions for in-depth study should be followed by plenary sessions in which groups share with the whole group the processes and conclusions that were reached in their small sessions. SR sessions often begin in plenary with brief presentations by knowledgeable participants of historical context, textual problems and overviews on each text that will be studied. It is common practice to begin a small session by reading the chosen scriptures out loud and then a text from one or sometimes two texts from different traditions are focused on. Following on that, small group sessions will address the text from the other traditions and also reflect on the relations between the scriptures. Time is also needed for reflection on the insights gained and attempts to draw these insights together into patterns and conclusions.

Each session requires a convener and this person should have both knowledge of SR theory and experience in SR practice. Note takers are also needed. Egalitarian principles of speech must be respected and protected. This means that the voices of women and men, senior and junior members, critical text scholars and theologians, and representatives of the different traditions are treated equally. To safeguard the cardinal rule of an egalitarian speech situation the convener may have to exercise her authority and intervene in the discussion to quiet a particularly strong voice or bring out a quiet one.

No single religious framework and no single methodological approach to the scriptures is privileged. It is the scriptures that hold the place of privilege and they and not the convener or individual participants are to be placed at the center of discussions. When scriptures are placed at the center they readily become sources of insight, community, and guidance. Respect for the scriptures, however, should not limit interpreters from subjecting them to text critical analyses. However, text critical methods are often turned to early in SR sessions to clarify issues of language, history, and the context and then study moves outward to more general and comparative forms of analysis. As mentioned in the above rules, later sessions of SR include reasoned and critical reflection on the free-flow dialogue on scripture. It is helpful for note takers to share the results of smaller sessions with the larger plenary group. Final sessions in plenary will then involve attempts to pull together the variety of interpretive discoveries for discussion of SR as a second order reflective endeavor and for conversations on the practical applications and implications of SR.

What if we do in our 1ST SR session a focus on passing on faith to youth? A problem we all share.

3

MAKING DEEP REASONINGS PUBLIC

NICHOLAS ADAMS

This essay will make six claims. These claims arise from reflection upon the practices of scriptural reasoning, in which members of different religious traditions meet together for study of their sacred texts. First, scriptural reasoning does not try to ground its own possibility. Its attempts at theory (such as this essay) are not attempts to explain how it is possible, but more modestly and usefully to describe its practices in an ordered way. Second, scriptural reasoning approaches metaphysics as an account of what is taken to be true, not as a means to demonstrate necessary truths. Third, scriptural reasoning relies on the luck of the moment. It is not minutely planned, executed and policed, but opens itself to surprising possibilities which are not prepared in advance. Fourth, scriptural reasoning models a practice of learning traditions' languages. Fifth, scriptural reasoning values and promotes friendship above consensus and agreement. Sixth, scriptural reasoning is a practice of making deep reasonings public. I will conclude that scriptural reasoning is a kind of reparative reasoning which addresses some of the acute needs of today's society while seeming to refuse certain imperatives that often accompany the academy's approach to such needs.

First, the question of grounding. One of the goals of rationalist philosophy has been to explain the grounds of thinking; that is, not only to acknowledge that thinking has grounds but to specify those grounds and even to demonstrate that they are necessary. This goal is not restricted to thinking in any narrow sense, but extends to any enterprise including problems in moral theory. For example, one of the most pressing problems in contemporary moral discourse is how mutual understanding is possible between members of significantly different traditions. This question matters because without

Nicholas Adams
School of Divinity, The University of Edinburgh, New College, Mound Place, Edinburgh EH1 2LX, Scotland, UK

mutual understanding there can be no real conversation let alone argument, and without argument there can be no agreement. Agreements are necessary for the establishment of, and more importantly the legitimacy of, laws. The characteristic rationalist response to this problem has been to try to explain the grounds of understanding. This means not only acknowledging that understanding has grounds of some kind, but specifying them and grasping them fully by means of theory. The legacy of German Idealism makes itself felt strongly here in any speech about "reason" or "rationality". One can claim, for example, that there is a universal reason that underlies and unifies all the various forms or rationalities that different cultures express. The rationalist quest then becomes that of cataloguing these various forms and discovering the universal reason that underlies them. Alternatively one can claim that all reasoning is grounded in tradition. The rationalist quest then becomes that of cataloguing the various traditioned reasonings displayed by different cultures and discovering the ground of tradition that unifies them. The problem with these quests is that they fail. Despite enquiries by some of the most impressive minds of the last two hundred years, there is no convincing account of universal reason or a satisfactory "theory" of traditioned reasoning. The characteristic response to these problems has been either to shift to a mode of enquiry that hypothesises about grounds, rather than discovering them (as one sees in the work of Jürgen Habermas) or to give up on the notion of grounds (as one sees in a good deal of postmodern anti-theory). Thinkers who give up on the notion of grounds tend to use concepts like "incommensurability" when dealing with philosophical topics such as "forms of life" (Wittgenstein) or "lifeworld" (Husserl). It is possible to form sentences such as "our culture and your culture embody different forms of life, and these are incommensurable; therefore there can be no real argumentation between us". Admittedly there are tangles involved in the use of a term like "incommensurable", whose focal meaning is found in the philosophy of science, and "form of life", whose focal meaning is found in discussions of language. But perhaps all that is intended in this kind of claim is the idea that different forms of life have different basic assumptions, and that proper argumentation requires shared basic assumptions at least at some level. These tangles become more severe if one moves away from a notion of basic assumptions, which sounds like a list of propositions, towards more nuanced accounts of rival narratives. One now might say that different cultures teach the art of judgement through different narratives and formations of identity, and that because we have no access to a master narrative that unifies these differences, members of traditions can only rehearse their own narratives in turn, perhaps listening charitably to each other, but never entering into argument. In such an account the public square or public sphere (or whichever geometrical shape one chooses) is a space where participants stand merely waiting their turn to speak, and having spoken, can do no more.

This is not the place to try to diagnose the intricate problems associated both with searches for a unifying reason nor postmodern contentments with successions of narratives. My own view is that because understanding between members of different cultures actually happens, there must be something that grounds this understanding. However, for the same reason that thinking cannot grasp the grounds of thinking, it is fruitless to try to specify this ground or conceptualise it in theory beyond the bare claim that there must be a ground of some kind. This is a lesson learned from the philosophies of Schelling and Schleiermacher as explained by the British philosopher Andrew Bowie, and for reasons of space these will not be rehearsed here.[1] Such a line of argument can be developed to indicate an agreement both with the German Idealists who claim that there is a unity of reason, and with French thinkers like Foucault who claim that any attempt to specify this unity is indistinguishable from a ruse of domination, because to grasp the unity that underlies all diversity is to be able to "place" all opponents and dissenters. Instead of attempting such diagnosis, I wish merely to draw attention to the empirical claim in this chain of reasoning: understanding between members of different traditions actually happens.

Scriptural reasoning is a practice which displays examples of such understanding. In the study of scriptural texts from three traditions (Jewish, Muslim, Christian) participants come to the table with different narratives, different philosophical practices, different presuppositions, and even different scriptures. In the course of study there are disagreements and agreements over a wide range of issues, from the plain sense of the text to the practical implications of certain interpretations. It is possible that this claim is false, and that what one actually has are only apparent arguments, and that in fact one has merely a succession of narratives which may or may not be consonant with each other on certain issues. Adjudicating this question is a difficult matter which will not be pursued here, but if it is seriously doubted that there is understanding and argument between members of different traditions in scriptural reasoning, this matter will need to be properly researched. For now I wish to claim, without defending the claim, that there is understanding and argument between participants in the context of scriptural reasoning.

Scriptural reasoning is a practice which can be theorised, not a theory which can be put into practice. More accurately, it is a variety of practices whose interrelations can be theorised to an extent, but not in any strong sense of fully explanatory theory. Those who practise scriptural reasoning tend to be aware of this, and of its philosophical implications. If one of the problems in (some) modern philosophy is the quest for, rather than the acknowledgement of, grounds then scriptural reasoning exemplifies an attempt to repair this problem. It is possible to describe scriptural reasoning in a way that is content to acknowledge that there must be a "unity of reason" or a "ground of being" or "condition for understanding" without requiring the further step of specifying that unity, ground or condition, or attributing necessity to any philosophical findings. Scriptural reasoning is a practice which invites theoretical description, because it is so interesting, but however sophisticated such theoretical description becomes it will never amount to the "grounding" of scriptural reasoning. Rather, one can be satisfied with the "fact" of scriptural reasoning, and only subsequently attempt to make sense of it.

Before leaving this question, it is possible to indicate some rival claims that might be made about the practice. It might be claimed on the rationalist side that there are, in fact, certain specifiable grounds that render understanding possible. These include common philosophical apprenticeships, common traditional practices and common theological commitments. It is *only* these instances of "overlapping consensus" which render understanding possible in scriptural reasoning, and without them it would fail. On the postmodern side it might be claimed that the claim of understanding is illusory, and is itself a ruse of domination. It suits (some) participants in scriptural reasoning to describe their discussions as occasions for understanding and argument, but this is in fact because misunderstandings and radical differences of view are routinely ignored. I take the view that anyone who believes they grasp the grounds of understanding is in error; this does not preclude the use of such an error as a ruse of domination, nor does it rule out tradition-specific speculations (as opposed to rationalist "graspings") about what the ground might be.

Second, the question of metaphysics. In contemporary discussion there is some confusion about the meaning of "metaphysics" or "the metaphysical". On the one hand metaphysics concerns the nexus of background narratives and commitments that structure our knowing. This includes our sense of the order, or the whole, of things, as well as specific items of dogma. We can call this "taking-as-true" metaphysics, and it is associated with concepts like Jacobi's *Fürwahrhalten*, Peirce's A-reasonings or Husserl's lifeworld. On the other hand metaphysics is associated with a rationalist project of securing our knowing through intuition or demonstration of some kind. It is associated with claims that certain truths are "self-evident" or some variant. In the light of the previous discussion, we might call this "grounding" metaphysics, and it is associated with Descartes' intuitions, Spinoza's geometrical method or Fichte's attempt to discover the necessary grounds of subjectivity. These two kinds of approach to metaphysics are distinguished in this little taxonomy, but it is quite common for particular chains of reasoning to mix them up. For example one might proclaim a commitment to "taking-as-true" thinking, with a corresponding rejection of rationalist projects, while at the same time claiming authority for one's own intuitions. Perhaps this arises because "grounding" metaphysics often dithers between appealing to intuitions or demonstrations, as in Descartes'

Meditations where the thinker intuits the meaning of "God", but seeks to demonstrate the existence of the thinking "I". Descartes is in error because what he seemingly intuits is in fact an inherited part of his tradition, and what he seemingly demonstrates is in fact presupposed.

Scriptural reasoning practises an emphatic "taking-as-true" metaphysics, and tries to cure itself of any tendencies towards "grounding" metaphysics. It treats intuitions and demonstrations as useful and informative claims, but never as guarantees. What one takes as true is indeed metaphysical in the sense that it structures and informs one's knowing: there is no getting around it. This does not make it a guarantee of the truth of one's claims. To acknowledge that one *takes* something as true is to renounce guarantees or self-evidence. What, then, is the status of a "something" that one takes to be true? There is room for argument over this. One can call it a "basic assumption" or a "fundamental narrative", as I did in the previous section. One can even call it an hypothesis. The latter is especially intriguing as it implies that it might be tested in various ways. Whatever the status one gives it, one cannot avoid taking things as true. Whether any particular something must unavoidably be taken to be true by everyone is an interesting question; what seems clear that some something must be taken to be true by someone if there are to be any claims, and any chains of reasoning, at all.

Scriptural reasoning is practised by members of different traditions, and that means that its participants take different things to be true. What, then, is the status of the other's metaphysics? If one calls it a "basic assumption" or a "fundamental narrative" this works quite well. It is an act of courtesy to acknowledge another's different takings-as-true, which are very likely incompatible with one's own. If one calls it an hypothesis then interesting things happen, because such things are, at least in principle, open to being tested in various ways. One can test coherence or comprehensiveness. Even more strikingly, one can test implications: what kinds of practice seem to follow from such takings-as-true?

Treating takings-to-be-true as hypotheses may seem counter-intuitive. After all, basic beliefs are things that people live by and die for. It seems strange to suggest that someone might live by and die for an hypothesis. What is intended here, however, is a useful contrast between hypothesis and guarantee. There may be a better contrast for getting at the different kinds of status that takings-as-true hold. Many Christians would claim to live by faith, rather than by hypotheses or guarantees, and this suggests that the contrast between the latter two kinds of thing may need revising if it is to be of use in discussions involving members of religious traditions, at least those involving Christians. The main point here is twofold, and does not depend on such revision: for scriptural reasoning, another's takings-as-true are openly acknowledged as different and one's own intuitions or demonstrations are neither self-evident, nor do they count as guarantees. This means that members of different traditions may discuss and learn from each other's chains of reasoning that follow from these takings-as-true, and without putting an end to dialogue in advance because one "knows" that such discussion is futile. Admittedly, discussion of such chains of reasoning would be banal if they invariably went their different ways, with each tradition pursuing its own isolated arguments. Among the interesting features of scriptural reasoning are the surprising convergences and divergences that appear between and within traditions in response to the sacred texts being studied: they do not invariably go their separate ways. Although this "fact" throws into doubt certain kinds of talk about incommensurability, we must leave this issue to one side. It may merit further research.

The kind of metaphysical model one holds arguably influences, strongly, the quality of argument and discussion between participants who have different takings-as-true. Treating intuitions and demonstrations as useful tools, but not as self-confirming guarantees, enables all kinds of surprising discovery which might otherwise seem ruled out in advance. It is now worth wondering a little about the kinds of surprise to which scriptural reasoning is open.

Third, the luck of the moment. A strong quest for grounding, which I have said is typical of some forms of modern philosophy, is sometimes intended to serve a model where theoretically secured results can be put into practice. In the case of scriptural reasoning, one can imagine that this might take the form of an attempt to discover the conditions for the practice and then to seek to establish and enforce these conditions in order to maximise the efficiency of its success. One would not even have to be committed to a strong quest for grounding for this to take place. One could have a more relaxed philosophical programme at the same time as a more urgent intent to commodify the practice. Here, one would merely need to notice which conditions for scriptural reasoning tend to yield the most effective results, through trial and error, and then establish and enforce these conditions in a way that successfully promotes the offered "product". My second claim is that the rationalisation of scriptural reasoning has not followed this course. It is true that over time, it has become possible to notice which conditions for scriptural reasoning tend to promote the best practices. By best practices I mean the most fruitful discussions, the deepest and most generative engagements with the scriptural texts and the most profound occasions for learning from each other about participants' traditions of reasoning. It is also true that there is a "Handbook of Scriptural Reasoning" and even "rules" of scriptural reasoning produced by members who have authority within the groups who practise scriptural reasoning. It might look as though the worries that scriptural reasoning conceals its practices of domination are groundless: it seems to display these dominations all too clearly!

Interestingly, scriptural reasoning does not exhibit the desire to control behaviours and commodify its practices. One of the features of scriptural reasoning that make it interesting is the constant surprises that it holds, even for experienced participants. The most fruitful discussions and most generative interpretations of scripture are not necessarily those that occur when most attention has been paid to arranging the optimum conditions. Texts in a tradition which members of that same tradition might view as over-interpreted, or just plain obvious in their meaning, often generate extraordinarily rich discussions and elicit deep insights into more than one tradition. Perhaps it is to be expected that investigating what one takes to be obvious is likely to yield telling information about those for whom something is obvious, but it is nonetheless surprising how *generative* and not simply *informative* these investigations prove to be, and often for all those involved in discussion. By generative I mean practices which invite further discussion, and which yield further insights into the text and its possible range of uses to address practical problems. The important point is that the choice of text is not something that needs to be forced in order to promote success.

Choosing texts for scriptural reasoning is in fact something that is not as controlled as one might anticipate, and this is a useful illustration of scriptural reasoning's general openness to luck. The choice of texts is often delegated to a small group, sometimes as small as two or three persons. Their task is to select two or three texts from each tradition, i.e. from Qur'an, Tanakh (usually Torah), New Testament, which broadly relate to a topic for investigation, such as hospitality, leadership, debt, prophecy and so on. Once these texts are selected, the selection may be discussed briefly with others to check that important texts have not been omitted from consideration. The selection may be revised. The final selection is then presented to the study group or groups. The process is relatively informal and it is rare for there to be strong disagreement about which texts should be studied. In a situation where there is a desire to dominate discussion, one would expect there to be strong bids for control over the selection of texts, given the ways in which such initial decisions might shape discussion. What one actually sees in scriptural reasoning is a willingness to take responsibility for ensuring that proper consideration of the available texts takes place in advance, but not a desire to forbid or insist on the discussion of certain texts. This is seen not only in the initial stages of choosing texts, which as I have said is relatively informal, but also in the actual study itself. It is open to any study group to decide which texts to study together, and for how long. It is thus possible for a group to devote a full ninety-minute session to one short text of three or four lines, or to consider three or four texts which each extends to many verses. No one person or small elite determines in advance how this is to happen: all participants seem willing to see what will happen as the discussion unfolds.

Scriptural reasoning shows itself shaped more by luck than planning. There certainly is planning, but not the kind of planning that seeks control over outcomes. More precisely, the outcomes that planning serves are very general: the best practices I referred to earlier, such as deep and generative interpretations of texts which yield insights into texts, persons and traditions. A concrete example of what scriptural reasoning does *not* do may illuminate this further. It would be possible to plan a study session on the theme of land and dispossession, with a view to getting members of different traditions together in order to promote peace and mutual understanding between those whose traditions are currently making rival bids for occupancy of the same geographical spaces. It would be possible to choose the texts very carefully, perhaps ruling out the potentially most inflammatory texts. It would be possible to choose the groups very carefully, perhaps ensuring that particular, potentially inflammatory encounters were prevented. It would be possible to have the groups led by experienced and charismatic persons with a clear idea of the outcome of the study session, and who might guide discussion if it seemed to depart from the charted course. It would be possible to do all these things, but they would be wild and innovative departures from the normal practices of scriptural reasoning. There might be an occasion when it might be judged appropriate to restrict the range of possible outcomes in this way, but it would be very much against the spirit of openness to luck and surprises which scriptural reasoning exhibits. In some ways, the more anxious one might be about the possible outcomes of scriptural reasoning, the more insistent one might have to be that openness to luck and surprises is vital to scriptural reasoning. Choosing "dangerous" texts is not to be undertaken lightly, and arranging groups in which there is a real possibility of enmity between participants surely needs to be given responsible prior consideration, but if it is anxiety that closes down possibilities in advance, then it is probably very bad scriptural reasoning.

This openness to luck is a possible candidate for a piece of shared theology: shared between all three traditions that currently engage in scriptural reasoning. More recent vocabularies of randomness and accompanying technologies of control, in relation to weather or crowd control, are at some remove from vocabularies of surprise and accompanying techniques of patience and hope. Surprises can be both welcome and unwelcome, and hopes can surely be disappointed. Randomness, on the other hand, is meaningless, whether it brings good things or ill; and control is not so much disappointed as successful or unsuccessful. To be open to luck in the study of scripture is to give up control in favour of patience and hope, and to view outcomes not as the result of random factors but as the endless flow of surprises made possible by . . . by what ever makes such surprises possible (texts? persons? relations? God?). How precisely one might specify this possibly shared theology is a question I do not propose to investigate here. It is enough, for the time being, to note that there is a shared openness to luck, and that this shapes the quality of discussion in scriptural reasoning.

There is one final point to be made about openness to luck. To establish control in the face of anxiety is to indicate a desire to establish a priority of the past over the future. Anxiety codes the future negatively, as an uncontrollable realm of threat and possible disaster. Control codes the soon-to-be-past positively, as a realm of preparation and enforced security. The future is thus not encouraged truly to be the future, but is to some extent determined by the past, and becomes merely the continuation of what is already the case. The more this nexus of anxiety and control determines one's practices, the more the past will be a site of enforcement and violence, and the more the future will be simply more of the past. Such a model presupposes a strong and narrow doctrine of efficient causality, where forces work upon objects, and the only variations are unforeseen or random intrusions into the operation of causality. Scriptural reasoning practises a different relation of the past and future, and a different model of causality. To be open to surprises is to deny that the past causes the future in a strong sense. To describe something as a surprise is precisely to deny a narrow conception of causality. In some ways surprises are descriptions of events that give the future priority over the past. It is not merely that "we did not see it coming", but that there was nothing to see until it came. With respect to a politically sensitive practice like scriptural reasoning, where the histories of the three traditions have each other's blood on their hands, and bones underfoot, this is a significant matter. If there are surprises then the past is allowed to be the past, but it cannot wholly cause the future. There may be surprises in the future that have not been prepared by events in the past but which occur as it were uncaused, unanticipated, unlooked-for. Friendship is made possible not only by repairing the past, if that is even possible, but by being open to the future. A past that is viewed from a perspective of surprising friendship is in some sense a different past from one viewed from enduring enmity. I do not wish in this context too hastily to make a connection between openness to surprises and eschatology, because the histories of eschatological vision in the three Abrahamic traditions are significantly different from one another. The openness to surprises in each of the traditions seems by contrast quite similar to one another. Historians rarely study the future. It seems to me that scriptural reasoning is, in a strange way, one of a number of religious practices which makes this study possible.

Fourth, the question of learning languages. Languages can mean all sorts of things in the context of scriptural reasoning. At the most obvious level, it means the original languages in which the texts were written and transmitted: Hebrew, Arabic, Greek, together with the languages of their commentaries, such as Latin. But it can also mean the patterns of usage, shapes of thinking, ways of describing and judging. One learns the languages of other traditions not with the goal of inhabiting them but in order to hear the deep reasonings in what others are saying. These deep reasonings concern things like kinship rules, eating practices, poetry, folk songs and the languages of elusive desire. The joy of learning another language is the discovery of these things, expressed in fascinatingly unfamiliar ways. Particular languages house histories of wisdom. For members of two different traditions to understand each other on a particular point, they might attempt to converse in a third language that is native to neither. That will work, at least to a degree. But if they wish to understand each other's histories of wisdom, they must learn the other's language. Our children are sometimes, regrettably, taught in school that learning other languages is useful because they will be able to close a sale more rapidly if they speak the "target language". Again, that will work. But we need to teach them that learning other languages makes possible the forming of friendships within which one learns each other's histories of wisdom. We might also acknowledge the inherent beauty of learning languages: it is a good with its own integrity.

Scriptural reasoning is less about the transmission of information contained in texts and more about the establishment and deepening of relations between persons with respect to texts. Learning languages, in the thick sense outlined here, is a central part of that enterprise. No particular approach to learning these thick languages need claim a monopoly. What are needed are excellent models for learning languages. If one looks at the techniques employed in educational institutions, one sees quite proper concerns with grammar and literature and with spending time in the culture about which one is learning. In the case of the three Abrahamic religions, however, it is not enough to learn the grammar of a language and read its literature. It is not enough for students of Islam to learn Arabic and read the Qur'an, although these are necessary. In order to hear the deeper reasonings of Islamic life one needs to hear the interpretation of Qur'an. But even this is not yet relational: it would be sufficient to read a book of interpretation such as a commentary, or perhaps hear a lecture. In order to establish relations between persons with respect to texts, one needs practices which enable multiple interpretations, tested against one another, in contexts in which there is a flow of conversation and argumentation. But even this way of putting things gets things backward. I only make this claim because I am *already* familiar with scriptural reasoning, which in fact performs these practices, and it is probably unnecessary to abstract from this in order to articulate a need which scriptural reasoning seemingly just happens to address. Perhaps it is simpler just to make the claim that establishing relations between persons with respect to texts is a good model for learning languages: the nuts and bolts of grammars and texts and the thicker, deeper reasonings embodied in a language's traditions. There may be any number of such good models. I wish to claim that scriptural reasoning is one of them.

To substantiate this claim, or at least make a start, it is worth drawing attention to some of the things that occur in scriptural reasoning study. The typical study is oriented to at least one text in each of the three Abrahamic traditions. There is also typically at least one person from each of the traditions. There are thus typically at least three texts and three persons engaged in study. If scriptural reasoning were a teaching environment, one would expect the Jewish scholar to expound the Hebrew, the Christian to expound the Greek and the Muslim to expound the Arabic texts. It might be a question of proceeding person by person, text by text, perhaps with questions for clarification. But that is not quite what happens in scriptural reasoning. It is not necessary that a participant introduce her tradition's text. It so happens that discussions have been found to be fruitful if she does, and this is surely not surprising, but it is nonetheless neither necessary nor insisted upon. Instead of the one-by-one procession of speakers, the group will choose to focus on one of the texts, and all participants will engage in its interpretation, generally beginning with the plain sense, and usually with an expert in the language clarifying points where translations are being used, which is almost always. (Few individual participants in scriptural reasoning have a deep triple mastery of Hebrew, Greek and Arabic.) Once the plain sense has been satisfactorily established, or its obscurities deemed to have been satisfactorily identified, understanding this to mean satisfactory for the time being, the discussion moves on to questions concerning how the text might be interpreted to address particular situations either in the past or in the present. In the case of the topic of debt, for example, the questions raised at the time the texts were produced are both different and similar to the questions one might raise today about the relation between misfortune, slavery and God's will for God's people. How one interprets prohibitions on charging interest, the status of strangers vis-à-vis family members, the permissible levels of destitution one may tolerate before taking remedial action and so forth have not ceased to be relevant in the twenty-first century. In interpretive discussions of this kind, the relations of expertise and intellectual authority are interestingly mixed. Some may have a deep knowledge of how a text has been interpreted, others may have a thorough grounding in the range of meanings associated with particular words and concepts, and others still may have a wide-ranging grasp of comparative economics. It is thus a most interesting kind of learning environment.

Scriptural reasoning is not merely an occasion for forms of expertise to be displayed, but an opportunity for relations to be formed and deepened.[2] This kind of insight tends to be couched rather reluctantly in some educational climates. To speak of relations between teachers and pupils, lecturers and students, tends in many people's minds to suggest first and foremost improper relations involving abuses of power and transgressions of social boundaries. This is a remarkable and damaging phenomenon. It is true that there are few betrayals more serious than breaches of trust and distortions of authority in education. Yet it is also true that the reason why these betrayals are serious is that these relations matter. In the university where I work in Scotland, it is increasingly normal for staff to direct students to specialised welfare provision, rather than for staff to take personal responsibility for a student's welfare. This specialised welfare provision is made possible by skilled and dedicated staff, but the division of labour between "education" and "welfare" ensures that those who hold responsibility for welfare have no prior relationship with students in need, and no reason or occasion to continue any relationship established when the student is no longer in need. The split between education and welfare permits and testifies to a further split between information and relations. It is badly one-sided to say that today's education is about information *rather than* relations, but it should be a source of worry that our class sizes are growing as institutions expand, at least in Britain. In the case of the study of religions this is a disaster. To study a different religious tradition is not merely the acquisition of information about that tradition, viewed as an object for inspection. Religions are "living traditions" not only in the sense that they endure and change over time, but in the sense that they are embodied in communities of persons. To get to know a tradition is to get to know those who embody and transmit that tradition. The educational question is how to model best practice in these complex forms of getting to know—*connaître* and *kennen* rather than *savoir* and *wissen*. Scriptural reasoning offers an excellent model because of the ways its practices foster the formation and deepening of relations between persons with respect to texts. A split between information and relations makes little sense in scriptural reasoning, as one's goal is the whole complex of operations involved in learning another's deep languages of tradition, and not simply the acquisition of a commodity-like information. Similarly, the best use of information in scriptural reasoning is its being directed to the purpose of deepening the study of the text: it is not instrumentalised beyond that.

Fifth, friendship rather than agreement. This talk of relations has tilted the discussion away from an impersonal description of learning toward the ways in which participants interact with each other. This raises further questions about what the goals of scriptural reasoning are. The aim of scriptural reasoning is to study texts as deeply and as wisely as possible. It is not the aim of scriptural reasoning to generate agreement between members of different traditions. This is somewhat surprising. Most forms of inter-religious dialogue place an appropriately high value on consensus and agreement. Very often the problem in the world which motivates a particular inter-religious dialogue requires consensus or agreement in order for the problem to be addressed satisfactorily. For example, it may be that one needs to decide what the content of the study of religions should be for thirteen year old pupils in schools. One might arrange a forum for inter-religious dialogue in order to come to an agreement about how best to decide this kind of question. Scriptural reasoning is not opposed to consensus and agreement but these are not its goals. Scriptural reasoning values friendship above consensus.

Friendship is a difficult category to use well in discussions of study. It is tempting to think of friendship as a private matter. Friends are those we welcome into our homes late at night, accompany on adventures (even minor adventures like shopping), invite to weddings. We do not necessarily study with our friends; we study with colleagues. Colleagues have the tact to leave our homes before it gets late, and we generally see them at funerals rather than weddings. With this kind of taxonomy it is very difficult to produce a good account of more public kinds of friendship, and it is significant that in the Christian tradition such discussions struggle badly with the narrowness of English and often seek to recover Greek distinctions between *eros, philia and agape*. A language closer to that of Quakers is perhaps needed to grasp more public and unsentimental forms and descriptions of friendship. Scriptural reasoning displays the characteristic of a society of friends, in the public sense. It fosters friendships of an unsentimental kind between participants, and if for some it has been accompanied by adventures, meeting late at night in people's homes and going to weddings, this is not primarily because it has generated private friendships but because it has called into question the privacy of certain kinds of religious practices. The problem with friendship is in some ways the same as the problem with religious life in the contemporary world: *both* have come to be described as private matters.

The friendship promoted by the practices of scriptural reasoning is just as little private as the religious life those practices presuppose and knowledge of which they seek to deepen. This has implications for the role of consensus and agreement within scriptural reasoning. Because the goal of scriptural reasoning is the study of texts, which I have glossed as the formation and deepening of relations between persons with respect to texts, its success is not tied in any strong way to the generation of consensus or agreement. The "*chevruta*" study sessions (and *chevruta* just means a group of friends) are often most fascinating, and sometimes hilarious, when disagreements persist. I do not mean the kinds of disagreement that rest on incompatible basic assumptions or rival narratives, although these are appropriately common too. I mean the deep disagreements that arise over how best to interpret a text in the context of the contemporary problems that motivate the study of that text. Two kinds of disagreement seem to me worthy of note. The first is when disagreements between members of the same tradition are voiced in the company of members of other traditions. There needs to be a significant level of trust between participants before it is safe for Muslims to voice their internal disagreements in the presence of their fellow Jews or Christians. "In house" disagreements are normally shielded from public scrutiny except in times of crisis. Scriptural reasoning has as one of its goals the establishment of such trust. It is thus quite common for disagreements between members of the same tradition to erupt strongly during scriptural reasoning, and I take this to be both a sign of a kind of friendship between members of different traditions which is tacitly acknowledged, and a sign that agreement is not the motor of scriptural reasoning. The second is when disagreements between members of different traditions are voiced in an open and serious way. Disagreements between members of different traditions are the normal state of play in the public sphere: it is what one expects, given the different histories, languages and practices embodied in those traditions. It is, however, a rather different kind of disagreement that arises in scriptural reasoning, because these differences are not at the level of "cultural diversity" but differences of interpretation of sacred texts. These kinds of disagreement are of different types. It is possible for a Christian to disagree with a Muslim over how to interpret a passage in the Qur'an, or for a Jew to disagree with a Christian over how to interpret a passage in the Torah, or for a Muslim to disagree with a Jew over how to interpret a passage in the New Testament. In the first case, the Christian is dealing with a text that is not authoritative for her, but which is authoritative for the Muslim. In the second case, the Jew is dealing a text that is authoritative for both him and the Christian. In the third case, both the Muslim and the Jew are dealing with a text that is authoritative for neither. These different kinds of relation to authority generate different kinds and qualities of disagreement. One might suggest that the handling of disagreements is one of the important ways participants in scriptural reasoning establish and acknowledge friendships. In a context which aims at consensus, disagreement is a problem to be overcome. In a context which values friendship, disagreement is a gift to be treasured. Scriptural reasoning is a practice that sometimes treasures disagreement as a gift.

Sixth, making deep reasonings public. By deep reasonings I mean histories of interpretation of scripture and histories of their application to particular problems in particular times and places. Deep reasonings are not merely the grammars and vocabularies of a tradition, but the relatively settled patterns of their use transmitted from generation to generation. Scriptural reasoning models a practice of making deep reasonings public, by offering a forum, in which mutual learning of languages takes place, unpredictably, among friends, to which an open invitation is extended to those who are interested to participate. Not all scriptural reasoning is emphatically public in this way, but its main annual meetings at the American Academy of Religion, for example, are open to all. The deep reasonings of the three Abrahamic traditions are admittedly not secret: many mosques, synagogues and churches willingly admit guests, and most scholars of the religions are willing to publish their work in journals. At the same time, the quality of public debate between members of different traditions, and no doubt between members of the same tradition, is dangerously low. Many issues that are discussed publicly are ethical, and include familiar questions over the beginning and the end of life, the extent of desirable or legal medical intervention, and the conditions for the public recognition or permissibility of certain social-sexual behaviours. If the deep reasonings of the traditions are not secret, they seem not to be very public when they might most profitably be so. Debates on the radio or television over religious attitudes to reproductive technology tend to be insufficiently informative about both religious attitudes and the technological details, and it is sometimes a wonder that such debates are considered at all worthwhile. The reason for this is doubtless the gloomy estimation programme-makers have of the patience of their audiences, at least in part. It may also be attributable to the lack of faith certain parties have in the persuasiveness of their traditions' deep reasonings. Because of the severe time constraints upon discussions made available through broadcast mass media such as television, other models are needed. Mass media tend not to make deep reasonings public; they tend to over-dramatise rival claims.

Given the religious difficulties surrounding foreign policy, school education and domestic and international law, it is surely a significant problem if the deep reasonings of religious traditions are not made public.[3] Here, emphasis can be appropriately shifted back onto questions of consensus and agreement. It is not the goal of scriptural reasoning to arrive at consensus and agreement, but any process which does have such a goal must reckon with the deep reasonings in religious traditions. There are a number of difficult questions that for reasons of space cannot be pursued here. These include representation: who has the authority to speak for a tradition? They include judicial power: who has the authority to adjudicate disagreements within a tradition? They include the competence of the press: how well informed are religious correspondents? They include coercive power: can members of religious traditions be compelled to share their deep reasonings? Any serious discussion of the formation of consensus and agreement in the public sphere must address these questions satisfactorily. Our concern here is with an earlier stage: the mere possibility of making deep reasonings public.

Scriptural reasoning is a model for making deep reasonings public because it fosters discussion between members of different religious traditions with respect to their most important sacred texts. Precisely because it is not primarily oriented to particular agreements or outcomes that are clearly identified in advance of study, it offers a resource for discovering deep reasonings in ways that are not subject to severe pressures of time or other constraints imposed by mass media. Because of its *chevruta* approach to study, it is not reducible to the transmission of information by religious experts. Scriptural reasoning is probably not the most efficient means for conveying such information, or for generating agreement on important issues of the day. But that does not mean it serves no purpose with respect to these important purposes. Rather, it draws attention to the prior formation that may be required for things like transmitting information or coming to agreement. The practices of scriptural reasoning suggest that making deep reasonings public is not primarily a matter of transmitting information or reaching agreement. Making deep reasonings public may be a matter of being open to surprises, and fostering forms of collegial friendship, by deepening relations between persons with respect to sacred texts. This process cannot be rushed. That means that the urgency of contemporary questions, and the urgent need for consensus, should not be allowed to force the pace of making deep reasonings public. It is the attractiveness of study, not the threat of political disaster, that offers the most promising conditions for this time-consuming but urgently needed process.

What can one learn from these six claims? The promise of scriptural reasoning may lie in its willingness to refuse certain imperatives at the same time as serving them. It refuses the theoretical imperative to ground itself, at the same time as offering a reflective practice that generates useful ad-hoc forms of theory. It refuses the imperative to control outcomes, at the same time as seeking the "lucky" conditions that yield precisely the outcomes that over-control both desires and prevents. It refuses a narrowly linguistic conception of language, at the same time as fostering practices of learning each other's languages which more fully contextualise questions of grammar and vocabulary. It refuses the imperative to generate consensus and agreement, at the same time as hosting forms of study which allow friendships to be established and deepened, and which are themselves the condition for consensus and agreement in the public sphere.

Scriptural reasoning is a "fact": it actually happens. It can thus be investigated, and not only by its own participants. Theoretical claims about it can be formulated, and not only by its participants. Its status in the academy, however, is interestingly precarious and fragile. Its participants do not, as participants in scriptural reasoning, claim any special theological or textual expertise, and this renders them vulnerable in an academy for which expertise is the goal of study, and in an educational milieu for which information is the most highly prized commodity. If scriptural reasoning is not about expertise or information, strong arguments are needed to justify why anyone might bother with it. This essay has attempted to outline the kinds of argument that might address some of these concerns. The stress on relations and luck is not intended to belittle or underestimate the importance of expertise and information, but to serve them better. This is not because expertise and information are the final indirect goal of scriptural reasoning, but because expertise and information are themselves merely tools for addressing real problems in the world. The most obvious of these problems are the damaged histories and relations between members of the Abrahamic faiths. Scriptural reasoning is a reparative response to these problems.

The problems bequeathed by rationalist philosophy are severe: it is still common for public figures to appeal to a basic identity that underlies the differences between religious traditions, and it is equally common for those public figures to attempt to describe that basic identity, with the result that dissenting voices are viewed as an obstacle to peace, rather than as disconfirmation of the identity thesis. It is also common for public figures to claim that there is no identity at all, and that if there is to be any meaningful interaction between members of different religious traditions it must be on the basis of some allegedly non-religious commitment such as democracy or economic benefit. The problem with this is that democracy is not part of the deep reasonings of any of the Abrahamic faiths, and they each explicitly rule out economic benefit as any kind of highest good. Scriptural reasoning is interesting because it makes no attempt to prejudge the actual points of coincidence and divergence between the different traditions. Instead it remains content with the fact that understanding is possible, and submits to the luck of the moment. Scriptural reasoning can thus be seen as an attempt both to repair problems in philosophy and to model best practice in the mutual learning of the deep reasonings of traditions: in public. It is precarious to the extent that it does not try to control and secure its own success. But it is for precisely this reason— namely that it reproduces the basic theological orientation to divine provi- dence found in each of the Abrahamic religions—that it may offer one of the most promising reparative approaches to the study of religions in the modern academy. Time will tell. If we're lucky.

NOTES

1   See Andrew Bowie, *Schelling and Modern European Philosophy* (London: Routledge, 1993) and *From Romanticism to Critical Theory* (London: Routledge, 1997).
2   I owe this insight to Susannah Ticciati; it is elaborated in one of her unpublished short papers on scriptural reasoning.
3   See Jeffrey Stout's timely argument for this view in *Democracy and Tradition* (Princeton, NJ: Princeton University Press, 2004), pp. 1–15. I owe the phrase "making deep reasons public" to Chad Pecknold; see his "Democracy and the Politics of the Word: Stout and Hauerwas on Democracy and Scripture", *Scottish Journal of Theology* Vol. 59 no. 2 (2006), pp. 1–12.

4

HEAVENLY SEMANTICS: SOME LITERARY-CRITICAL APPROACHES TO SCRIPTURAL REASONING

BEN QUASH

Introduction

In this essay I want to highlight four key marks of Scriptural Reasoning (SR). They are its *particularity*, its *provisionality*, its *sociality*, and its readiness for *surprise*. All four embody a certain resistance to finality—which is not (as I hope to show later in this essay) the same thing as a disregard for precision.

The way that the three faiths which currently do SR—Islam, Christianity and Judaism—are today configured in relation to one another is unprecedented. This is true both of their geopolitical configuration and of their configuration in the university. Their common recognition of problems in the contemporary situation (economic, political, environmental as well as scholarly) may also be unprecedented. Scholarly practitioners of these faiths—inhabitants of their respective traditions—now often gather under a single university roof, and may well read and be shaped by the same philosophical, ethical and hermeneutical currents of thought. All three see the capacity of what is thought and transmitted within their respective traditions to affect the peace of the world as a whole; they see the need for right and responsible reasonings. All three have been victims of a modern rationality (enthroned in many universities) that thinks itself "tradition-free" and claims universal validity, seeming to meet no resistances in the complexities of human experience or the uniqueness of particular pockets of historical circumstance and local variation. Many thinkers in the three faiths who now share in SR find this sort of rationality dangerously inattentive: it undermines truthfulness because of the sheer amount it is prepared to leave out of its descriptions (sometimes even concealing the

Ben Quash
Peterhouse, Cambridge CB2 1RD, UK

fact that there is a residue at all), and it is humanly destructive because it makes certain meanings, values and practices "invisible", or apparently indefensible—religious ones included.

SR is committed, then, to *particularity*. Muslims, Christians and Jews in SR insist that responsible thought only ever proves itself by the quality of attention it is able to pay to the concrete and the particular, by the adequacy of its descriptions of the world around it, just as by the adequacy of its descriptions of texts. They find a new possibility for cooperation in this insight, and in the common experience of having their wisdom disregarded or even suppressed by modern ideologies of knowledge. As far as SR is concerned, there is no reason to apologise for speaking from a particular place; there is every reason to acknowledge it. Unlike some forms of inter-religious dialogue, the members of SR speak confidently and enthu-siastically from their own distinctive viewpoints, finding in the specificity of their traditions, their scriptural texts and their convictions the energy that directs them into one another's company.

The *provisionality* of SR is symbolized by the image of a tent. We have called it the "tent of meeting"—a virtual space created by the scriptures and their readers when engaged in the practice itself. As with various "tents" depicted in the scriptures, this tent is not a permanent home for the participants; it is a mobile and temporary space, always determined by the specifics of texts and readers at a given moment of encounter. So the meeting place which is SR is not well symbolized as an unchanging edifice, immune to the influences of context and circumstance. And there is also something open-ended—provisional—about SR's resistance to propositional summation of the fruits of its reasoning. Whilst certain approaches to doctrine (in a Christian context at any rate) downplay its revisability, SR's concern with the power of the Abrahamic scriptures continually to unsettle their respective traditions and to foster inexhaustible discussion is another aspect of its provisionality. (I will return to a fuller discussion of this later in the essay.)

This links then to SR's *sociality*. It is an activity of irreducibly particular gatherings of *people*. They supplement one another's insights, and challenge one another's assumptions. The interrogative, argumentative and collabo-rative patterns of SR study depend on there being groups rather than individuals at work in response to the scriptural texts on the table. And SR both requires and enables a sensitization to those around us with whom we read, precisely as it fosters a process of sensitization to scripture (our own and others') to go on—partly because it is interested in the religious intentions at work in the reading of scripture, and not just in the texts as objects of historical interest.

And finally, SR is an activity open to *surprise*. The interrogation of one's own scriptures by other voices can have the effect of making the all-too-familiar texts of one's tradition "strange" once again. This heightens one's "pitch of attention" to one's own texts (to quote the poet Geoffrey Hill[1]), as well as to the texts of others. It can therefore lead one to a more vigorous engagement with the texts of one's own tradition, such that the practice of SR deepens a person's relationship to his or her own tradition through the agency of those of other traditions, which can act to unlock the "surprisingness" of texts we thought we knew in productive and generative ways.

In what follows, I aim to show how the virtues of SR as an activity that resists finality is one of its great merits—when the sort of finality being resisted is associated with "tradition-free" theory, or with claims for the superiority of "monological" description and definitive propositional statement. I hope to reinforce this positive construal of SR's critically imaginative, sociable and surprising character by comparing it with certain discussions encountered in a more literary-critical frame of reference. The key discussion partners I have chosen to work with are the "theological dramatic theorist" Hans Urs von Balthasar, the Russian literary theorist Mikhail Bakhtin, and John Beer, Professor Emeritus of English Literature in the University of Cambridge.

The point is to illuminate SR's implicit critique of certain inherited models of text study, of theological thought, and of the exercise of philosophic reason, by analogy with theories that have a literary focus. This will help to cast theoretical light on SR as a practice—though avoiding, I hope, the pretensions of "high theory" which lets its sense of how the objects of its study *should* be ordered take priority over the orderings—or resistances to order—of the objects themselves.

A justification for looking at theories with literary-critical dimensions in the context of this volume is that both literary-criticism and SR are interested in language and in texts as related (Beer's words) to "something we call 'life' . . . —whether it is the life of the individual or that of the culture".[2] Both presume that the way we relate to language and to texts—for example, in the face of the rise to overwhelming authority of scientific language—has effects for "the more immediate fate of human beings in the culture",[3] and both draw us back to the seriousness and complexity of the task of weighing words, as well as of assessing the validity of the workings of the human imagination at a time when it is thrown repeatedly into question.

Balthasarian Dramatics and Scriptural Reasoning

We turn to Balthasar first. Balthasar is a remarkable figure in twentieth-century theology because of the seriousness with which he took the literary (and especially the dramatic) tradition—using it as a source of categories with which to order his fundamental theology. In Balthasar's view, literary drama is a primary place in which human beings seek to orient themselves in relation to questions of ultimate meaning in their lives. Yet drama, for him, is always a patterning of *particulars*—patterned serially in time (in ways that may be analogically related to one another but that are never identically repeated or definitively summative). Balthasar's emphasis on the momentousness and irreversibility of historical action (both Christ's and ours) in what he calls the "theo-drama" of human creatures with their God issues in a positive evaluation of human finitude. A theodramatic sensibility, he alleges, should positively enhance our sense of the significance of each moment of time, and of the action of human agents in time. Drama, and especially the super-drama taken up and transformed in Christ, constrains Christians to acknowledge the fact that finitude and non-repeatable particularity can genuinely mediate the divine purpose. Or, to put it another way, finite people and possibilities can be the bearers of glory. This positive evaluation of particularity is exemplified in Balthasar's belief that the path to holiness—to sainthood—is not principally one of withdrawal from all the contingent aspects of personhood, but doing things that are uniquely one's own to do. Balthasar's use of drama thus shows the same concern with the concrete as can be seen in his theological aesthetics (*The Glory of the Lord*). As in the aesthetics, so in the theo-drama, what is aimed at is a more full entry into specifics, into *particularity*. Becoming holy as an actor in the theo-drama means becoming more distinctively *oneself*:

> For each Christian God has an Idea which fixes his place within the membership of the Church; this Idea is unique and personal, embodying for each his appropriate sanctity.[4]

Balthasar's insistence that revelation always occurs in the medium of the particular yields our first point of comparison with SR. There are of course significant differences between the "Abrahamic" religious traditions in their outlooks on revelation and its embodiment. Nonetheless, despite such differences, participants in SR from Jewish, Christian and Muslim traditions all view their scriptures in the expectation that the particularity of those scriptures (and the particularity of the groups gathered around them as listeners and readers) can in some profound way mediate the divine presence and purpose. Because it is a practice and not a set of concepts, SR acknowledges the inescapability of the linear and historical, the inescapability too of the limitations of physical, creaturely space, and of specific written words in texts. But, in line with the wisdom already internal to each participating tradition, SR *also* teaches that these "limits" of concrete human existence are not necessarily "tragic", and that they need not prevent the expression of the divine life itself, displayed in the ongoing activity and interactions of faithful people in obedient attentiveness to their identity-giving texts. In this respect, SR is a celebration of the revelatory power of particularity in something like dramatic form. It honours the embeddedness in histories and practices of its participating traditions as highly resourceful forms of specificity—not so much getting in the way as giving all of them things that are "uniquely their own to do" in the quest to discern and receive God's purposes.

With this celebration of particularity goes a certain honouring of the complex richness of meaning that emerges when texts are read for their own sake rather than for the sake of extracting a conclusion from them or putting them to work to achieve certain preconceived aims. I quote below a passage from a book by J. Neville Ward on prayer, called *The Following Plough*. It is very striking for the way in which what it seeks to say about poetry, as against prose, is very much the sort of thing that Balthasar would say about drama, and that participants in SR might say about the interpretations which are allowed interplay around the table (or in the "tent") when Jews, Christians and Muslims read together:[5]

> T. S. Eliot once said that prose is the language of ideals, while poetry is the language of reality. It is an idea that surprises people and makes them think at first that it is the wrong way round, that surely prose deals with reality, poetry with ideals. However, if you stay with it you see the kind of truth it has. Prose, using logical procedures as traditionally understood, is the appropriate vehicle for coming to a conclusion, making a practical recommendation, finding a solution to a problem. Poetry is the kind of language in which a whole situation is presented and its feeling communicated, so that you know what it means to see a certain segment of reality with your whole feeling self, to contemplate a person or an object sympathetically enough for it to exercise its full force upon you. Pages of prose could be written to set out what Blake's poem "The Sick Rose" is about, but, however full such treatment might be, something, indeed the all-important thing, eludes that procedure. You can find the poem real, and presumably share something at any rate of the experience of the poet, only by living encounter. You have simply to read the poem and you will come face to face with it.[6]

Neither drama, for Balthasar, nor SR, for its participants, is going to lend itself easily to the tidy business of "coming to a conclusion, making a practical recommendation, or finding a solution to a problem". The monological character of much prose may make it a thoroughly useful vehicle for presenting a series of events as a *fait accompli*, and for suggesting a finished product from which all the intermediate disagreements and conflicts have been ironed out (another way of characterizing such a style—which, following Hegel and Balthasar, I have developed elsewhere—is as "epic"[7]). Prose, in Ward's terms, is thus a genre good for instrumentalised uses. But much is sacrificed thereby. Drama, meanwhile, is the kind of genre in which "a whole situation is presented and its feeling communicated". And SR has this quality too, which is why it is so hard to capture in written summary form. Susannah Ticciati recognizes this in her essay when, following Eco, she discusses the "indefinite array of associations" that the texts (read symbolically) open up for their readers. These are not to be foreclosed. Just as was the case when reading "The Sick Rose", so in the interpretative activity of SR: "the symbol can never be left behind in favour of its interpretation".[8]

What, for Ward, seems to characterize poetry most certainly characterizes drama for Balthasar. It finds its realization through calling its audience to a "living encounter". Something *authentic* is opened up by this encounter (Ward calls it the "all-important thing"); something that we reach when (for example) *sympathy* is allowed a role in our knowing activity, thus enabling a new quality of knowledge—perhaps even, in some cases, a special kind of knowledge not attainable in any other way. It enables one to see a part of reality "with one's whole feeling self". For Balthasar, though, the theological value of poetry too is limited.[9] It would not surprise him that its commendation here, by Ward, is in the context of a book of devotional writing. Poetry of the sort Ward is referring to works with the perspective of immediate feeling and individual association. It is what Balthasar (again borrowing categories from Hegel) would call "lyric" in its generic character: it works by the individual's integration of metaphors, images and associations, and this can have the consequence that the shared, public world of experience and action is either assimilated or excluded from consideration. Balthasar says that this "lyricism" results in "a romanticism remote from reality" and in the Church produces a pious but largely "affective" theology.[10] Drama's appropriateness to the expression of Christian theology, meanwhile, is demonstrated in the interaction of individual persons with one another, and with the collectively-held content of Christian faith. The "truth" of this revelation is a truth that discloses itself not only in terms of life and decision, but also incorporation in a community.

Our examination of Balthasar's use of the category of drama has helped us to see SR as a fundamentally "dramatic" practice—a practice that does not seek a "finished product from which all intermediate disagreements and conflicts have been ironed out" (see above), and which is irreducibly communal. SR shares these features with the sort of Christian theology Balthasar aims to commend in his work. Indeed, my experience is that a "theodramatic" *Christian* theology like the sort Balthasar wants is often directly served by SR activity, because of the way it enlivens in Christian theologians an appreciation of the sociality of religious reading and interpretation (the fact that theological knowledge cannot be divorced from relationship with God and others; from sympathetic, "living" encounter). SR seems to serve the "internal" quality of theological engagement of the other two of its participating traditions in a comparable way—that of Jews and Muslims as well as of Christians. It (re-)emphasises for each tradition the fact that sociality around scripture is at the core of its shaping of religious identity, while at the same time extending this sociality (and therefore perhaps also those identities) to a new compass.

Incorporation in a community of living encounter is not only one of SR's preconditions, it is also its *modus operandi*. Once again, Ticciati's essay captures this well, especially her concluding remarks on the way that scriptural interpretation in community (SR activity *a fortiori*) entails a new discovery by each person of a centre that is outside herself (in my terms, this is a surpassing of the merely "lyric"). The text can no longer be read as a reflection of oneself; the encounter with the text can no longer be merely and enslavingly dyadic, such that I exhaust its meaning and it exhausts mine. Ticciati's suggestion is that SR breaks this vicious hermeneutical circle, for it brings us face to face (literally, in the facing of other interpreters) with what she at various points calls a surplus of signification—one that can resist and interrupt my "humanly constructed identity".[11] The theodramatic character of SR is, on this account, embodied in the claims of *other readers*. The creativity of SR thus happens paradigmatically *in community*, as our imaginations are sparked by the unexpected insights of others.

We close this section, then, helped by Balthasar to recognise patterns of resistance in SR that are comparable to the patterns of resistance enacted in his theological dramatic theory. We find a comparable affirmation of *particularity* as capable of revelation; an affirmation of *provisionality* in the chastening of epic (or prosaic) modes of reasoning and expression; and an affirmation of *sociality* in the chastening of lyric ones.

We turn now to our second "sympathetic" theorist: Mikhail Bakhtin.

Bakhtinian Theory of the Novel and Scriptural Reasoning

In turning to Bakhtin's claims for the novel, we in one sense continue a response to the question of genre raised with the help of J. Neville Ward in the previous section—asking whether there might be other genres than drama that get beyond the "monological" and instrumentalised uses of prose, and (when it is divorced from community) the enslaving self-referentiality of lyric. We also continue to ask what insights these critical explorations of different literary genres (and their adequacy in illuminating different aspects of human experience, and in serving different human purposes) can offer to a theory of SR. The section that follows will therefore find itself maintaining a concern with the qualities of particularity, provisionality (or open-endedness), sociality and surprise that are ineradicable from human life in a concretely historical world; qualities which SR honours (while some literary and philosophical approaches—not to mention some theological modes of reasoning—do not).[12]

Bakhtin thought there had been a widespread failure of literary criticism to do justice to the novel in its own right. Poetry seemed to him to receive extensive treatment as a form of literary "art", while the novel was treated as debased and hybrid, haphazard in its use of the purer forms of the language of "poetics", heavily diluted with "non-" or "extra-artistic" discourse. Bakhtin, by contrast, called the novel the "genre of genres", and attempted to redress the injustice done to it.

He did this first by celebrating the very thing the literary critical establishment (in his view) disparaged: the novel's affirmation of the aesthetic value of the ordinary—its use of everyday speech. Vigour and creativity, both social and individual, are sustained and renewed precisely in and through such everyday speech, he argued. This in fact is where I imagine his defence of the "prosaic"[13] quality of the novel would lie if J. Neville Ward's critique of prose were put to him (the critique of prose as using "logical procedures", for instance). Bakhtin frequently attacks the sort of "monologism" that would frame the superabundance and indeterminacy of novelistic facts in the terms of a unifying explanatory theory. The multiple meanings generated in the movement and interpenetration of people's everyday communicative activity (meanings that the novel so sensitively registers) cannot be exhaustively mapped. No all-encompassing pattern is exhibited by them. They represent a myriad "tiny and unsystematic alterations", all of which contribute to the continued making of language and culture, and they do so, often, in wholly unpredictable ways.

Second, Bakhtin celebrates the novel's unfinalizability. Again, a contrast with Ward's criticism of prose emerges here. Unfinalizability is for Bakhtin that which most nearly shares the character of "real historicity".[14] It is a concept that reflects his commitment to ethical responsibility and his belief in the manifold possibilities present to us in every moment in our real lives in time (a reality which the novel can honour and reflect). Unfinalizability safeguards the reality of individual and social creativity and freedom in the midst of unfolding processes and events in time. Every reality "is only one of many possible realities; it is not inevitable, not arbitrary, it bears within itself other possibilities."[15] There is room here for human agency and choice, in shaping what comes to pass in the ongoing development of the world's story.

And finally, dialogue, which for Bakhtin reflects the "nonself-sufficiency" of the self.[16] "Life by its very nature is dialogic", Bakhtin writes. "To live means to participate in dialogue: to ask questions, to heed, to respond, to agree, and so forth. In this dialogue a person participates wholly and throughout his whole life: with . . . eyes, lips, hands, soul, spirit, with his entire self in discourse, and this discourse enters into the dialogic fabric of human life, into the world symposium."[17]

In the view of Gary Morson and Caryl Emerson, real dialogism as Bakhtin advocates it will "incarnate a world whose unity is essentially one of multiple voices, whose conversations never reach finality and cannot be transcribed in monologic form". The unity of the world will then appear as it really is: "polyphonic".[18] The world is depicted enthusiastically by Bakhtin as like a great and chaotic medieval fair or Rabelaisian carnival, in which the merging and hybridization of languages is the healthy and creative norm. Images of perpetual surplus abound here. All the participants supplement each other, each having the richness of a unique field of vision, but each profiting from the bounty of the vision of those around her, which is necessarily additional to her own, and helps to fulfill (though never to finalize) her own sense of herself.

Bakhtinian theory carries within it a strong critique of a certain model of Idealist thinking—of the exaltation of a pure universal subjectivity, a single "field of consciousness", capable of comprehending all things together (itself included). Such Idealism is a means of rendering rationality monological, in Bakhtinian terms, and of making the raw material of the empirical, human world fit its organizing concepts. As a mode of protest against monologism, Bakhtinian theory is also, it seems to me, pre-eminently a dramatic vision, and it is defined over against the epic one, just as Balthasar's dramatic vision is. It is a dramatic vision, even when talking about the novel, because it is concerned with the encounter and interpenetration of discourses. A dramatic approach to the characterisation of reality can combine many styles. It, like the novel, can be a "style of styles, an orchestration of the diverse languages of everyday life into a heterogeneous sort of whole".[19] And if its characterizations are good, it does not finalize the lives and thoughts of its characters and the events they undergo, but evokes the "endlessly forward momentum"[20] which, for Bakhtin, also characterizes historicity.

It is worth emphasizing that Bakhtin was aware of the difference between his vision of diversified polyphony, and mere *cacophony*. He did not suppose that a lot of random, unconnected voices all speaking at once was to be celebrated as a blow against monological form. He sought literary theory capable of appreciating the immeasurably important reality of voices that genuinely *interact* in time—and he did allow the language of unity (*always provided* it presupposed diversity, rather than seeking to deny or suppress it) to have a place in this regard. Admittedly, he leaves such ideas rather vague, but they are of great importance. They have something to do with the way that "[i]n conversations with independent participants arguing intensely about matters of great concern to them, the whole may have a unifying spirit, regardless of the divergence among positions".[21] We may lack an easy vocabulary for that kind of unity, and that may be one reason why we lapse quickly into scepticism about its possibility. Where static unities are concerned, we can always give them the name *structure*, and we discriminate between kinds of structure. But there is value in searching out appropriate terms and metaphors for "the unity of event, and for the different kinds of "eventness" we have experienced".[22]

SR seeks to encourage just such "dialogization, and conflictual interaction" as Bakhtin advocates. The imaginative labour of SR experiments with activating and developing some of the latent potential of the "heteroglossia" represented by the sacred texts of the different Abrahamic traditions, the wisdom their worlds of language and thought may prove able to impart in the right situation. The Scriptural Reasoner, like the novelist and the playwright, can draw "dotted lines"[23] between texts that in everyday life have not yet entered into a profound dialogue—and some of which have, and have more to say to each other.

Conflict between texts will be a valuable element of this process. Part of what stimulates the energetic labour that is SR are the tensions that arise (or the gaps that open up) between the texts being studied. The texts—especially when read in each others' company—present difficulties of interpretation. But (in a rabbinic vein, which itself positively celebrates the *intra*-scriptural challenges of the Hebrew Bible), SR tends to see the *inter*-scriptural challenges of reading across Jewish, Christian and Muslim traditions as signs of the generosity of our scriptural texts, and not simply as regrettable problems. Why talk about "generosity" in this context? Because debate over the texts creates a community of argument and collaborative reasoning. The texts are together *creative* of a community of discussants. And this may be a more desirable, flexible and time-sensitive "product" of the texts than any body of doctrine would be. The participants in SR are not asked to come to agreements that can always be summarized in propositional terms. They are not first and foremost concerned with agreement on "doctrines". High quality argument may in the end be a better "product" of SR (if that is a suitable term to use at all) than any agreed statement would be, and a more desirable thing to transmit to those who enter the tradition which this practice generates. I sometimes catch myself imagining what it would mean for my own church (the Anglican Communion) if it saw its task not so much as achieving agreed statements as improving the quality of disagreement, and if it saw part of its best and most generous legacy to future Anglicans as being the transmission of these high-quality debates. To be given a debate might be as enriching as to be given a doctrine. That is after all what is achieved by the passing on of midrash in Judaism. (There is an illustration here of one of the things the activities of the *tent* are able to offer back to the activities of an individual religious *house*.) What is taught here is that dramatic tension between a plurality of perspectives is not always a sign of failure in the human appropriation of truth; it may be the disclosure of a deeper level of truthful reality than our rational minds are accustomed to allow us to appreciate.

It is time to conclude this section. In doing so, we may see that Bakhtin's categories have much to offer a theoretical articulation of what SR represents as a practice. SR rejoices in the "heteroglossia", if not quite of a "world symposium", then at least of the diversity of its Abrahamic religious traditions; the "perpetual surplus" of perspectives that is embodied in their texts and in the speech of their adherents. It has something robustly "colloquial" about it, too—by which I mean its interest in native forms of expression that can enter into unapologetic and often very entertaining interplay, rather than in some standard form of academic discourse by which such native speech is disciplined and to which it is told it should be aspiring. It finds creative life in the everyday speech of the traditions—an insight into the inner dimensions of these traditions as brought to the surface in their non-defensive self-expression. And this fact of the traditions "being themselves" in the way that they speak is celebrated by the other traditions at the table, such that one of SR's effects is one which Bakhtin would thoroughly approve—namely, to "reaccentuate the discourses of ordinary life" (see above).

Perhaps the most intriguing suggestion that Bakhtinian theory offers to SR is, as we have seen, the suggestion that really interesting unity is "not the unity of a single proposition, however complex";[24] it is instead some sort of "unity of event". I have indicated that Bakhtin attributed deep importance to experiences of "dialogic" concordance (for example, "the unified 'feel' of a conversation"), and he indicated his belief that when we meet such unity and appreciate it properly, we are nearer to understanding the "unity of 'truth' ". There is an ongoing need for SR to defend theoretically the value it finds in the "feel" of its conversations (and the very intense experiences it has of such "unities of event"). It is not concerned, as I have said, with propositional agreements. But it lives from achieved moments of " 'dialogic' concordance" that are as much to do with a growth in relationship between the people involved, with a concomitant mutual attunement to the concerns and habits of thought each participant has (which is why really good SR study only takes off after two or three days of intensive work with texts in small groups), as it is to do with intellectual insights or conceptual convergence.[25]

Bakhtinian theory has helped once again to bring into sharp focus the indispensable role played in SR by its multiple participants, in their irreducible *particularity*, in the *sociality* of their dialogical encounters, and in the unforecloseable *provisionality* of their ongoing conversation.

We now turn to our final interlocutor.

Against Finality

In the opening section of this essay I indicated four "marks" of SR on which I wanted particularly to concentrate. We have spent a good deal of time already looking at its *particularity*, its *provisionality* and its *sociality* in a way that has aimed to give them theoretical illumination by analogy with the theories of Hans Urs von Balthasar and Mikhail Bakhtin. The fourth mark, less developed so far, is *surprise*, which is related to both of the others inasmuch as (i) the open-endedness of the practice (its thoroughgoing historicality) means that it is never wholly programmable in advance—and hence it is always capable of surprising; and (ii) the presence of genuinely diverse readers and their readings in new social combinations means that texts previously thought familiar become newly, and surprisingly, strange. Though it has already been implicit (and lightly touched on) in our examinations of the unpredictability of "drama" and of "polyphony", the category of surprise will therefore be the explicit concern of this final section.

In discussing it, I will draw on a short but richly illuminating essay by John Beer, delivered as his Inaugural Lecture in the University of Cambridge in 1993, and entitled *Against Finality*.[26] It is a remarkable survey of a great sweep of the English literary tradition, from Shakespeare to Pound, Woolf and Eliot, with especial interest in Milton and Wordsworth. It also becomes, through exquisite reading of these writers, a meditation on large issues to do with the way that English-speaking culture has reflected on meaning and possibility in human life through a finely balanced task that involves sometimes *fixing* and sometimes *freeing up* the meaning of language.

Beer quotes Virginia Woolf, writing in her diary in 1940. Her concern was with "inventing a new critical method" with which to do better justice to her own literary art and its responses to the world, and she is inspired in this by the language of Shelley and Coleridge and their ability to get somehow to the heart of things in the way they write. What is so interesting from the point of view of SR is that she does not suggest that the answer is achievable simply by an elimination of all multivalence in the use of language:

> How delicate & pure & musical and uncorrupt [they] read. . . . How lightly and firmly they put down their feet, and how they sing; & how they compact; and fuse; and deepen. I wish I cd invent a new critical method—something swifter & lighter & more colloquial & yet intense: more to the point & less composed; more fluid and following the flight, than my [Common Reader] essays. The old problem: how to keep the flight of the mind, yet be exact.[27]

In describing the literary challenge in this way, Woolf represents (as Beer shows) an age-old tension: "the intensity that is generated by a need to bridge the gap between precise weighing and valid imagining".[28] It is, as she says, "the old problem", and it is heightened in the modern period by the continual pressure exerted on language by the new sciences—the natural sciences—which look to language to mediate authoritative interpretation in unambiguous usages. (Once again, something like J. Neville Ward's category of the "prosaic" rears its head.) This expectation has ramifications in other academic disciplines, too—such as the historical sciences. Beer remarks how:

> an implicit argument . . . can be traced throughout the nineteenth century between a dominant party inspired by Carlyle, demanding statements of finality that would lead to decisive action, and a few

more ruminative writers, such as Tennyson in *In Memoriam*, who combined their acceptance of brute fact with the keeping of a mind open to every possibility.[29]

If the history of letters is an ongoing conversation between "weighers" and "imaginers"—between devotees of finality and devotees of possibility—there are nonetheless those who strive to capture both sorts of "devotion" in their writing. Woolf, as we have just seen, is one of them in her simultaneous concern to be "more to the point" and yet "less composed; more fluid". Another is Wordsworth, and yet another is Milton. Beer reflects on Wordsworth's creative use of "moments of unbalance" in his poetry,[30] and highlights in particular the way he often sets together and weighs apparently "incompatible experiences" (often in the use of a single word or phrase whose disparate meanings cannot be rendered simple),[31] thus positioning himself in an extraordinary role of *accountability* to the (presently, at any rate) *irresolvable*. In this accountability to the presently irresolvable, the vocation of *weighing* is expressed in the accountability—which cannot be irresponsibly vague or casual, but which cannot be decisively exact either (as that would be irresponsible in a different direction). And the vocation of *imagining* is expressed in ongoing openness to the irresolvable, and particularly in a readiness yet to be surprised by it. For example, in the poem written a few years after the death of his young daughter ("Surprised by joy—impatient as the Wind"), Beer discerns in the use of a single word ("vicissitude") how Wordsworth's desolation at a loss—which at one level he regards as absolute—allows itself to be disrupted in the subtlest of ways by a "lingering sense" that the physical world is not in the end the real one—this sense also "witnessed to . . . by his regularly placing the Immortality Ode at the end of his collected poems". This refusal of absolute finality in a matter of life and death:

> always . . . kept alive in him the sense of a Miltonic "perhaps". Perhaps the most bitter of desolations, including even the one described here, might yet open out into a quite different ordering of things.[32]

In Milton's *Paradise Lost*, the account of the War in Heaven is a similarly poised evocation of a "perhaps" that brings dramatic surprise liberatingly into view. The war is, in Beer's terms, itself one between weighers and imaginers—"an allegory of the working of that supreme poetic imagination which made Milton . . . the hero of his own poem".[33] The "weighers" in this instance are the rebel angels, whose terms "were terms of *weight* / Of *hard contents*, and full of *force* urg'd home".[34] They are, of course, crucial to the poem's dynamic—but "they have not fully grasped the semantics of heaven, by which terms of weight can be overcome by arguments of light".[35] Eventually comes the moment when God the Father's chariot appears, driven by the Son:

Attended with ten thousand thousand Saints,
He onward came, farr off his coming shon...

This is a magnificent moment of surprise, especially for the loyal angels who have "succeeded in standing fast against those who were trying to impose their own version of finality".[36] The divine Son is "by his own first seen", and, as Milton tells us, in that moment "them unexpected joy surpriz'd". There is an especial attractiveness in the fact that what is shining is "His coming!"—not a mere object, but a happening, an event. As Beer puts it, "in those words simple light is overcome by illumination".[37]

SR shares with much of the literary tradition a concern to reflect on the possibilities for meaning and action latent in language and in texts. It is a mode of scriptural study that is positioned unusually because it has a relationship both to the academy (which has a strong set of principles about how religious texts are to be read responsibly as *historical* texts) and to communities of faith (which look to these texts to speak to them in the present and shed new and surprising light on their contemporary quests and dilemmas). In the present environment, and especially to those in the academy, it may seem that SR is an activity only for "imaginers", who in a rather playful way conjure "perhapses" from their texts in order to surprise and entertain each other. If true, this would be a concern with surprise for surprise's sake. The "weighers", looking on with a measure of worried disapproval at these irresponsible antics, would on this account be the historical-critical scholars, and they would be right to be worried, for the reading activity of unanchored imaginers would more than likely be mere eisegesis.

In fact, I think that this would do an injustice to SR, which is much more concerned (like Virginia Woolf) to find a new critical method that is both "exact" and yet *also* allows for the "flight of the mind". Its sense is that texts which by their traditions have long been regarded as communicating divine self-disclosure (their traditions having lived in this expectation—without disappointment—for centuries), have to be read in a way that allows for the surprising possibility that they may still "speak" in the present in ways not reducible to what they have "said" before. They may be the vehicles for a "coming" analogous to that of the Son's chariot in Milton's vision—an event of illumination. The marks of a good reading will be not only its semantic precision, or its awareness of the context of a text's composition, but also (to echo Woolf again) its "delicacy", its ability to "sing", its capacity to "compact and fuse and deepen" by its resonance with the experience of its readers. This will often come about through moments of "unbalance", in which the text does not do clearly what we expected it to, or what we thought it *ought* to do. But none of this is to say that exactitude is of no account. One of SR's greatest debts is to rabbinic midrash, whose "seeking" of meaning in the text is classically embodied in a concern for the *"peshat"* as well as the *"derash"*. The quest for deep senses of scripture—the quest after "valid imagining", in Beer's terms, which allows the present to be illuminated by hidden resources in a text that often emerge as surprises— cannot be divorced from careful and accountable attention to its plain sense. Attention to the plain sense of texts is not something that is considered optional in SR; as in midrash, a strong grasp of the plain sense is a necessary preliminary to the opening up of deep sense readings—and the plain sense is never left behind even when the sense deepens and takes on, for example, what my own Christian tradition would call allegorical, tropological, anagogical and other meanings.

In sum, our borrowing from John Beer enables us to say that the participants in SR are weighers as well as being imaginers. They are weighers, but they like to introduce "perhapses". And as Beer says:

> One needs only articulate one or two possibilities . . . to see the extraordinary subversive power that can be generated by that lightest of words: once introduce it and the discourse of finality bearing down on its opponents, is transformed into an invitation to debate and to the mutual exploration of possibilities.[38]

SR invites Jews, Christians and Muslims to just these things—to debate and the mutual exploration of possibilities. Beer remarks in his essay that one of the drawbacks to certain kinds of literary theorizing is that if one carries on with them for too long literary texts can lose their power to surprise—and it might be said that certain narrowly historical or heavily doctrine-laden modes of reading scriptural texts has just the same effect on *them*. SR acts as a corrective to such modes of reading, in the service of (Beer's words) "that best sort of surprise which opens out a new dimension in what we thought we thoroughly knew".[39]

Conclusion

SR creates a ground for meeting between the Abrahamic faiths which is not neutral (justified by some fourth rationale external to the three) but which invites the participants to be themselves in pursuing an activity they are all familiar and at home with within the life of their respective religious traditions: the reading of scripture. I hope this essay will have helped to illuminate some of the key marks that help it to achieve what it does. Because they all read scripture, the resources for dialogue thus open up from *within* each of the traditions, as the participants pursue an activity native to those traditions (this is the mark of *particularity*). The difference is that this reading is interrupted and illuminated in new ways by taking place in the presence of readers from the other two religious traditions (this is the mark of its distinctive *sociality*). These others are invited to co-read, to ask questions and become contributors to the process of suggesting possible answers to the questions (an ongoing process—this is the mark of *provisionality*). And one of the common consequences of this is that the texts open up unexpected meanings for those whose sacred texts they *are*, even at the same time as participants from the other Abrahamic traditions learn more about a text that is *not* theirs (this is the mark of *surprise*).

As well as a form of scholarly resistance to the restrictiveness of certain dominant modes of intellectual enquiry, SR offers a new paradigm of inter-faith encounter; a genuine alternative to the idea that all religious systems are instances of a universal type, which asks them to find common agreements at the level of concepts (whether ethical or metaphysical). Its new paradigm is marked by a concern with the "internals" or the particularities of the Abrahamic religious traditions. It stands against the pretensions of "tradition-free" rationality. The concern with the irreducible particularity of texts and practices of textual interpretation in the three faith traditions—and the refusal to synthesize particularities or prematurely to generalize across boundaries—can be seen as a model of respect for particularity in other areas too: the irreducibly particular liturgies, art-forms, histories, polities and so on of the Abrahamic faiths. In various ways, these topics of study are places where the "internals" of the faiths are notably "externalized". The challenge is to relate to them in such a way that their inner dimensions of intentionality and their deep rehearsal of identity are not lost to view. With its respect for people and texts, and their unprogrammable interactions in time—and with its concern for the religious meaning the texts have in the present (their generative power to open new possibilities of thought and action) as well as what they may have meant in the past—SR goes a long way to meeting the challenge. And, as I have indicated, it does so in a way that has far wider implications for how the pursuit of truth is justified and practised in the modern West—which is why Balthasar (the great critic of the Enlightenment's neglect of the claims of beauty, goodness and concrete particularity in favour of "pure" universal concepts) and Bakhtin (with his vigorous opposition to the all-synthesizing claims of the Idealist philosophical tradition), as well as Beer (with his evocation of the creativity of "moments of unbalance"), have proved such sympathetic conversation partners in this essay.

NOTES

1 Geoffrey Hill, "What Devil Has Got Into John Ransom?" in *The Lords of Limit: Essays on Literature and Ideas* (New York and Oxford: Oxford University Press, 1984), pp. 128–129;

he is himself borrowing the phrase from John Crowe Ransom. My thanks to David Mahan for pointing me to this essay.

2 John Beer, *Against Finality* (Cambridge: Cambridge University Press, 1993), p. 5.

3 *Ibid.*, p. 20.

4 Hans Urs von Balthasar, *Thérèse of Lisieux: The Story of a Mission* (London and New York: Sheed & Ward, 1953), p. xii.

5 I have pursued an analogous line of argument with reference to this passage in an essay expounding Balthasar's dramatics entitled "Real Enactment: The Role of Drama in the Theology of Hans Urs von Balthasar" in Trevor Hart and Steve Guthrie (eds.), *Faithful Performances: Artistry, Embodiment and the Enactment of Christian Identity* (Aldershot: Ashgate, 2006).

6 J. Neville Ward, *The Following Plough* (Cambridge, MA: Cowley Publications, 1984), p. 111; I am grateful to Anna Williams of Cambridge for pointing me to this book.

7 Ben Quash, *Theology and the Drama of History* (Cambridge: Cambridge University Press, 2005), pp. 41–42.

8 See p. 408.

9 This is something I have shown at greater length elsewhere: cf. "Drama and the ends of modernity" in Lucy Gardner, David Moss, Ben Quash and Graham Ward, *Balthasar at the End of Modernity* (Edinburgh: T&T Clark, 1999), pp. 145–159.

10 Hans Urs von Balthasar, *The Word Made Flesh: Explorations in Theology I* (San Francisco: Ignatius, 1989), p. 208.

11 See p. 409.

12 The section that follows is indebted to a discussion of Bakhtin that is also developed in my essay "Real Enactment" (see note 5 above).

13 See Gary Morson and Caryl Emerson, *Mikhail Bakhtin: Creation of a Prosaics* (Stanford, CA: Stanford University Press, 1990), pp. 27ff.

14 *Ibid.*, p. 47.

15 "Epic and Novel" in *The Dialogic Imagination: Four Essays by M.M. Bakhtin*, ed. Michael Holquist, trans. Caryl Emerson and Michael Holquist (Austin, TX: University of Texas Press, 1981), p. 37.

16 "Towards a Reworking of the Dostoevsky Book", Appendix 2 in *Problems of Dostoevsky's Poetics*, ed. and trans. Caryl Emerson (Minneapolis, MN: University of Minnesota Press, 1984), p. 287.

17 *Ibid.*, p. 293.

18 Morson and Emerson, op. cit., p. 61.

19 *Ibid.*, p. 17.

20 *Ibid.*, p. 184.

21 *Ibid.*, p. 256.

22 *Ibid.*

23 *Ibid.*, p. 247.

24 *Ibid.*, p. 237.

25 That said, there may be a further task to be undertaken (as Nick Adams points out when discussing SR in his study of Habermas) in distinguishing between the sort of consensus articulated in Habermas's theory of communicative action and theories like it (where participation in shared modes of rationality provide the key to convergence), and the sort of consensus SR is ready to acknowledge as the gift of the divine Other. Cf. Nicholas Adams, *Habermas and Theology* (Cambridge: Cambridge University Press, forthcoming), chapter 11.

26 See note 2.

27 Entry for 22 June 1940, in Anne Olivier Bell (ed.), *The Diary of Virginia Woolf*, vol. 5, (London: The Hogarth Press, 1984), p. 298; cited in Beer, op. cit., pp. 17–18.

28 Beer, op. cit., p. 20.

29 *Ibid.*, p. 4.

30 *Ibid.*, p. 37.

31 *Ibid.*, p. 30.

32 *Ibid.*, p. 38.

33 *Ibid.*, p. 39.

34 John Milton, *Paradise Lost*, vi, 620–621 (Beer's italics).

35 Beer, op. cit., p. 40.
36 *Ibid.*, p. 41.
37 *Ibid.*
38 *Ibid.*, p. 2.
39 *Ibid.*, p. 2.

5

SCRIPTURAL REASONING AND THE FORMATION OF IDENTITY

SUSANNAH TICCIATI

In this essay I seek to explore the practice of Scriptural Reasoning as it pertains to the *formation of identities*. More specifically, I will ask how it can be a locus for the formation of *Christian* identity. If it is not to dissolve into a neutral ground for the meeting of the three "Abrahamic faiths", justified by some fourth rationale not generated from within any of the three,[1] then it must be a practice in which members of each of the three traditions are led deeper into their *own* traditions: in which Jews learn how to be better Jews, Christians how to be better Christians, and Muslims how to be better Muslims. My primary task, therefore, as a Christian participant of SR, is to explore the ways in which SR informs Christian identity: to explore, in other words, a Christian rationale for SR.

How might the practice of SR, in which Jews, Christians and Muslims participate together in a shared reading of their sacred texts, be for the Christian a genuine expression of the Christian vocation? And why might this practice be particularly timely and important today? I will seek to address these questions by asking what is involved for Christians in learning to inhabit the "strange new world within the Bible",[2] reading the biblical story as their *own* story, and so discovering the biblical world as the locus of their identity. If this is how Christian identity is formed, how are Christians to relate to those who read the Bible differently or to those who do not read it at all? This question only arises with any urgency because of the implicit but crucial claim that this strange new world has *universal significance*. As the story of the redemption of the whole of creation in Christ, it pertains not just to Christians, but to all those to whom the gospel is proclaimed: to the whole of creation.

Susannah Ticciati
Department of Theology and Religious Studies, King's College London, Strand, London WC2R 2LS, UK

Perhaps the most obvious (and no doubt also the most common) way to interpret this universality is evidenced in the attempt to inscribe all others into the biblical world, indifferent to, and even against, the grain of their own self-understanding. I will argue, however, that a proper understanding of the *strangeness* of the biblical world entails a rather different interpretation of its universality. More specifically, I will argue that the strangeness of this new world is misunderstood when it is identified with the strangeness, for example, of a remote culture, a strangeness which can in principle be overcome when inhabited fully. I suggest, rather, that the biblical world is *inherently* strange, and so remains strange even to the one who finds her identity within it. For it is the story of radical dispossession: of the loss of one's life in order to save it.[3] This has far-reaching implications. In short, I will argue that the world of the Bible, as a world which can never be possessed, cannot be equated with any particular appropriation of it, but that its strangeness is, on the contrary, embodied in the Bible's *resistance* to interpretation. And I will suggest further that this resistance to interpretation finds indispensable embodiment in the resistance of others to inscription within its universe.

In the context of SR, this means that the Christian will be truest to the identity she is given within the biblical universe, not by trying to inscribe members of the other traditions into it, but by being attentive both to their different readings of the Bible, and to their alternative sources of identity—both of which resist inscription into her Christian universe: in other words, by being attentive to their otherness as Jews and Muslims.

My argument will be rooted in reflection on the biblical story of the Burning Bush, read implicitly through a Christian lens. And this reflection will at certain points be illumined by comparison and contrast with the Qur'anic version of the same story.[4] The argument's hinge will be an analogy between the burning bush and Scripture, such that we may learn from the nature of Moses' encounter at the burning bush something of what may be involved in the reading of Scripture. To come to grips with what happens at the burning bush I will draw on Umberto Eco's semiotics, and in particular his account of *abduction*.[5] I will then seek to pinpoint more specifically the semiotic phenomenon at stake in the story insofar as it is illumined by Eco's account of the "symbol".[6] The parallels drawn will show up even more important differences. This semiotic account of the occurrence will allow us, further, to read the continuation of the story in Exodus 3 and 4 as an unfolding of what has happened at the bush. More specifically, the mission given to Moses will be understood as a reconfiguration of his identity brought about by his encounter at the bush.

By understanding Scripture, by analogy with the burning bush, as *symbol*, it will be possible to draw conclusions from the nature of Moses' transformation about the nature of the identity formation involved in the reading of Scripture. I will then ask what practices of reading Scripture might best make room for this kind of transformation. That is, I will ask what it means practically to read Scripture as symbol, approaching it as Moses approaches the burning bush, and being open to the kind of reconfiguration of identity undergone by Moses in Exodus 3 and 4. My suggestion that SR is such a practice will be reached, not as a timeless solution to a perennial theological problem, but as a response specifically to the situation Christians—and Christianity—find themselves in today.

Miracles

> There the angel of the Lord appeared to him in a flame of fire out of a bush; he looked, and the bush was blazing, yet it was not consumed. Then Moses said, "I must turn aside and look at this great sight, and see why the bush is not burned up." (Exodus 3:2–3)[7]

Here we have what the modern reader, perhaps with a weary and disenchanted cynicism, would call a *miracle*. But let's look more closely at what is involved in this encounter. Moses' attention is attracted by something that has disturbed his field of vision. He turns to examine the disturbing phenomenon in order to make sense of it, to reintegrate it into his world. But what is this world in terms of which all must be explained? It is, first and foremost, a human world. It is the human being who does the explaining. In modern parlance, it is the world defined according to "the laws of nature"; but this is so only insofar as we remember that these laws are *human* constructs, implemented to explain the world, to turn an alien, uncomprehended terrain into a place one can call home: a place one has made one's own.

The Qur'anic version of the story provides us with a further insight into this human world:

> Has there come unto you the story of Moses?
> When he saw a fire and said unto his folk: Wait! I see a fire afar off. Peradventure I may bring you a brand therefrom or may find guidance at the fire. (Surah 20.9–10)

Here, Moses' reaction to the fire is not simply one of curiosity (indeed, the miraculous nature of the fire has entirely vanished); the significance of the fire is that it may be used for the people's end (either as the source of a brand, or insofar as it is a sign of a gathering of people who could offer guidance). The fire is still part of Moses' human world, which is not disturbed until Moses actually reaches the fire. And this human world, it would seem, is one of means to end. It is about *use*.

Returning to the biblical story, might we say that the world in which Moses is at home—the world in which burning bushes are consumed—is the world of human *use*?; and that inexplicable phenomena—"the breaking of the laws of nature"—are reality's *resistance to use*?[8] On this understanding, science, in its more or less sophisticated forms, is the attempt to turn an inexplicable world into a usable one. Establishing causal connections between diverse phenomena, it lays down workable rules for living: "If I do this, then that will happen." It domesticates reality. Miracles, according to this scheme, are occurrences which cause us to come up against the limits of this scientific capacity. This makes for a *relative* definition of miracle: something outside the limits of Moses' scientific capacity might not be outside the limits of ours; we may have developed sophisticated enough techniques to explain non-consumable bushes! In other words, miracles are relative, not to reality and its "laws", but to the humanly constructed world with its laws. This is not, however, to undermine the miraculous in the miracle. That there are limits to our scientific capacity—the capacity to make reality our own—is itself to be taken seriously as indicative of the fact that there is more to reality than human construct and use. Miracles are signs of this *excessive* nature of reality.

Abduction

This may all be described in semiotic terms. For this purpose I will draw on the work of Umberto Eco, who develops a triadic and inferential semiotics in the tradition of C. S. Peirce, which itself can be traced back to St Augustine.[9] The bush appears out of the ordinary to Moses only within a certain frame of reference—one according to which fire implies consumption. Indeed, in order to turn the raw sensory data into a meaningful perception, Moses must see the fire *as* that which consumes. Only then does he see it *as fire*; it would otherwise just be a red haze. His perception of the burning bush, in which a mere sensation is turned into a "perception invested with meaning", is therefore a semiotic event (even if one so automatic that it is normally ignored), one in which the red haze signifies fire.[10] At the root of this event is a process of inference, or more specifically, of *abduction*. This involves the positing of a context (the array of associations Moses has with "fire") within which the sensation gains meaning (the red haze, when understood in terms of these associations, is seen as fire); or more precisely, as Eco puts it, the hypothesising of a rule of which the datum in question is understood to be a case (p. 40). In this case, the pre-existing rule according to which Moses makes sense of that which he sees is the rule, "If there is fire, then something is being consumed." Only then does the sensory datum become meaningful to him, and only then does the fact that no consumption is occurring become odd.

Eco argues that such inferential labour is at work in every semiotic event, even those which appear to be based purely on equivalence (esp. pp. 39–43). In other words, whenever I understand something as a sign of something else, it is not just a matter of my substituting for the sign a content to which it is held to be equivalent ($p \equiv q$). Rather, I must interpret the sign by positing a context within which it gains its meaning. "The understanding of signs is not a mere matter of recognition (of a stable equivalence); it is a matter of *interpretation*" (p. 43). Eco gives the example of the utterance of the word "cane" in an excited voice, and points out that "in order to understand whether it is a Latin imperative («sing!») or an Italian holophrastic indexical proposition («dog!»), I must hypothesize *a* language as a frame of reference" (p. 40). Eco defines this process of abduction more specifically as "the tentative and hazardous tracing of a system of signification rules which will allow the sign to acquire its meaning" (p. 40).

But if all meaningful perception of the world around us involves semiosis (as implied above), then what this means is that the process of abduction is the most basic and pervasive way in which we orient ourselves within the world. The negotiation of our place within the world, in other words, involves the constant back-and-forth between our interpretations of reality and reality's resistance to our interpretations. A break is therefore effected between these interpretations and the reality that resists them. From this theoretical consideration, then, we reach the same conclusion that was implied in Moses' encounter with the "miraculous" burning bush: reality exceeds our interpretations of it; or as I put it before, reality exceeds human use.[11] Alternatively—to anticipate what will be of paramount significance in my argument below—the fact that a sign only ever signifies within a humanly posited context, and therefore only ever *for someone*, implies that it could always signify differently for someone else. The resistance to my own interpretation afforded by such an alternative interpretation of reality is therefore itself a sign of reality's excessive nature.

But what of the human side of the process? To explore this, it will be helpful to outline Eco's distinction between three different types of abduction. In many—perhaps most—cases, the abductive process is quasi-automatic, following from one's contextual circumstances in an unreflective manner. Eco refers to this sort of abduction as *overcoded*, pointing out that in such cases the rule is already given and it is just a matter of deciding "to recognise the Result as a Case of that Rule" (p. 41). *Undercoded* abductions occur, by contrast, when "the rule must be selected among a series of equiprobable alternatives" (p. 42). And even less determined than these are "*creative abductions*, in which the rule acting as an explanation has to be invented *ex novo*" (p. 42). In all of these types of abduction the identity of the interpreter is at stake, albeit to varying degrees. We arrived above at a distinction between a humanly constructed world and reality in excess of (and resistance to) this world. But the humanly constructed world is precisely that which is posited, altered and reconfigured in order to make sense of the reality that resists it—in order to turn an inexplicable world into a usable one, as I put it above. It is that which is hypothesised, in other words, in the abductive process. Our human worlds consist, therefore, in the abductions we make. And it is in these worlds that our identities subsist. So depending on the nature of the abductions we make, our identities will be more or less reconfigured as we try to make sense of the reality we encounter from day to day and moment to moment. Overcoded abductions will leave our human worlds more or less in place, whereas creative abduction has the potential to reconfigure their landscape considerably.

The Symbol

In the light of this, what can we say about Moses' encounter with the burning bush? What is the nature of the abductive process—or indeed failure of it—involved here? What sort of semiotic phenomenon are we dealing with? This may be approached by considering Eco's account of the symbol, which in many respects provides a model for the burning bush. Equally interesting, however, will be the ways in which the burning bush diverges from Eco's symbol.

Recognising that the word "symbol" has historically been used to refer to a wide variety of different phenomena, ranging from the whole of semiotic activity through to all its subspecies, Eco seeks to isolate a "hardcore sense" of symbol (p. 133), taking his starting point in the proposition that the term is classically used where there is "a certain *ineffectuality*" of signification (p. 132)—where rules for interpretation are lacking. He goes on to define the symbolic mode more positively as a "specific semiotic phenomenon in which a given expression is correlated to a *content nebula*" (p. 144). The correlation is not purely conventional (i.e. based on culturally determined rules), but motivated, drawing on the qualities generally associated with the signifier in a particular culture— what Eco calls the interpreter's "encyclopedic competence" (e.g. p. 142). However, the motivation is undetermined insofar as it is unclear which qualities of the symbol are to be selected as relevant for its significance. The signification of the symbol is therefore uncoded. It signifies, rather, by evoking within the interpreter an indefinite array of associations. Moreover, because it cannot be definitively interpreted, its content being rather "a *nebula* of possible interpretations", the symbol can never be left behind in favour of its interpretation: "The symbol says that there is something that it could say, but this something cannot be definitely spelled out once and for all; otherwise the symbol would stop saying it" (p. 161).

Once Eco has sufficiently pinpointed the properly symbolic mode as distinct from other semiotic phenomena, he puts us (by way of historically paradigmatic examples) before a fundamental alternative: between mysticism and deconstructionism. The symbolic mode proliferates in both (indeed in the latter, everything becomes symbolic, conventional meaning being dispensed with as delusory), but whereas in the former the truth expressed by the symbols is understood to "[lie] outside" the activity of signification (p. 155), being "extrasubjective and extracultural" (p. 163), the only truth in the latter is the play of deconstruction itself; there is no outside (p. 155). The mystical option, which Eco takes seriously but which he will ultimately distance himself from, is filled out in the further following ways: symbols, in this line of thought, are "considered as the vehicle of a transcendent Voice who speaks through them", as expressive of "a Truth", and so as "the voices of Being" (here Eco is following Ricoeur) (p. 147); and later, symbols are described (from a Heideggerian point of view) as "[showing] the true voice of Being. . . . [T]hey do not speak only of themselves; they reveal something else and something more" (p. 154).

But neither does Eco want to yield to deconstructionism. While opting for a fully secularised account of it, he is nevertheless at pains to retain and develop a delimited sense of the symbolic mode as something which "requires a specific semiotic strategy" (p. 157). Against the deconstructionist move, he claims that "not everything can be a symbol" (p. 157), and therefore that textuality does not just degenerate into the play of differences and displacements. Positively, he describes the symbolic mode as a case of *textual implicature:*[12] it is engendered by the presence of a word, sentence, object, gesture etc., in a context within which it seems to serve no function, thereby acquiring an emphasis it *"should not* have" within that context (pp. 157–158). Whereas the presence of a metaphor is indicated by falsity on a literal level, the metaphorical sense thereby *replacing* the literal, the symbolic mode is signalled by mere redundancy on the literal level; while there is not necessarily any absurdity on this level, there is, as Eco says, a feeling of "literal waste" (p. 161)—and in this sense it is like allegory. Unlike allegory, however, which "suggests its own key . . . [pointing] toward a portion of encyclopedia which already hosts the right frames for interpreting it . . . a symbol leaves the interpreter face to face with the uncoded" (p. 161)—and this is also something which distinguishes it from metaphors, which on the whole can be "disambiguated without vagueness" (p. 157). In sum, the symbol is signalled by the fact that it *"should not be there"* (p. 158). Its effect on the interpreter should be a sense of puzzlement and uneasiness in the face of its inexplicability, leading one to suspect "a *surplus* of signification" (p. 158). Symbols "reveal that they are there to reveal something else; it is up to the reader to decide what else" (p. 157).

The Biblical God

The parallels with the burning bush are not difficult to see. Might one not say that within the context of Moses' humanly constructed world, the burning bush, insofar as it cannot be explained, creates in Moses just that sense of uneasiness and puzzlement that the symbol engenders within its potential interpreter? Just like the latter, it *should not be there*. And just as the symbol's inexplicability on the literal plane causes the interpreter to look for its significance on another level, the inexplicability of the burning bush points to the excessive nature of reality. Surplus of signification in the case of Eco's symbol finds a parallel in this excessive nature of the reality inhabited by Moses. But even at this point differences are beginning to emerge. While the symbol retains meaning on the literal level, being inexplicable only in the sense of redundant, the bush is inexplicable in the stronger sense that it does not fit within Moses' context; it breaks its rules. The contrast is one between redundancy on the one hand, and inexplicability (in this stronger sense—the sense in which I will use it from now on), on the other.

But before drawing out the implications of this important difference, there are more parallels to be found when we consider the function of the burning bush within the story itself. As a miracle, its narrative function, it would seem, is simply to signal to the reader that something unusual is about to happen. It is the precursor to, and context for, Moses' encounter with God. One might say, in hindsight, that its inexplicability is a sign of the ultimate inexplicability of God, who radically exceeds Moses' humanly constructed world (something to which I will return later). In this sense, it has a narrative function over and above Eco's symbol. But beyond this negatively generated significance, it has, qua burning bush, no particular function within the narrative. We are left asking, Why a burning bush? Like Eco's symbol, it is in this regard redundant. And such a feeling of "literal waste" is, according to Eco, precisely what signals the symbolic mode.

This redundancy on the narrative plane is in some respects heightened even further in the Qur'anic version: the fire perceived by Moses is not even miraculous. While it still acts as a precursor to the divine voice, it has been stripped of the quality by virtue of which it could have functioned as a sign of the divine. But there is divergence from Eco's symbolic mode insofar as the narrative itself enacts this "making redundant" of the fire: Moses approaches it as something to be used, but as he does so he is pulled up short: "And when he reached it, he was called by name: O Moses!" (Surah 20.11). Seeing gives way to hearing and the fire, as part of Moses' human world, becomes irrelevant. His purpose is interrupted as the fire becomes the locus of an encounter with a reality that resists use. While the fire in the biblical story, even as part of the machinery of the human world, bore significance in relation to the divine by virtue of its inexplicability (and its continuing significance is confirmed and reinforced by the fact that God calls to Moses *out of the bush*), the fire in the Qur'anic story is rendered insignificant by the divine voice, which is all we are left with in Surah 20.11.[13]

The world of human use is superseded so radically in this story that virtually no room is left for its symbolic significance. The biblical story, by contrast, holds the burning bush in relation with the divine reality (even if only negatively by virtue of its inexplicability) in such a way that the possibility of its symbolic significance is opened up. And in one particularly pertinent respect within the interpretation I have been developing: just as the bush is not consumed, neither can reality be exhausted by human use. The "unconsumability" of the bush signifies the tenacity or resistance of reality in the face of human use. It has a particularity and uniqueness which exceeds its utilisation as a means to an end. The unconsumability of the bush signifies, in other words, the excessive nature of reality. From the continuation of the narrative we infer that this excess, signalled by the inexplicability of the bush, is rooted in the inexplicability or "excess" of God, to which the bush's inexplicability is a pointer. Thus the symbolic meaning may equally be elaborated along the following lines: just as the bush resists exhaustive consumption by fire, so the divine reality exceeds the human world, resisting human use. Once these connections begin to be made, symbolic elaborations may proliferate ad infinitum, in accordance with the "array of associations" evoked for the interpreter.

At this point it will be instructive to return to the comparison with Eco's symbol, and in particular the differences that open up. We recall that Eco's secular understanding of the symbol was developed as a way beyond the alternatives of a universal mysticism and a universal deconstructionism. Where, within this set of alternatives, does the biblical symbol fit? The most natural move would be to align it with universal mysticism. But it is precisely in the attempt to do so that the most interesting and important distinguishing marks of the biblical symbol come into view. On the mystical account, we recall, the symbol is the vehicle of a transcendent Voice—the voice of Being. It manifests, in other words, a Truth which lies beyond it. The divine reality of the Bible, by contrast, is that to which no expression or manifestation can be given: it is, rather, that which renders reality on the human plane, the reality of human use, inexplicable or *insignificant*. The burning bush, for which fire *no longer* signifies consumption, effects a break within normal semiotic processes.[14] If it "signifies" God, therefore, it does so only by virtue of its *insignificance*. The further *symbolic* significance it gains serves only to echo this negatively generated significance, the bush's unconsumability symbolising its resistance to human use.

By rejecting "universal mysticism" Eco has not yet rejected the biblical God: if Eco wants to be a true atheist, he has not gone far enough with his denials.[15] The divine reality he rejects—the symbolic contents understood as extratextual referents which are aspects of a universal, transcendent truth—is a far cry from the reality of the biblical God. Whereas the former is a timeless, universal truth to which all religious symbols ultimately give expression, the biblical God, as we have said, is one to whom *no expression* can be given. More than this, rather than unifying all reality by revealing it to be varying manifestations of the one, universal truth, the biblical God upholds creaturely reality in its intractable particularity and distinctiveness. In its "pointing" to a God to whom no expression can be given—the inexplicable God that we meet in the burning bush—creaturely reality is freed to be itself: the bush cannot be reduced to its existence for human use; reality cannot be reduced to its significance for Moses; the bush-in-the-story cannot be reduced to its significance within the narrative; and extrapolating from this, the story itself resists definitive interpretation: the scriptural text cannot be reduced to its meaning-for-us—it resists our use (but I will return to this later). At all of these levels, reality is more than its significance-for any particular interpreter. To put this differently, in its ultimate signification of *God* (which we have seen to be by virtue of its insignificance and inexplicability), creaturely reality signifies *nothing*, and is therefore established and affirmed in its existence as more than "sign"—and so as "thing".[16] Whereas mystical symbolic content abstracts from the concrete, embodied existence of the symbol, biblical symbolic content leads to its intensification: its signification of God is precisely what secures its substantial existence beyond the unstable, changing world of semiosis.

Whereas "mystical" symbolism, in its universality, leads to a dissolving of particularity, biblical symbolism upholds creaturely particularity in all its intractability. In this sense, it is closer to Eco's secular symbolism, whose symbolic contents remain *intracultural* "truths", "suggested by the co-text and by the intertextual tradition: the interpreter knows that he is not discovering an external truth but that, rather, he makes the encyclopedia work at its best" (p. 163). These intracultural and intertextual resonances are kept in place by biblical symbolism precisely as intracultural truths.[17] Thus by defining the religious versus the secular as the choice between extra- and intra-cultural truth, Eco has stopped short of a deeper, more subtle alternative. Unlike Eco's secular symbolism, biblical symbolism understands cultural or creaturely particularity to be rooted in the intractable and ineradicable uniqueness of the Creator, to which nothing can give expression. The surplus signification of Eco's symbol is exceeded by an even deeper surplus which cannot be converted into another level of human signification. And only this, finally, can prevent the dissolution of the concrete, embodied nature of the creature, in relation to which even Eco's "intra-cultural truth" is abstract. The decisive choice, on this account, is between the acceptance and rejection of this reality that exceeds *all* human, cultural meaning.[18] The prototypical symbol is that which signifies *nothing*. Eco's redundancy is taken to its limit.

Moses' Transformation

In the light of all this, what can we say about the nature of Moses' encounter with the burning bush—about the nature of the abduction involved? More specifically, what sort of reconfiguration of identity is brought about by Moses' encounter with the God who speaks out of the bush?

> But Moses said to God, "Who am I that I should go to Pharaoh, and bring the Israelites out of Egypt?" He said, "I will be with you; and this shall be the sign for you that it is I who sent you: when you have brought the people out of Egypt, you shall worship God on this mountain." (Exodus 3:11–12)

The bush brings Moses to an encounter, not with a piece of his reality, even a very significant piece, but with the ground of his reality in its entirety: with the inexplicable ground of his identity—Moses is who he is because God is with him. This ground does not change anything in particular; it changes *everything*.[19] In his encounter with the bush, Moses' humanly constructed world comes up against the intractable resistance of creaturely reality, what I have called its excessive nature. But in his attentiveness to this reality, Moses comes up, further, against the excessive nature of *his own identity*. All his normal abductive processes fail in the face of this miraculous sight. He cannot integrate it within his human world. He can only encounter it in his own excessive nature—to which it calls.

At the burning bush, Moses encounters the God of Abraham, Isaac and Jacob: the God of his ancestors (Exodus 3:6). He is pointed to the roots of his own identity. But the encounter is also the promise of a new future: Moses is called to participate in God's redemption of Israel from slavery in Egypt, a liberation in which they will receive again, indeed truly for the first time, their identity as the people of God. Beyond their identity as slaves in Egypt, they will receive an identity rooted in the God of their election—as the people of God. In and with this gift of past and future, Moses receives, beyond his own personal weaknesses and failings (cf. Exodus 4:1, 10–13), a place in the purposes of God: an excessive identity in relation to which his whole life is transformed. More concretely, Moses is given a voice to which the elders of Israel will listen (Exodus 3:18; 4:30–31), even against his own will (4:13). He is freed from the mute and enslaving identity of his own human construction in order to enact his role in the purposes of God.[20]

This takes the reconfiguration of identity involved in Eco's secular symbol onto a wholly new level. To recall, Eco's symbol, by virtue of its redundancy, leads the interpreter to look for another level of signification, on which its meaning is uncoded. As such, it gives maximal scope for creative abductions, triggering new associations and so reconfiguring the conceptual landscape—and crucially from our perspective—the identity of the interpreter. The biblical symbol, by contrast, involves on one level at least the failure of the abductive process. This failure (the burning bush's continued inexplicability), however, induces Moses to look for another level of signification, not in abstraction from the bush's concrete reality (as in Eco's symbol), but in the very concrete reality of which this bush is a part: the history and future of the people of Israel. Rather than looking beyond it for "transcendent" meanings, he is sent deeper into this primal narrative. Abstraction, or *conceptual* resolution, is therefore replaced by *lived reconciliation*:[21] by Moses' transformation and conversion. The excessive reality with which Moses is brought into encounter cannot be comprehended even by the most creative of abductions; it can only be "interpreted" by the conversion of a life. While the abduction reached to make sense of an Ecoan symbol brings about a reconfiguration of one's conceptual furniture, and to this extent a reconfiguration of one's identity, the "abduction" reached to "make sense of" a symbol of the biblical God brings about a transformation of one's whole life, giving one a new past and a new future: to repeat, it does not change anything in particular, it changes *everything*.

In short, the biblical symbol, as inexplicable or insignificant, does not lead to the formation of new conceptual hypotheses—for in the face of the biblical God these all break down—but to the transformation of a life. God's name, "I am who I am" (Exodus 3:14), has the purpose of undercutting all attempts to explain and define God; it points, rather, to the one God is in the history of his people. The only timeless, abstract definition of who God is, therefore, is one which tells you to look to how God has acted in the past and will act in the future. It calls one to pay attention to this particular history. To know this God, one must undergo the same transformation to which God calls Israel: from slavery to freedom. In sum, God calls not for explanation but for conversion.

Scripture as Symbol

I have so far explored the nature of this conversion as it is undergone by Moses at the burning bush. But if it is this same God that we hope, as Christians, to encounter in the reading of Scripture, then we may learn from the paradigmatic story of Moses at least something of what is involved in the Christian reading of Scripture; and more specifically, something about the nature of the scriptural formation of Christian identities. My drawing out of this parallel will be based more particularly on an analogy between Scripture and the burning bush. The bush is the element within the human world which Moses stumbles upon; it is the bush he must seek to interpret; and the bush is discovered to signal the holy ground on which he stands, and therefore to signify the God into whose presence he has been ushered. Similarly, Scripture is part of the human world, requiring interpretation; and insofar as it is understood to be the Word of God, it is understood, like the bush, to be a sign of this God, and therefore to induct one onto "holy ground". Its witness to God is what renders it *holy* Scripture.[22]

If this analogy is warranted, then Scripture, too, may be considered as a *symbol*, and more specifically, as a symbol of God. What, then, might be involved in the reading of Scripture as symbol? We recall that the burning bush signified God only by virtue of its *in*significance—by virtue of its resistance to interpretation. And this insignificance, establishing its creaturely existence beyond the changing world of semiosis, freed it ultimately to be itself. As symbol of God, therefore, the first thing to be said of Scripture is that it *resists* interpretation. In its signification of God it is established in its transcendence of any human significance that might be imputed to it. Hermeneutically what this means is that it must be read as that which *exceeds any particular interpretation*. It cannot be reduced to its significance for me (or for anyone else), just as the bush could not be exhaustively subsumed within Moses' world of human use. Paradoxically, therefore, by resisting interpretation—by signifying *nothing* (humanly speaking)—it becomes the generative source of ever-new interpretations (precisely because the "nothing" signified is God). Like the bush that is not consumed, it is never "used up" by its readers, but resists exhaustive "consumption" (and in this way the bush accrues another symbolic meaning). This allows it to remain a source for others in the future.

We may gather from all of this what sort of place Scripture should have within its community of readers. If, over and above all its particular human interpretations, it is essentially *in*significant within its community, then it may not be exhaustively converted into human use, but will resist conscription into our human projects. In relation to these it remains redundant and superfluous (to draw out the resonances with the Ecoan symbol). It cannot be utilised, as a key piece within the larger puzzle of reality, to explain or give sanction to anything. As itself *in*explicable, it will serve rather to disturb and disrupt—as did the burning bush. In sum, just as Moses' "interpretation" of the burning bush did not amount to any *conceptual* resolution, nor does the reading of Scripture ultimately involve conceptual resolution—either by underpinning a particular worldview or by informing a particular ideology.

What, then, positively, is the nature of the transformation it brings about in its readers? Again, we may look to Moses. Rather than receiving conceptual resolution, Moses received liberation for a new identity: an identity rooted in the God of his election. But this reception of new identity did not amount simply to a *tinkering* with Moses' identity to date. His identity in God exceeds any such humanly constructed identity just as God exceeds all human signification. It is not a matter, then, of new, ever more creative abductions, by means of which Moses may integrate within his world previously inexplicable data. Rather, as we have seen, the only form "abduction" can take here is the transformation of life: *conversion*.

By analogy, Scripture does not call for conceptual resolution, but for conversion: for reconciliation with God. The identity one receives in the

90 *Susannah Ticciati*

reading of Scripture, therefore, cannot be appropriated as an identity one
fashions for oneself (for all such humanly constructed identities work on
the level of conceptual resolution). Rather, as an *excessive* identity, it remains
a "centre" one is given beyond oneself—beyond the provisional centres one
constructs day-to-day—and therefore a hidden, apophatic centre. To bring
out the specifically Christian resonances of this, we experience in the
reading of Scripture the disruption of our existence as old creatures by our
encounter with the new creatures we already are in God. Our excessive
identities are the identities we have outside ourselves in Christ. And this
brings us to the heart of the matter. Read through the lens of Jesus' death
and resurrection, the biblical story is one which involves the death of the
old and the birth of the new; the relinquishing of one's life in order to save
it; the giving up of one's old identity and the reception of a new one. If this
is its shape, then the identity one receives by inhabiting it can never be
possessed: for it is, by definition, characterised by the continual relinquish-
ment of identity.

To receive an excessive identity, in other words, involves being dispossessed of one's humanly constructed identities. The formation of Christian
identity takes the form of this radical dispossession.[23] It is this which
constitutes the strangeness of the "strange new world of the Bible". The
excessive identity it bequeaths me, as something I may only receive by the
undergoing of continual dispossession, remains forever strange to me: it
never becomes my own. The more fully I inhabit the biblical world,
therefore, the stranger it becomes, leading me to more and more fundamental dispossession; or more positively, to the deeper and deeper reception of myself from beyond myself.

Universality and Scriptural Reasoning

Established by this discussion is a break between the biblical story in its
excessive nature, and any appropriation of it—which will never be more
than a human construct. This has far-reaching ramifications for the nature
of the universality of the biblical story. The most obvious way of enacting
this universality—the attempt to inscribe all others into the story—can only
ever succeed in absolutising my appropriation of it. For inscription involves
conceptual integration and resolution—the hallmark of humanly constructed worlds. The biblical story in its excessiveness, by contrast, is not
susceptible to such conceptual resolution. It calls, then, for an alternative
enactment of universality—a universality not on the conceptual level but in
embodied practices and the potential for conversion that they contain.

I have already argued at length that the biblical story is most honoured
as a symbol of God when its resistance to interpretation is registered. In the
context of claims for its universality, this resistance, I suggest, takes the form
of the resistance of others to inscription within its universe. But this

resistance must not remain theoretical; for it would then remain on the conceptual level, failing to bring about the kind of transformation we have talked about in terms of conversion. In other words, this resistance must be embodied by real others who read the Bible differently and even have alternative sources of identity. Such resistance will not be hard to find. Indeed, one need not even look beyond one's own gates: the readings of fellow Christians will frequently pose challenges to one's own readings, calling one to new appreciation of the excessive nature of the biblical story. But the others who are most likely to bring this challenge home will depend on one's context. Different contexts will call for different challengers.

My suggestion here is that SR has pinpointed one of the greatest needs for Christians in the contemporary context. A central problem for Christians in this context, I contend, is the temptation to substitute for the biblical story the Christian "religion". Once this substitution has been carried out, the universal becomes the *global*,[24] being enacted in the absolutisation of Christian meaning and the inscribing of all others into it, whether by an exclusivism which holds that this meaning can only be appropriated by those who convert, or by an inclusivism which holds it to characterise the world on an ontological level, affecting all whether they know it or not. While it has long been recognised that the term "religion"—which is in any case, so it is argued, a term of modern provenance[25]—does not do justice to the complexities of the great variety of traditions to which it is attributed, it is nevertheless the case that the secular logic of "religions" pervades the Western cultural imagination. When Christians mistake globalisation for the true universality of the Biblical story, they are buying into precisely this secular, totalising logic. Perhaps, then, the language of "religion" brings to particular cultural manifestation a more perennial theological problem— that of the difficulty of holding open the break between our humanly constructed identities and the excessive identities we have as creatures of God. Be that as it may, the question of religion continues to be a troubling one, even after it has apparently been successfully debunked—at least in theory.

And this is where the practice of SR finds its place. For the problem of how Christianity relates to "other religions" cannot be solved theoretically. And nor can it be solved *in general*. What I am suggesting is that the "others" who present perhaps the most pertinent challenge to Christian universality today will be members of other religious traditions. And this challenge will be all the more intensified by members of those traditions that read the same texts, or appropriate within their narrative identities the same ancestral figures—but differently. In Jews and Muslims, Christians are confronted by others who resist in particular, significant and intractable ways inscription into the Christian biblical story.[26] By paying attention to this resistance, both by reading their own texts in the company of these others, and by participating in close readings of the texts of these others, can it be that Christians will be brought to the kind of conversion undergone by Moses at the burning bush—encountering their inexplicable God in the inexplicable otherness of these others?

More specifically, might it be in such a practice of shared reading that Christians, like Moses, will be "given a voice" with which to express who they truly are, liberated from the enslaving identities of their past? Moses was freed from his enslaving past by being given a centre beyond himself. In this way he was enabled to inhabit the world as a world in which God acts: as more than his own human constructions. In the practice of SR, might one suggest by analogy that I find my centre outside myself as embodied by the members of the other traditions, in relation to whom Scripture is discovered to be more than its significance for me? Might it be quintessentially in such a way that I am freed from my own, self-enclosed readings of Scripture and that Scripture is freed again to be the locus of God's acts?

NOTES

1   See Ben Quash's essay, above, which describes some of the "marks" that distinguish SR from such a neutral endeavour.

2   To cite the well-known title of a 1916 address given by Karl Barth, reprinted in Karl Barth, *The Word of God and the Word of Man*, trans. Douglas Horton (London: Hodder and Stoughton, 1928), pp. 28–50.

3   For an account of the Christian story as one of dispossession, see Rowan Williams, "The Finality of Christ" in *On Christian Theology* (Oxford: Blackwell, 2000), pp. 93–106, where Williams also draws out implications for inter-faith dialogue. Substantial resonances with Williams's account will be evident in what follows.

4   Unfortunately I will not have space to pursue this intertextual comparison very far. The remarks I make more by way of suggestion nevertheless point to some significant ways in which the biblical and Qur'anic worlds diverge from one another, even while sharing some fundamental characteristics.

5   For which (at least for the purposes of this essay) I have principally consulted "Signs", Chapter 1 in Umberto Eco, *Semiotics and the Philosophy of Language* (Bloomington, IN: Indiana University Press, 1984), pp. 14–45.

6   Eco, "Symbol", Chapter 4 of *Semiotics and the Philosophy of Language*, pp. 130–163.

7   All biblical quotations in this essay will be taken from the NRSV. M. M. Pickthall's translation of the Qur'an will be used.

8   I am indebted to Mike Higton for this distinction between *use* and *resistance to use*, which he makes within a hermeneutical context. It is also developed hermeneutically by Rachel Muers in "Setting Free the Mother Bird: On Reading a Strange Text", forthcoming *Modern Theology* Vol. 22 no. 4 (October, 2006).

9   For such an account of the origin of triadic semiotics, see C. C. Pecknold, *Transforming Postliberal Theology: George Lindbeck, Pragmatism and Scripture* (London: T&T Clark, 2005), pp. 37–60.

10 Cf. Eco, *Semiotics and the Philosophy of Language*, pp. 32–33.

11 This alignment of "use" with "interpretation" echoes Augustine's parallel distinctions between "sign" and "thing" on the one hand, and "use" and "enjoyment" on the other. See *De Doctrina Christiana*, esp. Book I; see E. Hill, trans., J. E. Rotelle, ed., *Teaching Christianity*, (New York, NY: New City Press, 1996), resulting in a similarly semiotic understanding of the whole of the creaturely world (ultimately to be understood as a sign of God). The argument I develop in this essay is informed implicitly throughout by an

Augustinian semiotic. My explicit development of his ideas may be found in "The Castration of Signs: Conversing with Augustine on Creation, Language and Truth", forthcoming in *Modern Theology* 2007.

12 Eco is using "textual" here in a wider sense than merely *written* texts, as his later example of a wheel of a carriage at the door of a country house shows.

13 In this context, the miracles that follow (Surah 20.17–22) serve simply to underline further the redundancy—or perhaps better, relativity—of Moses' human reality. The "holy valley of Tuwa", in which Moses finds himself according to the divine voice (Surah 20.12), is a "place" where the solidity of the objective world becomes unhinged. (I am indebted to Willie Young for this phrase.) The effect of the miracles is radically to relativise its integrity and stability. The staff's significance for Moses lies in the uses it has for him (Surah 20.18). But beyond this human world it gains a surplus significance, as a "sign" of the divine (cf. Surah 20.23). This surplus significance, however, has no content: the arbitrary transformation signals only the divine *power*, the particular properties of staff and snake being irrelevant to the display. While they have importance from Moses' perspective *within* the human world, the power which upholds the human world in its entirety would appear to be indifferent to its particular contents.

By virtue of their different context, the "same" miracles as narrated within the biblical story (Exodus 4:1–9) serve not so much to relativise Moses' human reality as to convince Moses of God's power to act within this reality, overcoming Moses' impotence and enabling him to bring about that which he believes to be impossible (see esp. Exodus 4:1, 10–12).

14 The Qur'an is perhaps even more radical in this regard: the divine voice, rather than imputing the fire with another dimension of meaning, renders it irrelevant, superseding altogether the reality of human use. The miracles that follow signify the divine *power*, but this is precisely to signify *nothing*—that is, nothing in particular, the divine power being that which holds all particulars in being.

15 To echo Denys Turner's argument in *How to be an Atheist: Inaugural Lecture Delivered at the University of Cambridge, 12 October 2001* (Cambridge: Cambridge University Press, 2002).

16 To allude again to Augustine's discussion of signs and things in *De Doctrina Christiana*. See my "The Castration of Signs" for an interpretation of Augustine along these lines.

17 At this point an affinity may be noted between the account being developed here and the cultural-linguistic proposals of postliberal theology, such as that offered by George Lindbeck in *The Nature of Doctrine: Religion and Theology in a Postliberal Age* (Philadelphia, PA: Westminster Press, 1984), which also seeks to eschew a collapsing of particular, culturally specific truths into a universal truth to which they all ultimately point.

18 This account of God as beyond all cultural meaning resonates strongly with Rowan Williams's interpretation of the doctrine of creation *ex nihilo* in "On Being Creatures" in *On Christian Theology*, pp. 63–78. In critique of Sallie McFague and Rosemary Radford Ruether, he argues that God is beyond all cultural power: "[in the act of creation out of nothing] God does not impose a definition but creates an identity" (p. 68).

19 Cf. Nicholas Lash, *Easter in Ordinary: Reflections on Human Experience and the Knowledge of God* (Notre Dame, IN: University of Notre Dame, 1988), pp. 221–231, for a similar account of the difference God makes in the world.

20 The opposition between slavery and freedom alluded to here is explored further along similar lines in Rachel Muers, Chad Pecknold and Susannah Ticciati, "For Freedom Christ has set us Free: Galatians, Semiotics and Abusive Relations" (Unpublished MS).

21 I am indebted for this distinction—which will remain crucial in what follows—to Paul Janz. See his *God, the Mind's Desire: Reference, Reason and Christian Thinking* (Cambridge and New York: Cambridge University Press, 2004), e.g. pp. 174–177 and 198, where he draws the distinction between finalities of resolution and non-resolution. He has subsequently developed this in terms of the distinction between "conceptual resolution" and "causal reconciliation".

22 The drawing of such an analogy is reminiscent of the Christological interpretation of the burning bush prevalent among the church fathers: the bush, like Christ, is a place at which the human opens out onto the divine. The Christological foundations of my interpretation will be drawn out more explicitly below.

23   Cf. Rowan Williams, "The Finality of Christ", in which Williams talks about dispossession—which he argues to be a fundamental pattern of Christian discipleship—more specifically as our dispossession of "the God who is defined as belonging to us and our interests". He continues: "To be a Christian is to claim that the Jewish story with its interruption and repristination in Jesus is the most comprehensive working-out of this moment of dispossession—a religious tradition generating its own near-negation" (p. 104). His attack, in this essay, is on the same "totalized" or ideological universality which I will critique below, characterised by him further as "tribalized and self-protecting religion" (p. 104).

24   Cf. the distinction made between the universal and the global by Eric Santner in *On the Psychotheology of Everyday Life: Reflections on Freud and Rosenzweig* (Chicago, IL: The University of Chicago Press, 2001), esp. pp. 5–7.

25   E.g. Michael J. Buckley, "The Study of Religion and the Rise of Atheism: Conflict or Confirmation?" in David F. Ford, Ben Quash and Janet Martin Soskice (eds.), *Fields of Faith: Theology and Religious Studies for the Twenty-first Century* (Cambridge: Cambridge University Press, 2005).

26   We may again note the resonance with Williams's account of inter-faith dialogue (although he roots this more specifically in a historical account of the origins of Christianity as an "episode in the political history of a religious people", involving a conflict over the true identity of Israel (pp. 96–97)): specifically, he claims that "Israel's resistance to absorption by the Church is a refusal to grant that the meanings of Israel are contained and subsumed in the Christian institution, and that refusal is essential for the truthfulness and faithfulness of the Church, tempted as it is to claim a distorted kind of finality" ("The Finality of Christ", p. 103).

6

READING THE BURNING BUSH: VOICE, WORLD AND HOLINESS

OLIVER DAVIES

Ancient texts need to be read anew. This study represents an attempt to sketch a new reading of an ancient text which has over the generations proved to be a foundational one for the articulation and development of Christian metaphysics. It thus both acknowledges the place of this text within the tradition and expresses a certain dissatisfaction with the metaphysical tradition itself, which today seems to many to have reached a condition of exhaustion.[1] The principle difficulty is the act of abstraction which underlies the metaphysical moment and which shifts the locus from real existence, which is to say from sensible reality, in which thinking is a part, to ontology, in which thinking becomes the whole. This abstractive stage can be characterised as a movement from real, sensible existence, which is always constituted within an irreducible openness to what exceeds it, by virtue of the givenness of the real, to a *conceptualised coherence* about the sensible real as such. Such a conceptualised systematisation always includes a totalising aspect, since this is a function of coherence itself. Through ontology, we seek to understand the nature of the reality of which we are a part by acts of abstractive reflection, which then become autonomous systems of conceptualisation. These are open to correction through the rules engendered by their intrinsic coherence: simply stated, these must gain in explanatory power without falling into internal contradiction or vagueness. The role of reflection within sensible reality is not like this however. Here thought is judged, or corrected, by further folds of givenness within the disclosure of the real. Human thought stands to be corrected by the contours of the real world, of whose unfolding we are an integral and constitutive part.[2]

Oliver Davies
Department of Theology and Religious Studies, King's College London, Strand, London WC2R 2LS, UK

In terms of its Christian exegesis, Exodus 3 has a long and detailed history which began with a move that was internal to Judaism itself. The Septuagint replaced the verbal structure of Exodus 3:14 (*ehyeh ašer ehyeh*) with a substantival reformulation (*ho ōn*), which redefined the conception of God away from one which is temporally expressed to one that stands outside time. The Vulgate rendering *Ego sum qui sum* retained the aseity of the Greek translation, which became important for the metaphysical thought of St. Augustine, and which remained the primary topos of Christian metaphysical analysis until challenged by neo-Thomist readings during the twentieth century.[3] Both the classical and the existential model have in common the prioritisation of a pre-existing philosophical model of existence (Platonic in the former case and existentialist in the latter case), which has found purchase in the text of Exodus itself. As we approach this text again, therefore, it becomes imperative that we seek to set aside any such preformed metaphysical thinking. If we wish to be addressed once again by this text, then it must be read, as far as is possible, *on its own terms*.

Our point of entry into the text, which describes Moses leading Jethro's flock of sheep through the wilderness to Mt. Horeb, begins also with the memory that Moses had killed an Egyptian who was beating one of his kinsfolk, and that he fled from Pharaoh's power, like "every other political fugitive" in Brevard Child's phrase, when he discovered that this deed, committed in secret, was known.[4] From the very outset, therefore, we can see the presence of a political element in this most "metaphysical" of passages. The pericope also connects back to the lines which immediately precede it and which tell us that God heard the groaning of his people in Egypt, and "remembering his covenant with Abraham, Isaac and Jacob", God "looked upon" the Israelites and "took notice of them" (Exodus 2:23–25). This text is pregnant with the sense of divine action in the world and of human action in the world which is either ordered to, or in tension with, divine agency.

We learn that the angel of the Lord appeared to Moses at Mt. Horeb in a flame of fire out of a bush, which was not consumed, and that Moses saw it. But the following play on the root *r'h*, meaning "to see", is interesting. The occurrence at verse 2 probably means something more like "Moses was looking around and noticed the bush". In verse 3 this first occurrence of *r'h* as "to see" is contrasted with its next occurrence in the phrase "I must turn aside and look at this great sight". What we have here then are two depths or intensities of seeing: the one is general ("he was looking ahead or around") and has the sense of indeterminate seeing, denoting a field of vision. The second use of the root however is determinate seeing, for now something specific, this strange bush, fills Moses' visual horizon. The text suggests that he has left the path and is now focusing his attention upon it. This recapitulates the statement at Exodus 2:25 that God "looked upon Israel" and "took notice of them". The visual imagery of Exodus 2:25 is prompted however by the aural imagery of Exodus 2:23–24 (which speaks of Israel groaning and crying out in slavery and of God hearing them, and thus being prompted to the memory of his covenant with Israel), while Exodus 3:4 shows that the sequence in our text is reversed. Verse 4 contains the third and fourth occurrences of *r'h*, meaning "to see", when we are told that Yahweh "saw that he had turned aside to see" (that is, Yahweh saw that Moses was now looking at the bush more carefully). Only when he has seen this does God *speak* to Moses, calling his name twice from the bush, and eliciting the reply from Moses: "Here I am".[5] The movement from speech to sight at Exodus 2:23–25 is reversed therefore at Exodus 3:2–4.

So what exactly is it that this text is telling us? In the first place, it appears to show a remarkable degree of concern with overlapping or interrelated processes of seeing and hearing. The sensory movement depicted in Exodus 3:2–4 appears to be one of intensification. We progress, through inhabiting Moses' own sensory perspective as depicted within the text, from a general visual field, to a specific attentive act of focused seeing, then to speech and hearing. Specific acts of visual focusing always occur within a field, whereas acts of hearing are pin-pointed. Sound therefore conveys or can convey the particularity of space in a way that sight cannot. This is true above all of course in the case of the human voice. We generally turn to look at the person speaking to us; indeed failure to do this can arouse the suspicion of antagonism. Sound gives position and thus manifests the spatiality, or specific and thus specifically positioned materiality, of the human body. Indeed, it is often the sound of the voice which communicates to us human presence. It is with this principle in mind perhaps that Merleau-Ponty referred to the human body as "sonorous" and "like crystal".[6]

The meaning of this text seems to be that God has called Moses into relation with himself (following Moses' reply, they are now beginning to hold a dialogue), and has done so by triggering Moses' curiosity about something which is somehow out of the ordinary in the world. We may indeed assume that if Moses had not been generally looking around with some kind of openness of sight, at least sufficiently to notice something out of place, and if he had not then turned his attention to this, on account of what we might call curiosity, then God would never have addressed him from out of the bush and this dialogue would never have taken place. Curiosity about the world seems to play a key role in this, therefore, in a way which perhaps calls to mind the concern with discerning complexity in the world—which is one element in the Wisdom tradition.

What is it then that God first discloses to Moses in their conversation which comes about through this precise observation on Moses' part? It is the holiness of the ground on which he stands. This marks the second occurrence of the root *qdš* in the canonical bible, which suggests divine presence but also the separateness which is consequent upon it. Moses is being asked to consider that now, with the speaking of the divine voice from the bush, a new category has entered the world: a boundary to mark those places and spaces in which God is so present and those in which God is not so present. The divine presence in holiness is potentially dangerous, for Moses is told to "come no further" and to remove the sandals from his feet. God discloses himself as the God of Abraham, Isaac and Jacob, and Moses covers his face as he recognises with whom he speaks.

God's self-declaration to Moses, which is part of his self-naming, begins with a repetition of the divine intent given in Exodus 2:23–25. God is motivated by compassion for his people suffering in exile in Egypt, and he intends to lead them forth into the promised land. God tells Moses that he, Moses, will be the instrument for this liberation. When Moses expresses caution and self-doubt, and asks for God's name as a vouchsafe before the people, God gives him the name "I am who I am" (*ehyeh ašer ehyeh*). Rabbinic understandings of this phrase focus on the idea within it: "I shall be with you always", or "I shall always come to your aid".[7] God then says: "Thus you shall say to the Israelites, 'The Lord, the God of your ancestors, the God of Abraham, the God of Isaac, the God of Jacob, has sent me to you': this is my name for ever, and this is my title for all generations" (Exodus 3:15).

The name translated as "Lord" here is Yahweh. Its traditional connection with the verb *hāyāh* meaning "to exist" has led the commentarial tradition to argue that it is a name which particularly communicates the nature of God as Creator, as the one who calls all things into existence.[8] As such, it is the supreme name of God and, for Christians, it is the highest disclosure of the divine nature to humanity prior to the Incarnation. The speech relation between God who speaks within his creation and his human creatures who are gifted with speech began with God's commandment and blessing of Adam on the sixth day of creation (Genesis 1:28). The Burning Bush narrative marks the summation of that relation in that humankind, through Moses, are now called into a new and fuller intimacy with God which allows the giving and receiving of God's name, by which God, according to the Elohist tradition, will henceforth be known.

The modern readers of this text now find themselves in a predicament. We will have entered into this text through the eyes of the figure of Moses himself, drawing upon what is called the indexicality of the text. Indexicality is that linguistic structure which allows the reader (whose own world is likely to be far removed from that depicted in the text) nevertheless to enter into the textual world. We generally do so by imaginatively entering into the embodied, temporally and spatially fixed perspective of protagonists within that textual world. We know what it is to see and to hear, and, as we read this text, we see and hear with the eyes and ears of Moses. The text (and this text in particular with all its references to perception) allows and encourages us to do so. It is part of the story teller's art to make us, the listener or reader, feel that we are actually *there*, at that point in space and time, even bringing us to the point of forgetfulness regarding the real point in space and time which we actually inhabit when reading the text. In Paul Ricoeur's terminology, the world of the text is so constructed as to allow us to inhabit it vicariously and powerfully, despite our continuing existence in the—real—world of our own time and space. Thus the indexicality of the text (chiefly personal pronouns which can be exchanged between subjects and positional or relational words such as "now", "then" or "here") is a mechanism for allowing our real world and the world of the text to intersect with the consequence that, during the time that we are reading, we become virtually oblivious to the external, or non-textual reality of our ordinary empirical existence. Under the weight of reading, the empirical reality of our everyday world may well only "exist" for us through its mediations in the aesthetic character of reading itself, which is to say in that constitutive distinction between events which happen to us vicariously in the text and events which do or might actually happen to us in our real, non-textual world. This aesthetic relation is one of the imaginary, of play and of possibility therefore, which presupposes the *suppression* of our experience of the real, non-textual world, by the process of reading, at least for its duration.

The aesthetic principle of reading generally means that we can read this text, like any other text, enjoying it and then passing on to whatever it is that will next engage our attention. And yet, if the reader is a Christian (or indeed, a Jew or Muslim), then this particular text is not so easily read in such a way. The rules of reading Exodus 3:1–15, for someone who would wish to claim belief in the idea of God as Creator, are subtly though significantly different. And that difference comes into focus if we ask the question: "Whose voice is it that speaks from out of the Burning Bush? Is it a voice in the text, or is it also something more?" Just as we might say that the other textual voice, which is that of Moses, may stand in some real relation to the real voice of an historical Moses, shall we say too that the voice that speaks from the Burning Bush in our text may stand in some kind of real relation to something other, something historical: the voice of God perhaps really resonating at the foot of Mt. Horeb? Or to put it another way: shall we say that the name Yahweh disclosed here is a purely human construction, or shall we say that—whatever else it is—it is also and really a disclosive event?

Biblical theologians will be well aware that we encounter this problem in acute and extended form in the New Testament texts, but it appears that we encounter it in a particular way, indeed in a way that we might even call "metaphysical", in this particular text. After all, this text can itself become a Burning Bush for us too. The narrative delicately and systematically constructs for us a sense of the real. We see in our mind's eye Moses staring with all the force and energy of his being at this wondrous thing before him. This state of mind predicated upon a sensible experience is something to which we can all relate. Indeed, at this point the text may prompt us to recall or to imagine our most intense experience of the immediacy of the real, as the specificity of the here and now (the "here and now" is of course never generic but is always *this particular* here and now: yours and mine). We know what it is to engage with the here and now in the way that the text tells us Moses engaged with his here and now, by scrutinising so carefully, in his case, the conundrum of a bush that burned before him without being consumed. We can relate powerfully to this text therefore with respect to this posture and experience of Moses, even if we don't happen to believe that such a bush ever existed. In other words, this text "works" for us as a text, and does so subtly but powerfully, without forcing a commitment regarding our point of view on the credibility of the bush that burned. The same is not true, however, of the name of God. Even if we do not think that the name was disclosed to Moses, or believe that it was disclosed to him but not in this way, whatever we may think of the disclosure of the name, Yahweh remains an element in the tradition which has central importance for the Christology of the New Testament. It is not so easily set aside, or reduced to the aesthetic.

Another way to bring this complex sequence of readings and reasonings to a summary point is to ask the question: is this text not, firstly, bringing to our attention, at the reflexive level which is generic to all acts of reading, the simple reality of our embodied state: is it not textually reproducing for us the condition or awareness of existing at a specific point in time and space? And, secondly, is it not then telling us that it is at the very centre of the here and now that we shall hear the divine voice, receive the divine disclosure, discover the root of holiness? And, thirdly, is it not saying that if we are Christians, or believers in Yahweh, then we shall from now on have to understand that the relation between these two poles—the Creator, on the one hand, and the here and now as the spatial temporal coordinates of our ordinary embodied existence, on the other—is now irreversibly changed? Indeed, is this text not telling us that God exists as a disclosive possibility in the here and now, in the immediacy of these coordinates of ordinary awareness, and that nowhere else (not even at Mt. Horeb—unless that is where we happen to be), shall we find him?

We have made brief allusion to Paul Ricoeur's model of reading which understands the world of the text, that is the world that opens up from or before the text, to overlap with the ordinary world of the reader. We can think here also of the tradition of Hans Frei and George Lindbeck who understand the text of scripture to be world-absorbing in some sense. What I am proposing here, however, in the reading of this text, is different from both of these hermeneutical accounts. What I am suggesting is that the act of reading Exodus 3 draws us by means of the indexicality of the text into a new awareness of our own here and now. At the point at which God speaks to Moses from within the depths of his here and now, our own here and now (which is the here and now of an attentive reader) is addressed in its parallel potential as a site for the divine disclosure. A decision for the authenticity of the name Yahweh as revelatory (however this may be worked out in terms of historical referentiality, or authorial inspiration) of itself allows the reconfiguration of our own here and now (that is our here and now as reader, and as distinct from the here and now we vicariously experience through the figure of Moses) as the potential site of a divine speaking. In other words, this is not a text that lays claim to the world; it is not a text that generates a world that overlaps with our own ordinary world; it is rather a text which redefines for us our own relation to the everyday real, and—since reading is always a sensible act—does so *from within the world of sensible reality.* Rather than luring us away from our own ordinary reality into an alternative fictional or textual world, as we enter into this particular text we find that it spits us out and back into the everyday world of the real, but now with the discovery, if we have read this text according to its own laws, that that everyday reality is a place that might be and might become still a site of divine disclosure.

As a paradigm of the real, the Burning Bush pericope offers us the understanding that attentiveness to the given, to the sensible reality of the here and now, opens up for us the possibility that we shall discover the world, in its most elemental presence, as a place of divine speaking or disclosure. Moses' act of leaving the path and of studying the bush carefully (which Exodus 3 depicts as a free act of decision on his part) is a precondition, within the narrative, of God's speaking and eventual self-naming (and perhaps there may indeed be echoes here of the Israelite wisdom tradition with its emphasis upon studied engagement with the world's complexities as sign of the divine authorship). But the divine speaking itself is entirely sovereign and wholly outside the range of Moses' expectation. Indeed, he covers his face for fear of theophany. Although the voice appears from within the here and now, therefore, we cannot say that we ever get any grasp of its *location.* Just as the flame leaves the bush unconsumed, and therefore cannot be said to be located in it, so too the voice appears to emerge from within Moses' here and now but to have no location in it.

And the issue of non-location is a critical one. If God spoke in and through location, as a person might speak, then there would be a case for the view that God is either a *figure* within the text, as is Moses, or that God is already incarnate. But God does not speak through location (we have only the indeterminate "from within": God speaks "from within the bush"). The voice speaks without precise location, therefore, just as the bush burns without being consumed. And yet, the text presupposes that this is not an illusion: the voice really speaks and the bush really burns. Yahweh's voice is a laying claim to the real as divine self-communication, as divine bestowal, speaking "from within" the real, truly speaking, but nevertheless not as something within the world. Speaking "from within" the world, but as something, as Creator, that is not "of" or "from the world" (cf. John 8:23). The Burning Bush thus invites us to consider that the real which underlies or indeed governs the world of human sense perception and construction is itself taken up and taken over by the divine speaking.

But what are we to make of a voice that sounds within our world but is not "of" it, which, coming from some depth within it, eludes perception in itself? The implication is that we cannot grasp it in itself but only by receiving its effects. Those effects in our passage are to do with the principle of holiness, which is given when Moses is told that he is to take off his sandals, since the ground he stands upon is "holy". It is not the voice that is holy but the ground. The voice escapes holiness, just as the ground is not the revelatory divine. Holiness then is the key. It is the marker at the level of the perceived and constructed—we can begin to call that *culture*— that the voice has been truly heard and believed. Holiness is therefore a *cultural* category but it is one which gives the trace of the divine, whose source must lie beyond all perception and knowledge, though it comes to us precisely "from within" sensible reality. Holiness is the condition or state that we find the empirical or sensible world has when we have discovered and understood that what underlies it, or exists within it at its depths, is indeed the self-communicating divine.

With the theme of holiness, we begin to come to a point of closure with this text, or better, a point which can accurately be described as an *issuing out*. The passage which begins with a depiction of Moses' curiosity at a complexity in the world, redefines the empirical present of the reader as a place of possible divine disclosure which can, at any point, take on the character of the holy. We are thus forced to confront the ever-present possibility of holiness within the domain of our ordinary sensibility. In the reading of this passage we are likewise confronted with the regulative character of Moses' experience, since his narrated experience includes the disclosure of the Divine Name. The story of Moses and the Burning Bush has now become for us a generative and dominant narrative of human existence before God. This will oblige us to rest with the concept of "holiness" disclosed here, as passage to and marker of the reception of the Divine Name. And here we must recognise the pregnancy of the root *qdš* at Exodus 3:5. It appears to stand within the Priestly tradition and thus to designate the cultic separation which we have already seen at Genesis 2:3. But its place in the history of Moses' calling to serve God through his mission to his people, appears also to anticipate the ethical and political characteristics of the later Holiness Code, which we find, for instance, at Leviticus 19:1–18.[9] The speaking of the divine voice then has significance not only for setting Israel apart as the chosen people of God, but also for shaping the world as a place where Israel's destiny, and ultimately human destiny, before God may be fulfilled.

A Metaphysics of the World

We began this essay with some reflections upon the nature of metaphysics as an abstractive way of reasoning. We have become sceptical about such grandiloquent systems of understanding, pointing instead to the primacy of the particular over the universal and the enfleshed over the noetic. The pericope of the Burning Bush has held a central position in the articulation and development of deeply Christian species of metaphysics. The reading followed in this essay rejects abstractions and is therefore at an angle to these. And yet, too, there is something of the universal implied within it. We all exist in a "here and now", and we can all therefore be summoned to a reflexive awareness of that particular point in space and time that we inhabit, wherever and whenever we are. That condition is constitutive of the human as a creature within the world. But it is not reducible to any one experience or set of experiences that any person or group may have. Neither is it reducible to any one idea or set of ideas. In fact, it is properly transcendent since it is an awareness that can be realised from within any sensible particularity, though without ever itself being particularised. It is given as a possibility with every instant of being in this place at this time, but is only ever realised precisely within that particularity of the sensible real.

And so perhaps there is a sense in which we can relocate the narrative of Moses and the Burning Bush within a metaphysical tradition after all, though not as a moment that is itself abstractively "metaphysical". We can read it as speaking about the nature of the world, and of human existence in the world, which is a classically metaphysical departure. But this "enfleshed metaphysics" of the Burning Bush does so only reflexively, and from within the world, so that it must always inhabit the particular as the possibility of the greater realisation of the particular through attentiveness and "close looking". Thus, in the interstices between enfleshed particularity and a universalizable attentiveness of spirit and senses, the voice of God may speak to us *from within* the world, as Creator who cannot be *of* the world, summoning us to a holiness of awe and love.

NOTES

1   See the essays in the recent collection edited by Mark A. Wrathall, *Religion after Metaphysics* (Cambridge: Cambridge University Press, 2003).
2   What is of particular interest here is the point at which any ontological system claims to find purchase within empirical reality. Thomas Aquinas understands that to be the act of existence of the object known to consciousness, while Heidegger pursues more culturally and linguistically based presuppositions concerning the originary knowability of Being in *Einführung in die Metaphysik* (1935). The theme of vagueness, looking back both to traditional rabbinic exegesis and to the logical work of C. S. Peirce, has an important anti-metaphysical function in the scriptural philosophy of Peter Ochs, since it is only Scripture that can supplement the inherent vagueness of human reasonings, on his account see Peter Ochs, *Peirce, Pragmatism and the Logic of Scripture* (Cambridge: Cambridge

University Press, 1998). In Scriptural Reasoning therefore, vagueness becomes the essential instrument of a self-renewing dependence upon the scriptural word, which holds at bay the "metaphysical" impulses of any systemic practices of understanding.

3 Emilie Zum Brunn offers a helpful survey of Augustine's reading of Exodus 3:14 in *St. Augustine: Being and Nothingness* (New York, NY: Paragon House Publishers, 1988). Fergus Kerr gives an insightful critical commentary on Gilson's "metaphysics of Exodus" in his *After Aquinas: Versions of Thomism* (Oxford: Blackwell Publishers Ltd., 2002), especially pp. 80–85.

4 Brevard S. Childs, *The Book of Exodus: A Critical, Theological Commentary* (Philadelphia, PA: The Westminster Press, 1974), pp. 44–46. Childs stresses that Moses has to be sent back to Egypt "with a different authority and a new mission" (p. 45).

5 In the Hebrew text the final infinite "to see/look" in verse 4 is directly followed by "(he) called", intensifying the sequence.

6 Maurice Merleau-Ponty, *The Visible and the Invisible: Followed by Working Notes*, edited by Claude Lefort, trans. Alphonso Lingis, (Evanston, IL: Northwestern University Press, 1968), p. 144.

7 See Charles Touati, "Ehye ašer ehye (*Exode* 3,14) comme 'l'Être-avec' " in *Dieu et l'Être. Exégèses d'Exode 3, 14 et de Coran 20, 11–24* (Paris: Études Augustiniennes, 1978), pp. 75–84 and Georges Vajda, "Bref aperçu sur l'exégèse d'Exode 3, 14 dans la littérature rabbinique et en théologie juive du Moyen Age" in *Dieu et l'Être*, pp. 67–74.

8 For a bibliography on this theme, see Brevard S. Childs, *The Book of Exodus*, pp. 60–64.

9 Philip Jenson, "Holiness in the Priestly Writings" in Stephen C. Barton, ed., *Holiness: Past and Present* (London and New York: T&T Clark, 2003), p. 105.

7

QUR'ĀNIC REASONING AS AN ACADEMIC PRACTICE

TIM WINTER

According to a hadith of the Prophet, the Qur'ān "has an outward and an inward aspect, a limit and a place of rising [*maṭla'*]."[1] The mass of exegesis triggered by this and analogous scriptural proof-texts for the possibility of an esoteric reading of the Qur'ān is represented in summary form in a gloss by the Anatolian theologian Dāūd al-Qayṣarī (d.1350). The "outward" aspect, or "back" (*ẓahr*) of the scripture is "what is immediately apparent to the mind", and is the first-order exegetic sense accessible to ordinary Muslims as well as to specialists. Rational deduction from this plain sense produces second-order theological insights, which are the "inward" (*bāṭin*). The greatest theologians reach the "limit", represented by the most abstract texts of philosophical theology (*kalām*). Beyond this lies the "place of rising", a term suggestive of the splendour of sunrise, which is the knowledge triggered by contemplation of the divine speech, gifted by "unveiling" (*kashf*): a direct self-disclosure of God.[2]

Qayṣarī was a solidly orthodox figure, revered as the first professor of theology in the new Ottoman state.[3] In his college in Iznik he taught the major texts of Muslim theology in its twin orthodox manifestations of Ash'arism and Maturidism. Such a theology was, Islam being what it is, a scripture-driven exercise, eternally subordinate to the "back", or the supportive plain sense, to which all legal and theological reason was answerable. His fourth, frankly illuminationist category, he took to be no less scriptural; yet it was not taught in mosque or *madrasa*. For medieval Islam, a reading of scripture that was not subject to formal disciplines of philology, historiography, and learned consensus, formed no part of the schoolmen's curriculum.

Tim Winter
Faculty of Divinity, University of Cambridge, West Road, Cambridge, CB3 9BS, UK

Qayṣarī lived in times of transition (five years previously, his *madrasa* in Iznik had been a church in Nicea), and of a scepticism generated in part by the profusion of religions and sects in his vicinity. An honoured theologian-legist, he nonetheless acknowledged that formal theology is "a deduction from behind a veil",[4] confessing that "inductive monotheism [*al-tawḥīd al-istidlālī*] seldom delivers safety from doubts and ambiguities".[5] It is only God's friends, who are in receipt of direct illumination, who may safely call themselves monotheists. This uncertainty continued to preoccupy Ottoman thinkers, who from time to time attempted to reconcile the mystical and ratiocinative epistemologies, both of which were grounded in the Qur'ān;[6] but the illuminationist method of scriptural reading, despite its prestige, was never thought appropriate as a subject for university students. Instead, its proper place was the Sufi lodge, the *tekke*, site of what Weberians would identify as the charismatic religion that coexisted, at a distance but quite calmly, with the traditional piety of the *madrasas*.

Such a bifurcation was in certain respects akin to the cognitive dissonance which many modern theologians experience. The language of liturgy and sermon deployed in places of worship, particularly in charismatic contexts, is not always the obvious entailment of the finer work of the divinity schools, and scholar-theologians may find that their discursive assumptions about the origin, authority, and exegesis of scripture may fluctuate in complex ways as they migrate between class and congregation. Often this generates a Spinozan hermeneutic of suspicion towards theology in the secular academy, and a reciprocal devotional disdain for scholarship, and in particular for philosophical theology and scriptural criticism.

Classical Islamic civilisation did, however, contrive one method of overcoming this kind of polarity, and of integrating the direct experience of the living scripture into the formal academy. The Qur'ān had presented itself as an apologetic miracle, and as the theologies evolved came to be regarded as the principal proof of the Prophet's mission from God.[7] One aspect of this was taken to be the text's content, as a magisterially clear corrective to the errors of the polytheisms and monotheisms of the decadent age of its appearance. However it was the text's *literary* force which was taken to lie at the centre of the phenomenon of *i'jāz*, of the revelation's miraculous inimitability. The leading theorist of this quasi-aestheticist argument for God and His prophet was the Baghdad judge and Ashʿarite theologian al-Bāqillānī (d.1013), whose text *The Inimitability of the Qur'ān* is still widely taught.

Bāqillānī lived in an age no less turbulent than that of Qayṣari. Sceptics such as Muḥammad ibn Zakariyyā al-Rāzī (d. 925) had publicly condemned formal religion on the grounds that had the scriptures all been from the same God, their followers would not have descended into conflict. In place of scripture, Rāzī and his followers taught, human reason should be sufficient to distinguish right from wrong.[8] Against this background,

Bāqillānī begins by lamenting the times, and the inadequacy of the academic theology and scriptural hermeneutics of the day. "Everywhere," he writes, "heretics and unbelievers are challenging the foundations of the faith, and stirring up doubts, while the upholders of truth are few [. . .] Matters are as they were in the early days [of Islam], with some saying that the Qur'ān is the product of sorcery, or that it is poetry, or that it is mere fables handed down from ancient peoples. Nowadays people tell me that they compare it unfavourably with literature."[9] Responding to this failure of the formal theologians of the time to vindicate the truths carried in scripture, he embarks on a theological effort that is also literary: the text which he loves, and which had amazed the pagan Arabs four centuries earlier, can be studied formally so as to show it as miraculously replete, an aesthetic marvel so astounding that its divine provenance could not be rationally doubted. Literary criticism, grammar, rhetoric, and the entire sophisticated structure of Arab analysis of discourse were deployed as publicly verifiable supports for the presence of an aesthetic epistemology that pointed unmistakeably towards God and the divine origin of the text.

Modern academic practices of textual criticism are therefore not in principle wholly inassimilable by Muslim theology. The contextual analysis of the Qur'ānic text, arguments over the chronology of its pericopes, and the use of a variety of extraneous sources to unravel cruxes, are modern weapons with real medieval precedents. Indeed, there are historians who claim that the higher criticism which has so taxed believing Bible-readers is of Islamic origin.[10] Yet most Muslims in the academy are demonstrably alienated by conventional operating techniques in the philological wards. Most recurrently, Muslims point out that while Biblical criticism is carried out largely by Christian and Jewish insiders, the study of Muslim scriptures in the secular academy is carried out largely by Christian and Jewish outsiders; and this has contributed to the sense that the "higher criticism" is an alien and even an adversarial project.[11] Matters are not helped by a certain Orientalist paternalism: one leading academic account of the genesis of Islam's texts specifies in its introduction that "this is a book written by infidels for infidels".[12] If, as Gadamer believes, interpretation is a three-way activity, since the understanding (*verstehen*) of a text presupposes an understanding (*verständigung*) with another human subject on the meaning of that text,[13] it is easy to see why Muslim scholars have often found themselves ploughing a lonely furrow in the faculties, the victims of deeply sceptical reviewers.[14]

The arrival over the past fifteen years of larger numbers of Muslims in Western universities has both highlighted and eased this asymmetry. Muslims, like their colleagues, belong to their tradition in discrepant ways. Many are comfortable with secular interrogations of the integrity of scripture;[15] others reject the right of outsiders to work in the field,[16] while many others, perhaps the majority, are negotiating the relationship between the two styles of reading in ways as complex as those current among their Jewish and Christian colleagues. Here the academy, much more than the place of worship, is hospitable to gradations rather than boundaries, and allows a mutual fecundity, which, in the case of the Scriptural Reasoning project, has already progressed with striking results. The Muslim participation in the *Journal of Scriptural Reasoning*, which presupposes a high degree of comfort with academic paradigms, is much more substantial than that of most Islamic Studies journals, and has been able to platform some of the most significant Muslim theologians. Aref Nayed, Vincent Cornell, Basit Koshul, Muhammad Suheyl Omar, among others, are deeply involved in the movement.

The classical Orientalist *Vernunftreligion* may remain sceptical; but the *Journal of Scriptural Reasoning* is simply displaying its openness to recent shifts in hermeneutics to which Oriental Studies remain largely oblivious. The trajectory can readily be mapped. Dilthey believed that the genealogy of hermeneutics as a formal discipline can be substantially traced back as far as Lutheran zeal in refuting Tridentine strategies of scriptural appropriation, the *kairos* theme of the Reformation which ultimately made possible the "liberation of interpretation from dogma",[17] and hence from irrationality. Oriental Studies remains largely caught within this objectivist paradigm. With Heidegger, by contrast, interpretation became an "ontological event", a relationship between the reader and the text that cannot be distinguished from the text's content. The move has been implicitly reinforced by the many writers who have emphasised the subjective quality of the instruments which Dilthey held could permit a measurement or recreation of the interpretative experiences of others. The notion that one might persuasively model the ancient societies in which scripture was embedded has been widely challenged. The assumption that the outsider enjoys a privileged situation of neutrality (an axiom in much of Islamic studies) is under sustained attack.[18] Even classical logic has been the site of ambitious refinements that incorporate the role of the human subject, and seek to include a moral teleology.[19] Many would therefore concede Gadamer's prophecy:

> If, however, the ideal of the historical enlightenment that Dilthey pursued should prove to be an illusion, then the prehistory of hermeneutics that he outlined will also acquire a quite different significance. Its evolution to historical consciousness would not then be its liberation from the chains of dogma but a transformation of its nature.[20]

The inevitability of this paradigm shift is still bitterly contested, and indeed, Diltheyan scientism has been pushed even further in a positivist direction by the many thinkers who write in the wake of Emilio Betti. At another extreme, there is the continuing appeal of a totalising hermeneutic of suspicion as espoused by Derrida, which may not even permit the existence of the category of "scripture".[21] Yet Scriptural Reasoning, while located somewhere towards the end of late modernity, is usually committed to the effectively pragmatist view that as readers we experience ourselves as at least partially autonomous subjects, who would be unacceptably diminished by the counter-intuitive dogma which denies that there is a subject which reads. Scriptural Reading listens to Gadamer's scepticism about method, but is respectful of many methods, and is itself shaped by its continuing encounter with different methods and participants as well as with the text (which is why it bears no resemblance to fundamentalism, a quite different post-liberal option).[22] This has the invigorating consequence that our readings may be competitive: the text may not mean a single thing, but neither are all readings created equal; to use a Milbankian formulation, some scriptures may turn out to "out-narrate" others, and some methods may prove more persuasive than others in contemplating certain types of text. So Scriptural Reasoning, while admitting a certain postmodern reticence about final meaning, is by no means an intrinsically liberal method, and may turn out to be particularly hospitable to conservative thinkers who find that little is being communicated in academic or popular "dialogue" sessions driven by liberal presuppositions.[23]

Islam and Scriptural Reasoning

What might be the specifically Muslim experience of Scriptural Reasoning? Scriptural Reasoning (SR) is not a method, but rather a promiscuous openness to methods of a kind unfamiliar to Islamic conventions of reading. Although medieval Muslim exegesis could be as discrepantly hospitable in the paradigms it adopted as, say, Origen, contemporary styles of reading the text have for the most part passed it by. The Bible has been complicatedly part of the intellectual world which evolved into the academy within which SR typically takes place; the Qur'ān and Hadith have not. For the West, outside a few specialist circles, Muslim scriptures are largely *terra incognita*, or a backwater, associated by theologians with the culture which, through medieval Avicennism, influenced Europe for a while, before becoming isolated as an oxbow lake. For Muslims, Islam continued in fidelity to classical paradigms of faith, worship and devotion, while the Renaissance re-paganised European thought; and the Enlightenment secularised it. Muslims engaged in scriptural reading are therefore, in many cases, substantially medieval, and are generally proud of having providentially avoided the calamities of infidelity which have beset the West. But this very isolation places them at a certain disadvantage: they may find themselves, for instance, asked to clarify features of scripture which for them are elementary, due to the sheer unfamiliarity of Qur'ānic prophecy even to cultivated non-Muslims. A no less substantial inhibitor is the discovery that analytical tools developed in Biblical studies may prove inappropriate when investigating Qur'ānic texts; indeed, many Muslims hold that the entire Western culture of scriptural criticism, whether conservative or sceptical, is a reductionist Enlightenment or Protestant project which is apt to be culturally oppressive as well as philologically inappropriate when applied to Muslim sources.[24] The Qur'ān, after all, is accepted even in sceptical circles to have appeared over the course of a very few decades, and there is no question of identifying a *vorlage* for the text; it is simply unsuitable for the application of most methods of Biblical form-criticism. Hence as far as theology, or even society, are concerned, for Islam there cannot be a "return to Scripture" in Peter Och's sense, since the Qur'ān has nowhere been abandoned; and Muslim interlocutors in SR are much more likely to feel part of an unbroken tradition than advocates of a latter-day *ressourcement*. Unlike many Christians and Jews in SR, who come from societies wounded by a great divorce from scripture, Muslim participants are apt to come from societies wounded by fundamentalist misappropriations of scripture, and their appreciation of the insights and the moral teleology of the encounters will inevitably be very different.

Properly speaking, a Muslim may only interpret scripture after authorisation (*ijāza*) from traditional masters, who have themselves been authorised as part of an unbroken succession (*isnād*) stretching back to the Prophet himself.[25] Historicity is hence an axiom: no Muslim Bultmann has yet appeared at a SR seminar. Medieval exegesis, too, is authoritative, and Muslim scholars will, in theory, not use it unless they are accredited in the same fashion, this time as links in a chain extending back to the author of a given commentary. In this way, Muslims see themselves not just as interpreters but as para-witnesses to the scripture and to the exegetic cumulation. This imposes formal restraints on the reflections they are likely to offer. Muslims are not, however, required to be custodians of a univocal tradition. Medieval Muslims, like Jews and Christians, lived in internally diverse worlds; and like Jews, normally inhabited societies where more than one scripture was widely followed. Although the canonical form of the Qur'ānic text is not discernibly the product of an internal argument, but of an argument against other religions, the manifold difficulties of its language, and the immense and ambiguous body of hadith which supply its initial exegesis and *sitz im leben*, prohibit a single Islamic gloss on any given verse. Even the earliest major commentaries show this clearly.

Yet the Muslim freedom from Enlightenment constraints is very different from post-Enlightenment, postliberal freedom. Where, for Jews, premodern riches may be alive currently in smallish rivulets that escaped the Shoah, and where, for Christians, they might be found on Athos, to be brought home to the seminar room and unpacked, and jubilantly recognised, for Muslims premodern orthodoxy, liturgy, and scriptural reading are likely to exist in the nearest mosque. This will equip Muslims with an always discrepant voice at the seminar table. If SR tends to exclude the search for precision, and to celebrate an "irremediable vagueness" (Ochs), Muslims may demur: God need not choose to disclose himself only in playful obscurity, however successful that disclosure may be. First-order exegesis has the right to be true, rather than merely illuminating. "Fallibilism" is not a doctrine which is easily discerned as the way in which prophetic scriptures seek to be approached. Peirce's pragmatism will work, perhaps, for Māturīdīs, persuaded as they are of the consensual discernability of human florescence autonomously of scriptural definitions; but Ash'aris (and so perhaps the majority of Muslim theologians) are committed to a command ethic which will need to interrogate any arbitration between rival interpretations which is attempted merely on the basis of our perception of the humanity of their practical outcomes.[26] For Ash'aris, such a pragmatism can in fact be deconstructed, like the great edifice which Rawls erects on thin presumptions about "good people", or like Nussbaum's virtue ethics. Monotheism, taken seriously, means that God alone is the axiological source; human intuition is liable to set up rivals which may be idolatrous. What would an SR seminar have looked like in Nazi Germany, between, say, a Nazi biblical scholar and a Bosnian Muslim supporter of the Reich, in a world where definitions of human flowering were very different to those which currently prevail? Heidegger, after all, trusted his own *phronesis*.[27] There may be a progressist, liberal substratum here after all; in fact, a "hard" Ash'arism or Ḥanbalism of a type not uncommon amongst today's polarities might even interpret SR as yet another Americanisation of religion (not only Peirce, but also Dewey and William James are at work somewhere behind the scenes). As for the hopeful idea that psychomachy will naturally produce a love of the Other, one need only consider Ignatius Loyola's attitudes to Moors and Jews (examples in the Jewish and Muslim world are also not far to seek).

Yet where the vagueness entails an openness to a lack of closure, and nothing more than this, Muslims can and do participate energetically. As an internal validation, they may affirm the need to act in fidelity with the kerygmatic Qur'ānic address to Christians and Jews, who are called to love and affirm the Ishmaelite prophet, but also, in other texts, to uphold their own scriptures. Non-Muslim scripturaries are to be "disputed with in the most courteous way" (16:125). "O people of the Book" is a frequent Qur'ānic appeal, respectful insofar as the great bulk of the exemplary stories embedded in the text concern Israelites and Christians.[28] The Qur'ān is not a national polemic against rival ethnicities; on the contrary, it holds up the diversity of human "tongues and colours" as a sign of God (30:22). Generally hostile to Arab history and values, it is Arabic, but not Arab.[29]

This latent universalism and kerygmatic openness seems to have been a leading factor behind the growing Muslim participation in SR. Its consequences are not yet easy to discern. Even medieval Muslim encounters with other monotheists could bring about changes in exegesis, or at least an expansion of the boundaries of licit meaning.[30] The loose canons of SR are likely further to broaden Muslim interpretations, for instance by encouraging a reading of the Bible whose principal ambition is no longer to seek Muhammadan "foretellings" in the text,[31] but to consider it on its own terms, or, if that proves too "essentialising", on the terms of a community of its own interpreters. Internal Muslim differences are also likely to flourish, including esoteric-exoteric balances, Māturīdī, Ashʿarī and Shīʿī differentials, and gender-based disparities in the reading of the Qurʾān.[32]

The Muslim-Jewish Intersubjectivity

Although Scriptural Reasoning is comfortable with the tripartite "Abrahamic" category of monotheistic and historically-grounded traditions,[33] Muslim theology is probably more explicitly committed to the category than are either Judaism or Christianity. Afdal al-Dīn Kāshānī (d.1213), outlining his theory of scripture (the "sending-down") as the necessary catalyst for self-knowledge, is representative when he writes:

> [God] adorned the mark of these three sending-downs for three communities: the folk of the Torah, the Gospel, and the Qurʾān. Despite all the prophets, He said that only these three levels of sending-down should be kept standing. Thus He says: "O Folk of the Book! You are not upon anything until you uphold the Torah and the Gospel, and what was sent down to you from your Lord."[34] (Qurʾān 5:68)

The three-way dynamic helps to reduce binary polarisations, but it does carry a bias towards the "Semitic". Muslim-Jewish relations turn out to be privileged for several reasons which may relate to this traditional category. Both traditions are nomocentric, and have been the subject of analogous charges of "legalism", which may have influenced some textual critics.[35] Purity laws, for instance, comprise an important area of intertextuality between Torah and Qurʾān, and may be the subject of conversations that partially exclude Christian participation.[36] Jew and Muslim also converge when they read scriptural tales against a background of a very analogous valorisation of martial prowess and of human sexuality (again, both have on occasion been the subject of Christian critiques).

A further convergence which can emerge from SR sessions is that neither tradition is as manifestly committed to teleological views of history than is Christianity, with its proclamation of a radically new covenant. (For Islam, the messiah has come, but his role was to emphasise, in somewhat amended or even Masorti form, the timeless Law of Moses: no new "economy of salvation" is being launched.)[37] Hegelian notions of a progress from nature and image towards abstraction seem to be interrogated by Semitic naturalism, by the integration of the body and its functions into a liturgy which continues to satisfy modern needs, and, in the arts, by a primordial aniconism.[38] It is true that certain forms of liberal Judaism, rooted in Abraham Geiger's view of Tanakh and Talmud as early, primitive stages of human evolution, remain staunchly committed to ideas of progress; but the experience of the Holocaust has dented this, and encouraged a reversion, (sometimes formalistic, sometimes sophisticated, and sometimes both), to older patterns of "awaiting the day of the Lord".[39] Most Muslim and Jewish participants in the joint study of scripture will be alert to messianic references, but will not see the "Old Testament" as either the foreshadowing of full salvation (Augustine), or as the record of a process of moral advancement (Wellhausen), but as the complex memory of a people whose access to the divine was, from earliest times, already complete, a completion that was periodically wounded and healed. There is a *historia monotheistica*, but monotheism itself does not advance.

The cognate quality of Arabic and Hebrew, which frequently enriches the practice of comparative SR, is a well-established topos, having historically permitted substantial cross-fertilisation, as in the case of Muslim scriptural lexis with Hebrew cognates,[40] and also subsequently, as the Arab grammarians transformed rabbinic strategies of scripture-reading.[41] Still more theologically productive is the fact that both religions have cherished their scriptural languages as meta-languages, uniquely sacred vessels of a real presence, and have developed, and debated, doctrines of Torah or Qur'ān as the uncreated divine speech (*Torah min ha-shamayim; al-Qur'ān kalāmu'Llāh al-qadīm*). The power of the *bayān*, the discourse, expressed in a powerfully pure and consistent language, is itself taken to be evidence of God's unity, as Bāqillānī and his tradition saw, supplying a "kerygmatic ontology".[42] The "sending-down" of the "word made book", is composed of "signs" (*aya*); but these turn out to be unlike other signs, in that they are ontological reflections or even instantiations of the divine, a belief that triggered exuberant forms of letter-mysticism both within and outside the paradigms of Kabbalah and Sufism. Gadamer identifies Plato's *Cratylus* as the point at which the view of language as comprising icons rather than mere signs begins to decay, leading to the modern view that "the word is reduced to a wholly secondary relation to the thing".[43] Classical expressions of Judaism and Islam, by contrast, appear to revert to ancient iconic associations of signifier and signified,[44] which become the basis for a logocentric theology that is the polar opposite of Saussurean relativism.

The Argument from Beauty

If scripture is God's uncreated speech, then to recite it is to speak a miracle; even more, it is, as Bāqillānī insisted, to speak an apologetic miracle. Hence there is a strongly aesthetical aspect to SR engagement, and this is certainly congenial to Muslim concerns.[45] Most hermeneutical theory has stressed beauty as a potential indicator of truth (Gadamer's *Truth and Method* starts by mobilising Plato to defend this), and in recent years, in tandem with the decline in classical Kantianism and in reaction against postmodern dismissals of aesthetics as mere reification, there has been a revival of interest in aesthetics as a possible sign of truth. A well-known instance is Elaine Scarry's *On Beauty and Being Just*, which proposes that beauty offers a "radical de-centering", supplying both ethical intuition and access to timeless truths, which for her include political liberalism and social equality.[46]

Scriptural Reasoning has no doubt gained in credibility from the turn which Scary champions; yet in concentrating on the beauty and plenitude of scriptural language it represents a unique and highly concentrated case.[47] The three traditions, in their irreducibly distinct ways, experience Truth in the fullness of the text: not the text as meaning, but as reading. Consider Levinas, reflecting on a Talmudic passage, where it is shown that

> the statement commented upon exceeds what it originally wants to say; that what it is capable of saying goes beyond what it wants to say; that it contains more than it contains; that perhaps an inexhaustible surplus of meaning remains locked in the syntactic structures of the sentence, in its word-groups, its actual words, phonemes and letters, in all this materiality of the saying which is potentially signifying all the time. Exegesis would come to see, in these signs, a bewitched significance that smoulders beneath the characters or coils up in all this literature of letters.[48]

This is hard to distinguish from the deepest insight of *iʿjāz* theory: the Qurʾān is a literary, aesthetic argument for itself, which challenges (*taḥaddī*) present-day readers despite the apparent archaism of its diction and concerns, where the anachronic gap simply adds another fertile dimension to the productive interaction of its letters and sudden shifts in style and subject. The spoken miracle continues to speak thanks to the difficulty of its beauty.[49]

Qurʾānic Reasoning as Epistemology: Two Examples

> Had they established [*aqāmu*] the Torah and the Gospel, and what has been revealed to them from their Lord, they would have eaten from above them and from beneath their feet. (Qurʾān, 5:65–6)

The medieval commentaries offer divergent but "valid" (*ḥasana*) interpretations of this text. What is it to "establish" the Torah or the Gospel? It is to be faithful to God's covenant as set forth therein, such fidelity including a receptivity to the possibility that God might will to send a Gentile prophet. Alternatively, it is to apply the laws and commandments which those scriptures contain. Thirdly, it could mean that Christians and Jews are to hold up their scriptures "before their eyes", lest they slip in any observance. "What has been revealed to them" can refer to the new revelation of the Qur'ān, or to the books of the Prophets (*nabiyyīn*) such as Daniel. Such are the plain senses, as commended by the leading medieval Ashʿarite Fakhr al-Dīn al-Rāzī (d.1209).[50] A Scriptural Reasoning encounter would probably register these meanings, and then press on in unforeseeable ways to consider the consequences of "establishing" Scripture: prosperity, perhaps earthly, perhaps celestial; the metaphor of scripture as a "banquet" (*ma'daba*) to be savoured (as the Latins put it), with the *palatum cordis*;[51] the implication that faithfulness to scripture places human beings between heaven and earth (the verse continues: "Amongst them are a balanced people"). There would be no conclusion, despite the general enrichment and sense of respect for the fecundity of the text; however, there would probably be a consensus that the text is presenting scripture as the source and guarantor of a divine gift.

And when the Qur'ān is recited, pay heed, and listen with reverence, that you may perhaps receive mercy. (Qur'ān, 7:204)

Here the plain sense found by Rāzī focuses on the use of the imperative mood, and on the deduction, from the "perhaps", that both believers and unbelievers are being addressed.[52] The Sufi commentary of Ismaʿīl Bursevī (d.1725), affirms Rāzī's reading, but adds a reflection on scripture-reading as a source of mercy. The core liturgical habit of Islam is the fivefold daily prayer (*ṣalāt*), and the core of the *ṣalāt* is Qur'ānic recitation.[53] "Paying heed", for Bursevī, suggests the formal activation of a sense, while "listen with reverence" denotes an appreciation with one's "inward ear". This is not the *bāṭin* of Qayṣarī's schema, but the *maṭlaʿ*, the "rising-place". Bursevī cites another scriptural text, the hadith in which God says, "When I love My servant [...] I become the ear with which he hears"; so Bursevī observes that "whoever hears the Qur'ān with the ear of his Maker has truly heard it being recited", and adds a couplet from the poet Jāmī (d.1492):

For you to understand not one letter of the Qur'ān is no wonder;
The wonder is that your eye can be blind to the sun of His generosity.[54]

Considering a commentary of this order, an SR seminar might summon other scriptural resources, such as the passage where the Qur'ān speaks of its own "sending-down" as a "healing" and a "mercy" (17:82). A discussion on mercy (Ar. *raḥma*, with its Hebrew cognates) as the salvific fruit of worship might include, in the context of the "sending-down", the metaphor of rain (*raḥmet*, in some Islamic languages), and of the "healing" of the earth. Finally, the conversation might "fall" in the direction of the clear soteriological and epistemological intent of these texts. Does scripture purport to supply a sacramental source of knowledge intuited through recital and cantillation that is supra-rational but which cannot be ignored theologically? If so, will this yield simply another private *fides ex auditu* (the *sam'iyyāt* of *kalām*), or is it akin to the "hermeneutical ontology" towards which Gadamer worked (or does it resemble it only in its insistence on indeterminacy)? Does the miracle of holding the text point towards its exogenous origin, as in the Muslim legend in which Moses can only lift the tablets of the Law when he invokes the name of God?[55] And what of the intuition of fellowship experienced during the seminar, as the texts are tasted as a kind of ambivalent communion in three kinds. Do we find in this new fellowship of intersubjectivity, which is so often tangential to religious boundaries, something transcendent?[56] Nothing is sought to be proven; but a context and an energy for further work within one's own community have certainly been supplied.

NOTES

1   For this hadith see Gerhard Böwering, *The Mystical Vision of Existence in Classical Islam: The Qur'ānic Hermeneutics of the Ṣūfī Sahl al-Tustarī* (d.283/896), (Berlin and New York: Walter de Gruyter, 1980), pp. 139–141. The parallel with the Talmudist's four levels of meaning, *pesht* (plain sense), *remez* (allusive meaning), *derash* (solicited meaning), and *sod* (secret meaning) is evident.

2   Mehmet Bayrakdar (ed. and introduction), "Risala Fi Ilm at-Tasawwuf li Dâwud al-Kaysari", *Ankara Üniversitesi Ilahiyat Fakültesi Dergisi* Vol. 30 (1988), pp. 171–216; p. 199.

3   Mehmet Bayrakdar, *La Philosophie Mystique chez Dawud de Kayseri* (Ankara: Kültür Bakanlığı, 1990).

4   Qaysarī, *Risāla*, p. 210.

5   *Ibid.,* p. 210.

6   For an example in translation, see Nicholas Heer, "Al-Jāmī's Treatise on Existence" in Parviz Morewedge (ed.), *Islamic Philosophical Theology* (Albany, NY: State University of New York Press, 1979), pp. 223–256.

7   Muḥammad ibn al-Ṭayyib al-Bāqillānī, *I'jāz al-Qur'ān* (Cairo: Muḥammad 'Alī Ṣubayḥ, 1370/1951), p. 33.

8   Latimah-Parvin Peerwani, "Abū Ḥātim Rāzī on the Essential Unity of Religions" in Mohammad H. Faghfoory, (ed.), *Beacon of Knowledge: Essays in honour of Seyyid Hossein Nasr* (Louisville KY: Fons Vitae, 2003), pp. 269–287; see also P. E. Daiber, "Abū Ḥātim al-Rāzī (10th century A.D.) on the Unity and Diversity of Religions", in J. Gort, H. Vroom, *et al.* (eds.), *Dialogue and Syncretism: An Interdisciplinary Approach* (Grand Rapids and Amsterdam: Wm. B. Eerdmans Publishing Company, 1989), pp. 87–104. For the background see Josef van Ess, "Scepticism in Islamic Religious Thought" in Charles Malik (ed.), *God and Man in Contemporary Islamic Thought* (Beirut: American University of Beirut, 1972), pp. 83–88.

9   Bāqillānī, *I'jāz al-Qur'ān*, p. 29.

10   Hava Lazarus-Yafeh, *Intertwined Worlds: Medieval Islam and Bible Criticism* (Princeton, NJ: Princeton University Press, 1992).

11   See, for instance, Mohammad Khalifa, *The Sublime Qur'ān and Orientalism* (London: Longman, 1983). For a classic example, see the leading nineteenth-century British historian of Islamic origins, William Muir: "The turning point is the genuineness and integrity of our Scriptures; when that is proved, the truth of the Christian religion and falsity of Mohammedanism follow." William Muir, *The Mohammedan Controversy* (Edinburgh: T. & T. Clark, 1897), p. 54.

12   Patricia Crone and Michael Cook, *Hagarism: The Making of the Islamic World* (Cambridge: Cambridge University Press, 1977), p. viii.

13 Hans-Georg Gadamer, trans. Joel Weinsheimer and Donald G. Marshall, *Truth and Method*, second edition, (London: Sheed and Ward, 1989), p. xvi.

14 Conversely, the association of critical scholarship with Orientalist and hence implicitly imperial aspirations has intensified the difficulties of those working to confirm the integrity of the Qur'ān while developing theories of its deep appurtenance to its original Arabian context; this political inhibition is discussed, for instance, by Ömer Özsoy, *Kur'an ve Tarihselcilik Yazıları* (Ankara: Kitâbiyât, 2004), p. 98.

15 See, for instance, the various writings of Abdul Qadir Sherif.

16 ʿAbbūd Zakī al-Ghāmidī, *Mawqif al-Mustashriqīn min Kitāb Allāh* (Beirut: Dār al-Ghurabā', 1987).

17 Gadamer, *Truth and Method*, p. 176.

18 Francis Watson, *Text, Church and World: Biblical interpretation in theological perspective* (London and New York: T. & T. Clark, 1994).

19 Peter Ochs, *Peirce, Pragmatism and the Logic of Scripture* (Cambridge: Cambridge University Press, 1998).

20 Gadamer, *Truth and Method*, p. 177.

21 Wesley A. Kort, *"Take, Read": Scripture, Textuality and Cultural Practice* (University Park, PA: Pennsylvania State University Press, 1996), p. 4. The Algerian thinker Mohamed Arkoun follows this closely: Mohamed Arkoun, *Lectures du Coran*, second edition, (Tunis: Alif, 1991), p. 258.

22 It cannot be emphasised too often that Scriptural Reasoning bears no resemblance to the *alliance sacrée* between fundamentalism and postmodernism which is emerging in some quarters.

23 "The more one is firm about the classical points that divide us the better we know where we stand, and our discussion becomes surprisingly open and fruitful." Georges Anawati, "Vers un dialogue islamo-chretien", *Revue Thomiste* Vol. 64 (1964), p. 627.

24 Ismail Albayrak, *Klasik Modernizmde Kur'ân'a Yaklaşımlar* (Istanbul: Ensar Neşriyat, 2004), pp. 17–19.

25 For the *ijāza* system see Franz Rosenthal, *Knowledge Triumphant: the concept of knowledge in medieval Islam* (Leiden: E. J. Brill, 1970).

26 For the Ashʿarī-Māturīdī split here see Kevin Reinhart, *Before Revelation: the boundaries of Muslim moral thought* (Albany, NY: State University of New York Press, 1995).

27 The dangers are starkly illustrated in Hans-Georg Gadamer, *Reason in the Age of Science*, trans. F. Lawrence, (Cambridge, MA: MIT Press, 1981), pp. 88–112.

28 Özsoy, *Kur'an re Tarihselcilik Yazıları*, pp. 13–15. Christian stories held up for Muslim admiration include the legend of the Seven Sleepers and the "Companions of the Trench".

29 Or, if it is Arab, it is a document of radical auto-criticism and affirmation of the Other. The text's non-Arab nature allowed attacks on the Arabs, on Islamic grounds, by the likes of Abu'l-Rayḥān Bīrūnī (Edward D. Sachau, *Alberuni's India* [London: Kegan Paul, Trench, Trübner and Co., 1910], p. 185), and Abū ʿUthmān al-Jāḥiẓ, *Risāla fī fadl al-Turk* in ʿAbd al-Salām Muḥammad Hārūn (ed.), *Rasā'il al-Jāḥiẓ* (Cairo: al-Khanjī, n.d.), pp. 1–86.

30 See, for instance, the already-mentioned Abū Ḥātim Rāzī, whose consciousness of Christianity and of religious diversity impelled him to read Qur'ān 4:157 against the Muslim consensus, as affirming the reality of the crucifixion. Latimah-Parvin Peerwani, "Abu Hatim Razi on the Essential Unity of Religions", pp. 282–283.

31 This was the main reason for pre-modern Muslim Bible reading; see for instance ʿAlī b. Rabbān al-Ṭabarī, *The Book of Religion and Empire*, trans. Alphonse Mingana, (New Delhi: Kitab Bhavan, 1986).

32 Over the past few decades the number of Qur'ānic commentaries authored by women has grown rapidly; see for instance M. Akif Koç, *Bir Kadın Müfessir: Aişe Abdurrahman ve Kur'an Tefsirindeki Yeri* (Istanbul: Şule Yayınları, 1998).

33 "The proper Buddhist place to start the study of Buddhism is not the life-story of the Buddha at all, but through outlining straight away the Dharma." Paul Williams, *Buddhist Thought: A Complete Introduction to the Indian tradition* (London: Routledge, 2000), p. 23.

34 William C. Chittick, *The Heart of Islamic Philosophy: The Quest for Self-Knowledge in the Teachings of Afdal al-Dīn Kāshānī* (Oxford: Oxford University Press, 2001), p. 228.

35 This is probably a fair comment in the case of Julius Wellhausen, who worked extensively on the textual sources of both Judaism and Islam.

36   Jacob Neusner and Tamara Sonn, *Comparing Religions through Law: Judaism and Islam* (New York: Routledge, 1999). For a large but interesting generalisation about the relationship between universalism, law, and the monotheisms, see Huston Smith's introduction to Seyyed Hossein Nasr, *Ideals and Realities of Islam* (London: George Allen and Unwin, 1966), p. vii.

37   Mahmoud Ayoub, *The Qur'ān and its Interpreters II: The House of ʿImrān* (Albany, NY: State University of New York Press, 1992), pp. 149–150. The strictly non-chronological structure of the Qur'ānic text is, probably, a further sign of this non-progressism.

38   Some hold that the Qur'ān may best be seen as a form of literature older than Torah; see most notably Jaroslav Stetkevych, *Muhammad and the Golden Bough: reconstructing Arabian myth* (Bloomington, IN: Indiana University Press, 1996); cf. for instance p. 11: "Unlike the latter [Genesis account of Joseph] the Quranic rendition is not an ideology-saturated pretense of tribal history, and, for that reason, it is more detached and more archetypal— and thus closer to myth."

39   Peter Ochs, "The God of Jews and Christians" in Tikva Frymer-Krensk *et al.*, *Christianity in Jewish Terms* (Boulder and Oxford: Westview Press, 2000), p. 54.

40   Even during the Prophet's lifetime the Qur'ānic vocabulary was being explained with reference to Hebrew cognates: Ḥusayn al-Baghawī, *Maʿālim al-tanzīl* (Beirut: Dār al-Maʿrifa, 1407/1987), III, p. 22.

41   W. Johnstone, "Reading the Hebrew Bible with Arabic-sensitized eyes" in W. Johnstone (ed.), *William Robertson Smith: essays in reassessment* (Sheffield: Sheffield Academic Press, 1995), pp. 390–397.

42   See further Antoine Maqdiçi, "L'Ontologie kérygmatique de Paul Ricoeur: Approche arabe" in Gary Brent Madison (ed.), *Sens et existence: en homage a Paul Ricoeur* (Paris: Seuil, 1975), pp. 170–206, cf. p.188: Arabic "a été tellement parfaite, que le rhythme du discours, l'attitude qu'il provoque, la sensibilité qu'il crée, semblent être le travail d'un seul, l'Unique dans son unicité qui crée en exprimant et exprime en créant." See also Jacques Langhade, *Du Coran a la philosophie: la langue arabe et la formation du vocabulaire philosophique de Farabi* (Damascus: Institut Français de Damas, 1994), pp. 26–27.

43   Gadamer, *Truth and Method*, p. 414.

44   See, for instance, William C. Chittick, *The Heart of Islamic Philosophy*, p. 164; certain readings of the Kabbalah also readily sustain this view in a radical way.

45   And to most monotheistic concerns; although note that Calvin would repudiate any Scriptural Reasoning venture conceived on such principles, since, in his understanding "it was also not without God's extraordinary providence that the sublime mysteries of the Kingdom of Heaven came to be expressed largely in mean and lowly words, lest, if they had been adorned with most shining eloquence, the impious would scoffingly have claimed that its power is in the realm of eloquence alone." (Cited in Kort, p. 26.)

46   Elaine Scarry, *On Beauty and Being Just* (Princeton, NJ: Princeton University Press, 1999); for a thorough critique see Robert B. Pippin, *The Persistence of Subjectivity: On the Kantian Aftermath* (Cambridge: Cambridge University Press, 2006), pp. 273–277.

47   Aref Nayed criticises Gadamer for his desire "to see *hermeneutica sacra* only as a special application of a universal General Hermeneutics"; yet "sacred" and "profane" hermeneutics will not be so swiftly distinguished in the academy; neither should they be, unless we are to discount the possibility of discerning the transcendent in all texts not conventionally classed as scriptural. See Aref Ali Nayed, "Reading Scripture Together: Towards a Sacred Hermeneutics of Togetherness", *The Princeton Seminary Bulletin* Vol. XXVI, no. 1, new series (2005), pp. 48–53 or http://etext.lib.virginia.edu/journals/jsrforum/nayed-princeton.pdf.

48   Emmanuel Levinas, *Beyond the Verse: Talmudic Readings and Lectures*, trans. Gary D. Mole, (London: Athlone Press, 1994), p. 109.

49   Talip Özdeş, *Mâturîdî'nin Tefsîr Anlayışı* (Istanbul: Insan Yayınları, 2003), pp. 279–282.

50   Fakhr al-Dīn al-Rāzī, *Mafātīh al-ghayb al-mushtahir bi-al-Tafsīr al-kabīr* (Cairo: al-Maṭbaʿa al-Miṣriyya, 1933), XII, pp. 46–47.

51   See the hadith "the Qur'ān is God's banquet" (Abū Dāūd, Faḍāʾil al-Qur'ān, 1). For the "eating" of Christian scripture see Peter Norton SJ, "Lectio Vere Divina: St Bernard and the Bible", *Monastic Studies* Vol. 3 (1965), pp. 165–181, especially pp. 174–175.

52 Fakhr al-Dīn al-Rāzī, *Mafātīḥ al-ghayb al-mushtahir bi-al-Tafsīr al-kabīr* (Cairo: al-Maṭba'a al-Miṣriyya, 1933), XV, pp. 102–105.
53 Ismā'īl Ḥaqqī Bursevī, *Tafsīr Rūḥ al-bayān* (Istanbul: Eser Kitabevi, 1389/1970), III, p. 303. The hadith is from Bukhārī, Riqāq, p. 38.
54 Ismā'īl Haqqī Bursevī, *Tafsir Ruh al-bayan*, p. 305.
55 Al-Rābghuzī, *The Stories of the Prophets: Qisas al-Anbiyā, an Eastern Turkish Version*, eds. H. E. Boeschoten, M. Vandamm and S. Tezcan, (Leiden, New York and Köln: E. J. Brill, 1995), II, p. 347.
56 Here the seminar might ponder the hadith: "My love must come to those who love one another for My sake" (Muwaṭṭa', Shi'r, 16).

8

PHILOSOPHIC WARRANTS FOR SCRIPTURAL REASONING

PETER OCHS

Introduction

Scriptural Reasoning (SR) is a practice of philosophic theology that is offered as a rationally warranted albeit fallible response to the inadequacies of modern liberal *and* anti-liberal theologies whether they are adopted as academic projects or as dimensions of lived religious practice. In terms of everyday religious practice in the West today, SR may be characterized as an effort, at once, to help protect Abrahamic folk traditions (that is, of Christianity, Judaism, and Islam) from the cultural and theological effects of residual western colonialism *and* to help protect religiously pluralist societies in the West from reactionary, anti-modern movements within these traditions. In the terms of recent academic discourse in theology, SR may be characterized as *pragmatic, postliberal, scriptural,* and *inter-Abrahamic.*

SR may be labeled *"pragmatic,"* because it employs philosophic reasoning only to identify problems in its practitioners' communities of everyday practice and in the institutions that are expected to repair them. SR may be labeled *"postliberal,"* because it emerges as a response to problems in the projects of modern, liberal theology, in particular this theology's inadequate attention to problems in everyday practice. At the same time, SR is equally critical of anti-liberal theologies, or those that, rejecting the autonomy of human reason, argue for the opposite: grounding all projects of reasoning on a practice of "Christian reasoning" per se (or, comparably, of other confession-grounded reasonings).

SR enlists many "postmodern" strategies in its critique of the modern complex of liberal-or-anti-liberal argumentation, but it argues that standard postmodern criticisms do not apply to the SR practice of scriptural theology.[1] Briefly stated for want of space, we may say that the force of most

Peter Ochs
Department of Religious Studies, PO Box 400126, University of Virginia, Charlottesville, VA 22904-4126, USA

postmodern criticisms is captured in the critique of "foundationalism": or the effort to locate some truth claim(s), independent of inherited traditions of practice, on the basis of which to construct reliable systems of belief and practice. Most efforts of this kind come in the form of "intuitionism": or the belief that such truth claims may come in the form of discrete, self-legitimating cognitions.[2] SR tends to be distinctive among other postmodern and postliberal projects in its commitment to *reading scripture* as its formational discipline. It is unique, moreover, in its including *Christians, Muslims, and Jews* in this discipline while also honoring postliberal claims about the text-and-tradition specificity of any practice of knowing and acting in the world. How SR can achieve all these ends is the subject of this issue. Within that subject, the purpose of this essay is to illustrate a logical strategy for warranting and testing the work of SR. Beyond the limits of SR, this model is also offered as a more economical and less language-specific criterion for warranting and testing all postmodern criticisms of the failings of modernist projects or their equivalents.

A Logical Strategy for Postmodernism/Postliberalism

The logical strategy is, briefly put, to distinguish between the binary logics that help us recognize marks of both suffering and oppression and the triadic logics that help us recognize and recommend acts of repair and redemption. Lacking this distinction would render postmodern and postliberal projects more liable to replaying some of the errors they criticize in modernist philosophies or liberal theologies. It would tend, for example, to encourage postmodern critics to adopt the binary logic of suffering as if it were also a logic of repair. Once adopted as a basis for action, however, this binary logic would be indistinguishable from the logic of oppression, and postmodern efforts at repair would prove to be as oppressive as they were reparative. Among postliberals, the errant tendency would, most likely, be to assimilate the marks of suffering and of oppression: assuming, on the one hand, that the binary logics of modernity are marks only of oppression rather than also of suffering while, on the other hand, making assertions on behalf of Christian care for the oppressed through binary logics that also serve their oppressors.

The Logic of Suffering and the Logic of Oppression

One set of guidelines for summarizing all the postmodern criticisms of modernity is this:

(a) To note that every object of opprobrium (*totalité*, colonial oppression, substantialism, and so on) belongs to a mode of argumentation or belief or practice that can be adequately described in the terms of modern propositional logic or, in other words, in terms brought to a *reductio ad absurdum* in Wittgenstein's *Tractatus*.

(b) To note that, with the exception of extreme forms of postmodernism, the critique is aimed not at the logic itself but only at its misapplication, which is most often a matter of quantification or modality. In the first instance, modernists are said to err by misapplying universal quantifiers to finite domains of reference. In the second instance, they err by mis-categorizing actual or possible claims as necessary or impossible.[3] In Descartes' terms, each error may be ascribed to an act of asserting the will beyond the limits of warranted observation/cognition.

(c) To recognize that the grounds for this critique are often but not always apparent in the rhetoric of modernist argumentation. As a result, postmodern and postliberal criticisms often give rise to counter arguments that *accept* the standard of criticism but challenge the evidence for applying it to a given case. As if to say: "yes totalizing is bad, but I do not do it." Our logical contribution has the advantage of providing formal criteria that make it more difficult to defend against postmodern criticisms, since not only the defendant but also the postmodern plaintiff will, more often than not, appear guilty according to these criteria.

(d) To adopt, therefore, the following stages of criticism[4]: (1) any claims are suspect if they bear the quantifier "universal" or the modal character "necessary" or "impossible"; (2) all such claims remain suspect if they may be restated as a series of discrete propositions, each one of which can be readily inferred from another and each one of which obeys the principles of excluded middle and non-contradiction; (3) claims that remain suspect after step #2 are removed from suspicion *only* if they can be shown to be tautological (analytic in Kant's terms) in either of two senses: with respect to common sense conventions (dictionary definitions and matters of speech or of the media of argument); or with respect to any given system of beliefs or explanations. In the latter case, the claim may be restated as "universal (or necessary/impossible) for all adherents to the given system," but *as of indeterminate quantification and modality for all others*.[5]; (4) claims that remain suspect after step #3 may be adequately redescribed as *binary claims*, or claims that assert that "only X or Y are true claims about the world," that "Y is the contradictory of X $(Y = -X)$," and that, therefore "only X is true.[6]"

(e) To treat all binary claims as suspect.

What do we do with such binary claims? The next step in this logical guideline is to resist the temptation to identify "suspect" claims simply with "errant" claims. This identification is the source of many errors in postmodern and postliberal criticism, because it tempts the critic to make a binary assertion about a binary claim: that if the suspect assertion was "X", then that is prima facie reason for considering "-X" as at least a reasonable hypothesis.[7] The next step is, instead, genealogical: to label each binary claim a confused symptom of some as yet unarticulated problematic situation. This is a Deweyan move comparable to Foucault and also John Milbank's genealogical moves. There is error in the claim, but the error belongs only to the claimant or the school of inadequate reasoning that he or she serves. As every hermeneut of suspicion has suggested—from Nietzsche to Derrida—whatever is an error in the realm of formal cognition becomes a performance of (unintentional) concealment in the realm of history and social/religious life. A binary claim is prima facie a non-claim. But the fact that we are interested in it generally accompanies our own sense that the claimant is a worthy antagonist of some sort, whose claims represent a significant event in the idea life of our society or faith tradition. This means that the binary claim also has the pragmatic force of a mark of societal disruption: something is amiss. At the same time, our critique of this claim, up to step #4 above, is itself attached to a binary claim: "X is true or is not true." The fact of *this* binary should alert us to the pragmatic force of *our own interest in this "error"*: that something is amiss with us too. At the very least, our peace is amiss, since we now recognize something is wrong with our neighbor (this modernist). More likely, we also recognize something of our selves, let alone of our societal context, in our neighbor's error, so we realize that his/her error is something that implicates us as well. Our next move is as much for self-love as neighbor love: to look for ways to heal the condition that gave rise to the binary reasoning.[8]

With limited space, I suggest we look, for now, only at two reasonable hypotheses about what is amiss: suffering and oppression. Calling these "hypotheses" is a critical step in SR's approach to truth, displaying SR's refusal to replace modernist intuitionism with what would be an oxymoronic "post-postmodern" intuitionism. For SR, every discrete cognition by individual humans bears the public force of a probable claim or hypothesis. Following Charles Peirce, we may label the conscious or unconscious processes that lead to such cognitions "abduction", and we may note that abductions are warranted, ultimately, only by the long run of history.[9] In the short run, we have the limited warrants only of the community that shares our reasons for offering such abductions, and these reasons constitute the "presuppositions" that mark the particularity and finitude of our hypotheses. *To argue in this humble way is not to forestall faith or confident action in the world. It is, to the contrary, a sign of faith, for it means that we are unafraid to act and let God and the events of history judge and correct us. According to SR, theologians who seek "universal warrants" for beliefs and action prior to action display the same kind of anxiety or lack of faith that marks the Cartesian project.*

In this case, our hypotheses about suffering and oppression draw on two presuppositions. *The first is that our several scriptural traditions converge on this single command: we are to care for those who suffer. The second presupposition is that the logic of caring differs from the logic of suffering and of oppression. The first presupposition, which I will turn to now, displays the scriptural ground of pragmatism's critique of modernism. The second presupposition will enable us, in this essay's concluding section, to distinguish between SR's alternative to modernism and the alternatives offered by other postmodern and postliberal projects.*

We are to Care for Those Who Suffer

Prototypically characterized as "the poor, the stranger, the widow, the orphan, the other, the naked, the hungry, those who sit in the dust", these are all recognized as those who cry out in pain or those whose cries we should hear even if they are unable to cry out loud. We cannot and need not try to define what "suffering" means, beyond identifying it with "the reason for someone's crying out" and "the reason for me to see that something is amiss". For our scriptural traditions, our capacities both to suffer and to recognize suffering in others belong to who we are as creatures of the God who created heaven and earth. SR draws its critical practice, in part, from the tradition of philosophic pragmatism, because this pragmatism drew its rule of repair from out of the same scriptural sources. In Charles Peirce's words, "pragmatism is but a logical corollary of Jesus' words 'That ye may know them by their fruit.' "[10] From the command to care for those who suffer comes the pragmatic maxim for academics: that you may wield the sword of theoretical reasoning only for the sake of repairing institutions that fail in their work of helping repair suffering by repairing broken practices of everyday life.[11] Were it not for our prior commitment to the commands of scripture, we would have no irresistible warrant for choosing "care for those who suffer" as one of the indubitable purposes of our academic work as well as our interpersonal engagements.[12] Nor would we have sufficient warrant for adopting pragmatism as a primary resource for our critique of the modern academy.

Peirce's studies in phenomenology—or what he considered abductive speculations about the elemental categories of our experience of the world—help us link his pragmatism further to scripture's account of creation, suffering, and redemption.

Firstness and Creation. Peirce labeled the first of his three phenomenological categories "Firstness", corresponding to what he considered the irreducible element of spontaneity, originality, and freedom in every thing we experience in the world—and, *therefore*, in every conceivable dimension of the world itself. We say "therefore" because Peirce argued, against Kant, that the notion of "unknowable dimensions of the world", or *noumena*, was senseless, since we cannot have evidence concerning what we cannot know. He concluded that there was therefore no prima facie reason for our imagining that the elements of our experience are not also elements of the world per se. Both this conclusion and the notion of Firstness reflect Peirce's understanding of the phenomenological force of the Biblical doctrine of creation. "All reality," writes Peirce, "is due to the creative power of God. . . . In general, God is perpetually creating us."[13] In Peirce's reading, to be created is to be known by God and knowable by his creatures. Anything like "noumenal" reality could be attributed, if at all, only to God, but not to any aspect of the creation. God's activity of creating, furthermore, must be characterized by Firstness since this creativity is the prototype of freedom and spontaneity. As created, being is therefore, everywhere, touched by Firstness. If this is so, then modernity's mechanistic view of the universe is false, along with anything like Laplace's determinism.

To date, the evidence of natural science corroborates this feature of creationism. For example, quantum physicists have, now for a century, attributed chance behavior to sub-atomic particles. By-passing the limits of Newtonian mechanics, they have nonetheless successfully applied non-standard logics, probability theory and such mathematical innovations as matrix theory to recover strategies for rational behavior in a world of what we call irreducible Firstness.[14] These strategies open new areas of convergence or at least parallelism between the procedures of science and of scriptural interpretation in the Abrahamic traditions. One primary example is the place of irreducible vagueness or indeterminacy in both realms of inquiry. Early quantum theorists (Heisenberg and Bohr, or what is called the "Copenhagen" school of particle physics) argued that one could not simultaneously identify both the space-time coordinates (or the "particle-like" character) and the relative velocity (or the "wave-like" character) of subatomic particles. The physicist achieves precision with respect to one character only at the expense of precision with respect to the other. This phenomenon is related to another: the unavoidable influence that the observer—or the instruments of measurement—has on what is observed. This influence may at times be negligible in measurements of macroscopic phenomena, but it is always a factor in sub-atomic measurements. This is because the instrument of measurement is the very interference of another sub-atomic particle (such as photon or electron) with the particle to be measured. A resultant, third feature of measurement is what, after Peirce, we may label its *"abductive"* character: the fact that the product of measurement is meaningful for us only in relation to the specific conditions of measurement. For our present purposes, three of these conditions are of particular interest: *the material and formal conditions of measurement* (laboratory procedures or rules; and the physical make-up of equipment used); *ontology or mathematical-system* (in terms of what picture of the world the laboratory was set-up: typically some mathematical account of the sub-atomic environment to be observed); and *the specific questions asked or test performed.*

Now, consider the parallel phenomena in classical scriptural hermeneutics. I will refer to rabbinic scriptural interpretation as an example. The rabbinic sages regard the words of scripture (Tanakh, or what some call the "Hebrew Bible") as utterly authoritative but meaningful only by way of the act of reading. The latter condition may sound self-evident, but only to the ears of "intuitionists", to re-invoke the terms we used earlier for modern foundationalists who believe that they have direct or self-legitimating cognitions of the outer or inner worlds. For the rabbinic sages, reading is an *abductive activity*, which means that they read words of scripture the way quantum physicists measure sub-atomic particles. A reading of scripture is therefore meaningful only with respect to the specific conditions of reading. What we called *the material and formal conditions of measurement* parallel what the rabbinic sages considered *the many levels of study* requisite to scriptural reading. There are, for example, the capacity to use language in general; the capacity to read Hebrew in particular (Scripture may also be read in translation, but such reading remains derivative); years of learning how to read the Bible's grammars, syntax, semantics and also pragmatics (that is, its various patterns of context-specific meaning or force); then there is the depth of experience in life itself (since Scripture displays its meaning with respect to everyday life in this world as well as to features of life in the world to come: all of which entails multiple levels of biological, personal, social, political, and spiritual life, and so on). In the words of *Shammai* in Mishnah *Pirke Avot* ("Ethics of the Fathers" 1:15): "Make the study of Torah your primary occupation; Say little do much; Greet every person with a cheerful face."

For the rabbis, what we called the physicist's *ontology or mathematical-system* parallels the reader's elemental modes of relationship to God, to Torah, and to Israel.[15] Finally, *the questions asked or the tests performed by the physicist* parallel the immediate, real-life questions that the rabbinic reader must ask of Scripture in order for Scripture to disclose its meaning and force for this time of reading. Michael Fishbane refers to this feature of rabbinic reading the "exegetical construction of reality and the transformation of the culture into the images produced by that exegesis.... The world of the text serves as the basis for the textualization of the world—and its meaning."[16]

In sum, *rabbinic reading is abductive*, which means that each reading of Scripture as Scripture displays an element of Firstness or chance, newness, and spontaneity. A modernist critic might conclude that rabbinic scriptural reading is therefore "relativistic" or "purely subjective". A postmodern critic might conclude either that the rabbis were radical postmodernists *or* that they contradicted themselves when they asserted that Scripture is, nonetheless, authoritative in the way that it commands behavior. Postliberals who consider themselves "post-postmodern" might voice aspects of both these modern and postmodern criticisms: concluding that the rabbis were right to receive the divine word as ever-new but wrong to associate this newness with the particularizing conditions of local reading. According to SR, however, such modern, postmodern, and post-postmodern criticisms would misrepresent the meaning of abductive reading. All three criticisms reduce abduction to the either-or terms of a binary logic. Both modernist and postmodern criticisms would err in identifying non-determinism with subjectivism or relativism (one approving the result, one disapproving). A post-postmodern criticism would appear, in contradictory fashion, to assert features of both modernism and anti-modernism. In Cartesian fashion, it would appear to identify certainty or authoritative knowledge with the character of a discrete intuition and then to identify the rabbis' non-intuitionism with some variety of relativism. At the same time, the criticism would also appear, in anti-Cartesian fashion, to identify authoritative knowledge with participation in some life that cannot be identified through any series of discrete propositions. Rabbinic reading is also reading from out of a life rather than some set of propositions. But a post-postmodern critic would appear not to identify "life" with as this-worldly an activity as the rabbis have in mind. For this reason, the critic would appear to have in mind a life that is, somehow, also entered by way of intuitions—a notion that appears contradictory by SR standards.[17]

For SR, reading Scripture is abductive because all knowledge in this created world is abductive, and that includes our knowledge of God. As the rabbinic sages say, "God is known only in His actions": "R. Abba b. Mammel said: God said to Moses, 'You want to know My name? Well, I am called according to My work.' "[18] And this includes His on-going activities of creating worlds and speaking Scripture: "For in Your goodness, day after day, You renew the order of creation."[19] To know God through His actions is to know Him directly since He is in His actions. Peirce also recognizes this in his claim that "Thirdness [which is our knowledge of God in the world] pours in on us directly."[20] But to speak of knowing God only "through His actions" is the rabbis'—and the pragmatist's —way of saying that we know God abductively: knowing *that* He is there as certainly as we know anything, but knowing *of* Him only in relation to how and where we know and always subject to further refinement and correction. This means that our knowledge is "entangled": it doesn't come as bits of information there for anyone anytime to value but as parts of some greater whole, of which at any time we see and understand only some features with instructions about where and how to turn to see and understand more. Our knowing is a relationship, only partly cognitive, that leads us into further and further circles of relationship if we seek to pursue knowledge further. But to know something or someone in its Firstness is not yet to have been moved to seek knowledge or enter into relationship.

Secondness, Facticity, and Suffering. Firstness is only part of the story of creation. There is also the Biblical account of Adam and Eve and, with it, an account of error, sin, and suffering in the world. The narrative's move from "and it was good" to "and they were thrust out of the Garden" corresponds to the move, within Peirce's phenomenology, from the category of Firstness to that of Secondness: the irreducible element of pain, struggle, resistance, volition, and shock in the world. Once again, what Peirce sees in human experience he also attributes, per hypothesis, to the world, so that, just as Adam and Eve leave the Garden, so too may all created beings find themselves cast into a realm of struggle and loss as well as gift. But they cause pain and loss as much as they suffer it. For Peirce, the binary character of Secondness is not directional: to push the world or be pushed by it, either way we are dealing with an event of two-ness. Secondness is the category of fact, not value; there is no possibility in it, no quality of anything, since qualia are Firsts, and a Second is not a First plus One, but the negation of a First, its contrary. It just is, or they are—this non-relational pairing of two. For this reason, Peirce suggests that philosophers like Kant err when they label pain the quality of a feeling, like pleasure. For Peirce, pleasure is a feeling, but pain is something else: a mark of separation or change, a reason to flee something or a mark of having fled, associated in human physiology with many feelings, but not itself a feeling.[21]

To refer to Secondness is thus to introduce movement into a phenomenology, since Secondness marks *force* rather than quality: the realm of effects, not ideas. Cognition of a Second, such as Pain, is not the cognition of any quality but, rather, the registration of some *event*: *that* there has been some interruption, the shock of some No!—so that now something is different. This registration of difference is what we mean by an awareness of movement: something we characterized as "here" or "this" may now also be characterized as "not here" or "not this". Since there is no direction predicated of this difference, however, we can refer to the movement only formally—*that* it is the case, but without any further characterization. As we will explain in the next section, Peirce introduced the term *indexicality* to name this kind of bare, demonstrative reference, and he characterized each reference to a second as an index, or deictic sign. A cry, we will say, is an indexical mark that there is pain there, somewhere.

Thirdness: Hearing, Saying, Relating and Repairing. To hear a cry, however, and then to move toward it is to introduce some third thing we have not yet considered: it is to *represent* the cry as a *sign*, or as something that has some meaning for us. For Peirce, this is to invoke the phenomenological category of *Thirdness*: the irreducible element of representation, relationship, mediation, and love in the world. The Biblical story does not end with Adam-Eve's exile from the Garden; it begins there, so that all the rest of the narrative is, as it were, about how to get back in or how, in other words, to repair the condition of sin and suffering that underlay the exile. The knowledge that comes by way of reading scripture is the knowledge of how to get back in.

Peirce devoted much of his formal work to proving that a Third could not be constructed out of Firsts and Seconds, or that *relationship* comes only out of other forms of relationship. One helpful product of these proofs is Peirce's logic of relatives, a way of diagramming the different classes of predicates that accompany our judgments about the Firstness, Secondness, or Thirdness of something. Thus, Peirce suggests that judgments about something in its Firstness bear only "monadic predicates", such as "—is red", or "—is awesome" (where the *blank, —*, can be filled by some subject); judgments about something in its Secondness bear only "dyadic predicates", such as "—hits—" (X hits Y) or "—dwells in—"; and judgments about something in its Thirdness bear only "triadic predicates", such as "—gives—to—" (X gives Y to Z) or "—means—to—." In these terms, to observe that someone acted some way to repair suffering would thus be to make a judgment that bears a triadic predicate, such as "—does—to repair—" (X does Y to repair Z). When we report that someone cries, it often sounds like we are making a simple judgment of quality, like "—is red"—or, in this case, "—emits the cry-sound." But reports about cries generally carry the presumption that the cry is a sign of pain or suffering uttered with the hope that someone will listen to it and respond: thus "—cries about—to—". However incompletely uttered, a cry is thus a communication or representation of pain.

Diagrammed in the terms of Peirce's logic of relatives, a cry may therefore be characterized as an *indexical sign* of pain or suffering.[22] The force of such a sign depends on the world of signs within which it is received. By revising the terms we introduced earlier for comparing physics and rabbinics, we may now characterize such "worlds of signs" as the *semiotic conditions according to which we know the world and how to act in it.* For present purposes, we may note three sets of conditions: *material and formal* (the *language* through which we know the world), *ontological* (the *practices and relationships* through which we know the world), and *interrogative* (the space-time specific questions or problems to which our activity of knowing and acting now responds).[23] According to SR, *the ontological meaning of a cry is set by Scripture's model of creation and command*: in this world created by God, a cry means, *at once*, that someone somewhere is in pain; that there is also somewhere a redeemer, or someone who can and will respond to hear and heal that pain; and that we who are in ear-shot of the cry are obligated to hear it and join in the work of healing. To worship the creator God of Israel is to retain the hope that, ultimately, each cry will be heard and the conviction that each of us is obliged to share in the hearing. According to SR, *a cry is thus defined materially and formally as at once a sign of need and an imperative to act:* a fact that carries with it not only a value but also a behavioral command. This is why the cry is received, finally, as interrogative: *the conditions of command are necessarily here-and-now*, as if to say "you who hear this cry are obliged to inquire into and act in response to its space-time specific conditions". This is why, finally, the meaning of a cry cannot be defined once-and-for-all or atemporally or as a condition of "being in general": it is a condition of *this being*, here.

The Logic of Caring is not the Logic of Suffering and of Oppression

Sharing in a theme of David Ford's theology of wisdom, we have adopted the directive "Care for those who cry!" as a name for the maxim that guides SR's way of repairing the ills of modernism. Other essays in this collection describe and illustrate how scriptural reasoners practice this maxim. To conclude this essay, I want to recommend a logical criterion for distinguishing their practice from that of some competing projects of postmodern and postliberal criticism. The criterion is to distinguish between the dyadic logics of suffering and of oppression and the non-dyadic, or illustratively triadic, logics of caring for those who suffer and of repairing the conditions of suffering and oppression.

The two different logics are illustrated in Biblical narratives about suffering or oppression and about repair or redemption. As illustrated in the narrative of Cain of Abel, *the logic of oppressive behavior* requires only two elemental terms, so that every action or judgment made according to the logic either affirms one term or the other, and where to affirm one term means to deny the other:

> YHWH paid heed to Abel and his offering. Cain was much distressed and his face fell. YHWH said to Cain, "Why are you distressed. . . . Surely if you do right, there is uplift; But if you do not do right, Sin crouches at the door; its urge is toward you, yet you can be its master. Cain said to his brother Abel . . . (Gen. 4: 4–8)

We can map Cain's actions through a series of dyadic statements: Cain (1) gives an offering (2). God favors Abel's offering. God does not favor Cain's. Cain is angry. God says, "Do not be angry. You can control anger." Cain remains angry. Cain kills Abel. With one exception, no action toward an object is mediated by a third-something. The exception is that God offers guidance that could interrupt the two-part relation between Cain and his anger: if Cain had accepted the guidance, then we would have an action that could be mapped only through a triadic statement: God's Word (1) led Cain (2) away from his anger (3). Abel's fate can be mapped by the same logic: Abel's offering is favored. Abel is hated by Cain. Abel is killed by Cain.

This exception introduces a transitional moment between oppression and redemption. Here, the logic of attending to someone's oppression contains a moment that can be identified only through dyadic statements, but it opens as well to the possibility of three part relations:

He said, "What have you done? Hark, your brother's blood cries out to
Me from the ground! Therefore, you shall be more cursed than the
ground." ... Cain said to YHWH, "My punishment is too great to
bear!" YHWH said to him, "I promise, if anyone kills Cain, sevenfold
vengeance shall be taken on him." And YHWH put a mark on Cain ...
(Gen. 4:10–15)

Reading this text leads us to re-read the first one. God's warning to Cain
appeared as if dyadic: Do this or that will follow. But the warning is more
than dyadic, since Cain lives on, bearing a mark that re-directs this
warning, outward, to any who would want to kill Cain. The warning thus
becomes a third-something: (1) a sign of (2) Cain's on-going relations, at
once, (3^1) to God and (3^2) to any other human he may meet. But, just as the
warning *to* Cain converts into a protective mark *to others*, so too do we learn
that the act of "seeing the oppressor" is coterminous with the act of
"hearing the cry of the oppressed". In each case, seeing and hearing are
two-part relations (one either sees/hears or does not), but they open out to
the possibility of three-part relations. If one oppresses Cain, then God will
act against the oppressor: the act against Cain will also be a mark of the
divine-action-that-will-come. In this way, the life of Cain introduces a
general possibility into the world: that any act of oppression/being
oppressed is a sign that God *could* respond to that act.

Exodus 3 (or more fully Exodus 1–20) narrates God's redemptive activity
as an *actuality* rather than mere possibility. The result is a dense narrative
of indefinitely expanding circles of relationship and action, each element or
moment of which shares in the defining features of God's redemptive work
as a whole:

An angel of YHWH appeared to [Moses] in a blazing fire out of a
bush. ... He said, "I am the God of your father, the God of Abraham,
the God of Isaac, and the God of Jacob. ... Now the cry of the Israelites
has reached Me; I have seen how the Egyptians oppress them. Come,
therefore, I will send you to Pharaoh and you shall free My people. ...
But Moses said to God, "Who am I that I should go ... ?" And He said,
ehyeh imach, "I will be with you; that shall be your sign that it was I
who sent you." (Exodus 3:2–12)

While there is no space in this essay to unpack the riches of this passage
(and the rest of Exodus 1–20) as a narrative of redemption, we may, at least,
catalogue some of the features of redemptive work that are displayed in it.
According to SR, these are among the features we should look for in any
postliberal or postmodern effort to *repair* and not merely criticize the
failings of modernity. The most general feature I want to isolate is *the
continuity (or integrative character) of part and whole*: that is, the requirement

that every recognizable part or moment of redemption should share in the central features of redemptive activity as a whole. The following features should each illustrate this:

- *Continuity of the historical here-and-now (particular) and the eternal (infinite)*. Each moment of redemption must include the divine presence, the human presence in its space-time specific historicity, and the relationship that draws them together. In our narrative, YHVH appears in direct relation to Moses in the specific context of Israel's enslavement in ancient Egypt.
- *Continuity of past, present, and future*. While addressing the concrete details of this moment of oppression, the redemptive activity invokes and replays the prior history of God's relation with Israel, and it anticipates the near and distant future of that relation.
- *Continuity of hearing, speaking, interrogating, commanding, and acting*. Throughout the whole narrative, each of the dramatis personae—God, Moses, Israel, and/or her oppressor—are engaged in each of these activities.
- *Continuity of hermeneutical, reparative, and theophantic activities*. Each moment of redemption includes interpretive behavior (hearing words and interrogating their meaning), reparative behavior (in this case, caring for Israel), and divine-human encounters.
- *Transformation of dyadic into triadic relations, but all within the logic of triadic relations*. While, in this passage, the cry of suffering stimulates redemptive activity, the narrative as a whole suggests the triadic logic of redemption, rather than the dyadic logic of suffering. If, for example, we were to diagram the role of voices in the passages, we might refer to "(1) God speaking to (2) Moses for the sake of (3) Israel", but we would not have an instance of voices uttered outside of such a triadic relation. We do not hear the cry as mere cry, but only as what "reached Me so that I now do this". In sum, no recognizable part of the redemptive activity is dyadic.

Scriptural Reasoning as A Distinctive, Reparative Activity after Modernity

The reparative work of SR applies these features of the scriptural narrative to the practice of reading Scripture itself. For comparative purposes, the last two features are the most significant.

The continuity of hermeneutical, reparative, and theophantic activities. For SR, to encounter the divine presence is to engage in a practice of *reading* and of *interpretation*. To *read* God's disclosures means, in recognition of God's infinity and *our creatureliness*, to refrain from intuitionist claims as one would refrain from idolatry. While postmodernists tend to share in this critique of idolatry, some Christian, Muslim or Jewish postliberals may be perplexed by it. They may argue that the only alternative to modern secularism *and* postmodern relativism is a reaffirmation of truth claims under the aegis of a given revelation and the tradition that serves it. And they may understand truth claims to take the form of what we call intuitionist claims. For SR, however, a "postliberal intuitionism" would be oxymoronic for two reasons. Limiting itself to the terms of a binary logic, it would conceive of truth claims in only binary terms: a given claim is either true or it is false; our epistemology either allows for true-or-false claims or it does not and, if not, it is relativistic; if the universalistic claims of modern secularism are false, then the universalistic claims of religion should be true. . . . But to make claims like these is to overlook a third alternative: non-foundationalist truth claims, which are truth-claims that are non-discrete, non-universal, non-necessary and non-impossible. If we think only in binary terms, then the latter may appear to be relativistic. In the terms of SR, however, these are the claims of scriptural truth. A postliberal intuitionism would be oxymoronic, secondly, because it would reduce what should be the triadic logic of redemption to the binary logic of suffering-or-oppression. The postliberal critique of modernism, for example, identifies the binary character of modernist claims as *symptoms* of the fact that somebody somewhere is suffering and, most likely, somebody is also oppressing somebody else. To express a post-liberal alternative in binary terms, however, would be to replace the marks of one kind of suffering-and-oppression with the marks of another kind. A genuine alternative to modernism should neither complain to us about some other kind of oppression, nor impose itself on us as a new kind of oppression.[24]

The transformation of dyadic into triadic relations. Perhaps the single most telling mark of SR is that its practice of repair is also a practice of reading Scripture and its practice of reading also a practice of repair. One logical rule informing this practice is that no moment of reading or of repair should warrant the construction of dyadic judgments. This does not mean that our work will be without dyads—we cannot avoid suffering them in this world—only that our obligation is to read the emergence of any dyad in our work as a mark of suffering (and, potentially, of oppression) to which we must respond, again and again if necessary, in the name of the Redeemer. Practically, all this means that, when we Jews, Muslims, and Christians (or any sub-group, intra-denominational as well) sit together to study Scripture, we acknowledge that each word and text of each Scripture participates in a potentially infinite process of semiosis. As individual or collective readers, we lack the capacity and authority to make general (and thus binary) claims to forestall that process. At the same time, from out of the here-and-now of our historical condition, we also have the capacity and authority to give witness to how we suffer, individually or collectively, in the act of reading any word or text of any Scripture. *As a dyadic mark of suffering, this witness should stimulate the reading fellowship as a whole to practice the prototypical work of SR: reparative reading that, at once, opens the text of Scripture and the life of the sufferer, one to the other, until, between them, a third something arises that we call "scriptural reasoning" per se. This reasoning is the context-specific process of interpretation/repair/theophany that SR practitioners consider, at once, the redemptive activity of the God whose word is Scripture and the reparative work of this particular fellowship of readers here-and-now.* SR moves beyond postmodern agnosticism in its willingness to claim that, yes, we can encounter God here-and-now in the reading of Scripture. At the same time, SR protects itself from intuitionist dogmatism in its willingness to voice this claim only by way of judgments that are strictly *abductive* and that pertain only to the public fruits of any such encounter: judgments about the meanings, here-and-now, of this particular scriptural text in relation to this particular account of the social-historical moment. These judgments remain, at once, hermeneutical, reparative and theophantic: recommending ways of hearing God's word that may contribute to repairing both the textual and societal conditions of suffering that stimulated this particular project of reasoning.[25]

For SR, in short, God alone is the source of our hope that suffering and oppression can be repaired in this world, and God's Word alone is the source of our knowledge of where to turn for guidance in the pathways of repair. SR includes a family of claims about how best to turn the mind and heart to receive this guidance. Within circles of SR fellowship, I tend to warm to some such claims more than others, but I would also mistrust my own judgments and practices if they were not balanced by these others. This is because my own claims display the creatureliness of some finite *ego cogito*. SR gives hospitality to the *ego cogito*: honoring its place in God's creation and its contributions to our work of reasoning out of God's Word. But SR can neither reduce its overall work to what can be articulated within the activity of the *ego cogito* nor privilege the words of any individual thinker as true in themselves. Circles of SR fellowship generate *practices* of reading and reasoning that I believe are true to the God who is Redeemer, and I am prepared to offer philosophic and theological arguments on behalf of this truth. But, no one of these arguments can be true in itself—nor, all the more so, any one claim within those arguments. Like any reading of scripture, any claim by an individual practitioner of SR has the strength only of a strong abduction: it really points to what is really true, but only by way of the creatureliness of the one who did the pointing. To learn from the pointing—to understand and test it—is to share in the same fellowship of reading, interpretation, and discussion through which we encounter God's Word. The way we test our judgment about SR is therefore not different from the way we seek guidance from God's Word. There are no short cuts, nor should a person of faith require or ask for them.

NOTES

1 With apologies, I must, for want of space, write as if the reader shared my unstated assumptions about what these standard criticisms are and who offers them—from Dewey against the optical to Wittgenstein against foundationalism to Lyotard against master

narratives to Foucault against modernist and neo-colonialist uses of power to Derrida against presence to Levinas against *totalité*. I assume that, along with other forms of postliberalism (such as that of Hans Frei and George Lindbeck) SR shares, in part, in all these.

2   In his early, *Journal of Speculative Philosophy* papers of 1868–69, Charles Peirce identified Cartesianism with intuitionism, the assumption that there is a "cognition not determined by a previous cognition of the same object, and therefore so determined by something out of consciousness" [5.213: references are to *Collected Papers of Charles Sanders Peirce*, eds. Charles Harteshorne and Paul Weiss (Cambridge, MA: Harvard University Press, 1934/5)].

3   All forms of colonial, imperialist, and totalizing thinking extend to the "universal" claims that are appropriate to only a finite realm of evidence. Classic determinism imagined various empirical claims to be necessary or impossible, rather than probable/improbable and non-falsified.

4   The strategy here is to replace all those rhetorically dense and context-specific standards of criticism (against "foundationalism," and so on) with a nominalist-sounding suspicion of *all* general claims. This is, rather than strain to locate the crucial fault in each modernist claim, to put the onus on the claimant and say: all who dare to make general pronouncements must pass the following tests.

5   In short, this means that universals may be universal only within some finite domain of reference: such as all folks in this school, "universally"; or all claims made in this denomination. But no human can make claims, even on behalf of his/her religion, about its powers relative to some other belief or religion that has not been specifically examined. Only the Creator makes such claims, and scripture, as we will see, sets the rules for how to read them.

6   No human, in other words, is privileged to make claims about some character of all creation, so that, respecting the law of excluded middle, these claims also inform us about contradictory characters.

7   This is the "Cartesian" move: to assume that we cannot construct a model of what is true by conceiving the contradictory of what is false. Richard Bernstein does a profound job of showing how this "Cartesian" move restates feelings of over-generalized anxiety and over-generalized certainty in the rhetorical form of logical claims: see Richard Bernstein, *Beyond Objectivism and Relativism: science, hermeneutics and praxis* (Philadelphia, PA: The University of Pennsylvania Press, 1983).

8   This is the subject of my essay "Compassionate Postmodernism: An Introduction to Rabbinic Semiotics", *Soundings* Vol. LXXVI no.1 (Spring, 1993), pp. 140–152.

9   See, for example, Peirce's "A Neglected Argument for the Reality of God," in *Collected Papers of Charles Sanders Peirce*, 6.452–493.

10   That is, the warrants of both prophecy and rational inquiry are displayed in their consequences for public behavior in this world, rather than in self-legitimating intuitions, including those attributed to encounters with God. Peirce's claim may be found in his 1893 note on "How to Make Our Ideas Clear," in *Collected Papers of Charles Sanders Peirce*, 5.402n2.

11   To be sure, I use poetic license here to summarize a complex characterization of the Peirce-James-Dewey critique of unwarranted abstraction and unresolved argumentation in academic practice. The pragmatists do not insist that every act of theorizing prove itself in the field of practice: only that theorists have no warrant for making claims of truth or falsity except for claims tested by the work of repairing problematic situations or healing wounds in our actual social lives.

12   The Jewish Kantian, Hermann Cohen makes a strong case for this claim: that, while Platonic science provides Kantian ethics with its epistemology, Scriptural prophecy, alone, introduces the object of ethical knowledge (humanity encountered in its suffering) and its purpose (to end this suffering). See, for example, Hermann Cohen, "Classical Idealism and the Hebrew Prophets" in *Reason and Hope: Selections for the Jewish Writings of Hermann Cohen*, trans. Eva Jospe, (New York, NY: Norton, 1971). See discussions of Cohen in Robert Gibbs, *Why Ethics?* (Princeton, NJ: Princeton University Press, 2000), Chapter 13; and Peter Ochs, *Peirce, Pragmatism and the Logic of Scripture* (Cambridge: Cambridge University Press, 1998), pp. 292–295.

13 *Collected Papers of Charles Sanders Peirce*, 6.506–7, from "Answers to Questions Concerning My Belief in God", (c. 1906).
14 For a fine, readable introduction see John Polkinghorne, *Quantum Theory, A Very Short Introduction* (Oxford: Oxford University Press, 2002).
15 Knowledge, in other words, is *yidia*, or intimacy/intercourse, rather than *gnosis*, in the sense of cognition at a distance (or through identity). Intimacy means *relation*. "Truth", *emet*, is therefore an attribute of "reliability in relation", in that sense, "faith", *emunah*. In *this* sense, "truth is the seal of God".
16 In Michael Fishbane, *The Exegetical Imagination: On Jewish Thought and Theology* (Cambridge, MA: Harvard University Press, 1998), pp. 3–4.
17 I will assume postmodern and postliberal readers share my characterization of the kind of determinism that would lead modernists to criticize abductive reasoning as relativistic. And I assume readers attracted to Radical Orthodoxy share my characterization of postmodern tendencies to opt for this kind of relativism. In a survey of the postmodernists, for example, Frederick Bauerschmidt argues that postmodernism retains "with the modern a sense of the lack of reality of all representation, but it is no longer suspicious of received representations" [since that is all we have]": "The Theological Sublime" in *Radical Orthodoxy: a new theology*, eds. J. Milbank, C. Pickstock, and G. Ward (London: Rutledge, 1999), pp. 202–203. The post-postmoderns I have in mind are Slavoj Zizek and Alain Badiou. The latter's study of *Saint Paul: The Foundation of Universalism* (Stanford, CA: Stanford University Press, 2003) displays the kind of intuitionism I have in mind and, with it, a binary rejection of abductive, religious thinking—here, in the form of rabbinic legal reasoning. According to Badiou, "the law always designates a particularity, hence a difference. It is not possible for it to be an operation of the One: . . . no evental One can be the One of a particularity." "Legality" is, however, "always predicative, particular, and partial"; it is therefore always "statist", seeking to "control a situation" that cannot ultimately be controlled. (p. 76). "Jewish law" is therefore error, but so is "Greek wisdom": for the one reduces its object of knowledge to "elective belonging", while the other reduces it "to the finite cosmic totality" (p. 56). Grace alone redeems humanity, universally, from either reduction, free of any finite law; and this is Paul's message (p. 77).
18 *Exodus Rabbah* on Exodus 3:13.
19 From the "Blessings before the Sh'ma", in the rabbinic daily prayerbook.
20 Thus, Peirce writes that we "can know nothing except what we *directly* experience", and thus that our idea of God comes from direct experience. "Direct" does not mean immediate, however, in sense of mere intuition: it means that we directly encounter Thirds (triadic relations), that we encounter God's word as such as a Third, and that our understanding of that encounter comes, as all understanding comes, through temporal and social processes of reception, interpretation, testing, and so on. See "A Neglected Argument."
21 See Peirce's writings in phenomenology, for example, *Collected Papers of Charles Sanders Peirce*, 1.334–76.
22 David Ford has made "the cry" a centerpiece of his current work on Wisdom in Christian theology and in scriptural reasoning. His treatment of cry is a primary stimulus to this aspect of my essay.
23 The most thoroughgoing treatment I have seen of this pragmatic use of the interrogative is in Robert Gibbs, *Why Ethics?*, cited above.
24 Participants in both Scriptural Reasoning and Radical Orthodoxy may be challenged at times by the temptation of defending good scriptural readings by way of unnecessarily over-generalized, and thus dyadic, claims. Among Radical Orthodoxy folks, for example, much of John Milbank and also Catherine Pickstock's writing complements SR's critique of modernism and its general project of recovering scriptural faith. When arguing on behalf of the latter, however, they both tend at times to reach for universalistic warrants on behalf of their intuitions of Christ and against all possible alternatives. Thus, for example, much of Pickstock's *After Writing: on the liturgical consummation of philosophy* (Oxford: Blackwell Publishers, 1998) also serves SR, as illustrated in phrases like these: "because liturgical space, by its recognition of a transcendent, is not merely scalar, physicality is intensified as much or more by its continuity with a spiritual" (p. 231) and "by deliberately exposing the mechanisms of our 'reason'—as in our syntactic

performance in the *Credo* and *Gloria*—of that which we 'understand' of the Trinitarians relations and the economy of salvation, our apparent human pride is grounded in a supreme and doxological humility" (p. 227). But then the argument ascends, past humility and abduction, to universal/necessary claims based on intuitionism. With Milbank, for example, Pickstock argues not only for the plausibility, power and attractiveness of her formulations of gift ("thus, through Christ, every good thing in transposed into gift", p. 241) but also for the utter uniqueness of that "through Christ": "thus, with Christianity the optimum of meaningfulness and the optimum of living subjectivity coincide with the world" (p. 273). I believe this is a case of assimilating real possibility (a good abduction) to necessity: an unnecessary assimilation for one who writes in faith. One source of the excess can be seen in the tendency to over-draw criticisms of the postmodern, rendering the postmodern X not merely contrary to what we want but also contradictory, so that its negation is equivalent to the good: on the previously mentioned topic of liturgy, for example, she writes "whereas spatialization, in its postmodern consummation, renders absent every present, apostrophe renders present every absent" (p. 194). The latter is a useful abduction, but it becomes reified through the discussion of liturgy into a dogma. The resulting lack of testing leaves the excesses of *"every present"* unrefined to fit the contexts of liturgy as lived and not idealized. Milbank's' discussions of gift are comparable, if more strongly stated. His criticism of modern and postmodern models of gift contribute well to SR, as does his alternative when opposed as a strong abduction: that the Eucharistic "gift given to us of God himself in the flesh" is the "gift of an always preceding gift-exchange", which is the exchange of love between Father and Son, between Being and beings and between Christ and his Church. By participating in Christ, he argues, humanity thereby receives the gift of giving as well as of receiving. (See John Milbank, "Can A Gift be Given?" *Modern Theology* Vol. 11 no. 1 (January, 1995), pp. 119–161; pp. 150–152). But then Milbank extends his abduction into a dogma, as if the language of his claim represented a direct intuition of the divine reality and as if evidence were already given that no other tradition's formulation of gift were equivalent: this gift is given this way in Christ in a way that it could not be given in any other tradition or witness. This extra move leads him, like the post-postmodernists, to seek ways of trumping possible analogues in Greek philosophy and Judaism and then to condemn these where the analogues fail to live up to his model. (See n.17 above and John Milbank, "Can A Gift be Given?".) As unfortunate as are the fruits of these condemnations, the fruit is in this case not my real concern, but rather the logical seed: the effort to over-extend an otherwise helpful analysis and thereby render Christological claims in the form of Cartesian argumentation. Removed from this added packaging, Milbank's claims appear as admirable abductions.

25 Postliberal movements like Scriptural Reasoning and Radical Orthodoxy therefore have at hand an appropriate and effective way to reduce their dyadic tendencies and temptations. This is to turn written and oral discussions away from the presentation of universal claims and the defense of individual claims toward the on-going study of the meaning and force of God's Word for the specific contexts of our lives.

9

SCRIPTURAL REASONING AND THE PHILOSOPHY OF SOCIAL SCIENCE

BASIT BILAL KOSHUL

The goal of this essay is not to discuss the relationship between Scriptural Reasoning and modern social science exhaustively but to display the fruitfulness of an exchange between the two illustratively. The illustration will come in the form of demonstrating that an exchange between Scriptural Reasoning (SR) and modern social science can make a unique contribution to bridging the divide between religion and science. It will demonstrate this point by taking Max Weber's (social) scientific critique of rationalism, augmenting it with C. S. Peirce's pragmaticist philosophy and bringing the Weber-Peirce synthesis into conversation with the Qur'anic treatment of material reality.

More than three decades ago Robert Bellah observed that desiccation of contemporary culture could be directly traced backed to the increasing fragmentation of knowledge characteristic of the modern academy. He also noted that the origin of this fragmentation is located in the religion vs. science divide that opened up with the birth of modern physical/natural sciences and deepened with the birth of the modern social sciences. But at the end of his analysis he notes:

> I feel there are greater resources now for healing the split between the imaginative and the cognitive, the intellectual and the emotional, and the scientific and the religious aspects of our culture and our consciousness than there have been for centuries.[1]

Bellah was speaking as a sociologist about the resources present within the modern social sciences for bridging the divide between religion and science. In this essay a practitioner of SR brings the resources of the social sciences into conversation with resources in scripture, thereby complementing Bellah's undertaking.

Basit Bilal Koshul
Department of Religion, Concordia College, 901 8th St. South, Moorhead, MN 56562, USA

Before getting into the main body of the presentation, a few words on the structure of the proposed line of argument. Weber's contribution in the founding of the modern social sciences, more specifically the social scientific study of religion, has been widely acknowledged. But it is only in recent decades that his contribution in the area of the methodology of the social sciences has begun to receive the type of attention that it deserves. It is in the context of his discussion of the methodology of the social sciences that Weber offers a penetrating analysis of the concept of rationalism. Looking at his analysis of religion in light of his methodological insights puts his valuation of religion in a whole new light—revealing a much more nuanced and affirmative attitude towards religion than the one widely associated with the religiously unmusical Weber. The first section of the paper will offer a reconstruction of Weber's valuation of the relationship between religion and science. The second section will augment Weber's insights with Peirce's pragamaticism. The services of Peirce the philosopher are needed at this point because Weber's positive valuation of religion-science relationship is not so much a social scientific claim as a philosophical claim based on evidence from the social sciences. Not being a trained philosopher, Weber lacks the precise philosophical terminology as well as the philosophical authority in/on which to base his conclusions. Peirce lends Weber's position both the philosophical terminology and authority that it lacks. The third part of the paper will turn to the Qur'anic treatment of material reality to evaluate the Weber-Peirce position of the relationship between religion and science from within a scriptural tradition. This part will demonstrate that there is deep affinity between the social scientific/philosophical perspective on the one hand and the scriptural perspective on the other. I will conclude the discussion with some brief remarks on the relationship between the particular argument presented in this essay and SR in general.

Rationality and the World of Contradictions in Rationalism

What is "rational"? How is it distinguished from "irrational"? A particular, mythical self-understanding of the Enlightenment generates categorical answers to these two questions. Bellah notes that there is an Enlightenment myth that "views science as the bringer of light relative to which religion and other dark things will vanish away".[2] From this perspective:

"light" and "science" = "rational"
"dark" and "religion" = "irrational"

A look at Weber's understanding of "rational" and "irrational" shows that his views are not at all compatible with the Enlightenment myth. Weber describes the process of rationalization as following the "imperative of consistency" in the domain of thought and action.[3] It is only by pursuing this imperative that human beings can hope conceptually and practically to master the chaotic flux of experienced reality that is characterized by contradiction and ambiguity. In other words following the imperative of consistency is the only way to confer meaning (*Sinn*) on a reality that presents itself as meaningless. Insofar as all human cultures have been equally concerned with making human ideas and behavior meaningful, they have been equally "rational". Furthermore, when judged in purely objective terms, the degree of inner consistency achieved by one culture is virtually indistinguishable from that achieved by another. For these reasons, Weber is exceedingly cautious in using the rational vs. irrational dichotomy as the criterion for distinguishing modern culture from pre-modern or primitive cultures. For example, Weber notes:

> Magic . . . has been just as systematically "rationalized" as [modern medicine]. The earliest intentionally rational therapy involved the almost complete rejection of the cure of the empirical symptoms by empirically tested herbs and potions in favor of exorcism of (what was thought to be) the "real" (magical, daemonic) cause of the ailment. Formally, it had exactly the same highly rational structure as many of the most important developments in modern therapy.[4]

Consequently, Weber does not draw a distinction between modern science and primitive magic because one is "rational" and the other "irrational"— from a strictly objective position both are equally rational or equally irrational. Weber notes:

> Something is never "irrational" in itself but only from a particular "rational" vantage point. For the nonreligious person every religious way of organizing life is irrational; for the hedonist every ascetic organization of life is "irrational" even if it may be, measured against *its* ultimate values, a "rationalization."[5]

By noting that there is no objective difference between the rationality of primitive magic and modern medicine (or the rationality of the hedonist and the ascetic), Weber problematizes the accepted understanding of "rational". His observations at the end of chapter two in *The Protestant Ethic and the Spirit of Capitalism*, express the problematic in explicit terms:

> A simple sentence should stand at the center of every study that delves into "rationalism." It must not be forgotten that one can in fact "rationalize" life from a vast variety of ultimate vantage points. Moreover, one can do so in very different directions. "Rationalism" is a historical concept that contains within itself a world of contradictions.[6]

It is worth noting that Weber sees the concept of rationalism containing "contradictions" (in the plural) not merely a "contradiction" (in the singular.) The first contradiction is the fact that the ultimate goal of rationalization, attaining consistency, can be pursued from multiple perspectives that are clearly in tension with each other. This point is best illustrated by looking at Weber's typology of rationality that has been skillfully summarized by Stephen Kalberg.[7] One type is practical rationality that is most prominently displayed in the pursuit of mundane, practical interests. This rationality brings consistency to human thought and action from the perspective of the immediate, this-worldly needs and interests that emerge as a result of human interaction with material reality. Substantive (or value) rationality is another type and it is most prominently displayed in religious thought and behavior. It brings consistency to human ideas about the world and human action in the world from the perspective of ultimate values learned via revelation. A third type, theoretical rationality, focuses on the cognitive manipulation of ideas about material reality and gives rise to abstract concepts. This type of rationality is characteristic of the life of a philosopher. Finally, consistency in thought and action can be pursued with reference to universal rules, laws, or regulations derived from experimental manipulation of material reality. Formal rationality, as Weber calls this perspective, is the defining characteristic of modern science.[8] If a strictly objective definition of "rationality" is maintained, it is clear that practical needs, religion, the philosophical life and modern science are equally legitimate means for pursuing consistency in the face of experienced chaos. As Kalberg has demonstrated, this is a point that Weber emphasizes repeatedly and emphatically in many of his writings and throughout his career. At the same time, it is equally obvious that the four different perspectives are in tension with each other—a tension that leads up to and past contradiction into outright hostility. Consequently, the first contradiction in the concept of "rationalism" is the fact that the single goal of following the imperative of consistency in thought and action can be pursued from multiple, mutually contradictory perspectives. This contradiction in the concept of rationalism is on the horizontal plane.

There is a different, but related, contradiction on the vertical plane. From the Weberian perspective we cannot speak of the flesh-and-blood, lived practice of science as being composed solely of formal rationality. Similarly, we cannot speak of the actual practice of religion being the expression of value rationality, exclusively. The same holds for philosophy and practical interests. In short there is no such thing as pure "scientific rationalism", "religious rationalism", etc. For Weber, while formal rationality is dominant in the activity of science, theoretical, value and practical rationality types are always and inevitably present in the activity of science as it is practiced by the scientist. Weber explicitly recognizes the fact that something more than formal rationality is necessary in order to even conceive of science as praxis:

All scientific work presupposes that the rules of logic and method are valid; these are the general foundations of our orientation in the world;

and, at least for our special question, these presuppositions are the least problematic aspect of science. Science further presupposes that what is yielded by scientific work is important in the sense that it is "worth being known." In this, obviously, are contained all our problems. For this presupposition cannot be proved by scientific means. It can only be *interpreted* with reference to its ultimate meaning, which we must reject or accept according to our ultimate position towards life.[9]

The practice of science is not possible without the affirmation of the value-judgment that scientific knowledge is "worth being known". But Weber also notes that "belief in the value of scientific truth is the product of certain cultures and is not a product of man's original nature"[10] or of any "laws of nature". Consequently, there is nothing unscientific, irrational, or inhuman in rejecting the claim that scientific knowledge is "worth being known" in favor of non-scientific knowledge. Science can only describe the consequences of this decision by identifying the costs incurred and benefits forsaken by preferring non-scientific knowledge over scientific knowledge. For the sake of intellectual integrity, science should also describe the benefits attained and costs avoided by this value-judgment. The important point, for Weber, is that science cannot label the rejection of one value (including its own value) in favor of another as being "false", "wrong", "irrational", and most notably "unscientific".

At this juncture the question emerges about the rational grounds on which a particular value can be affirmed. Speaking to this particular issue, Weber notes:

Only on the assumption of belief in the validity of values is the attempt to espouse value-judgment meaningful. However, to *judge* the *validity* of such values is a matter of *faith*.[11]

This makes the problematic even more acute. In addition to the impasse created by the fact that the affirmation of the value of science cannot be justified scientifically, an additional impasse is created by fact that this affirmation has to be justified in palpably non-scientific terms—the affirmation amounts to an act of faith. In terms of Weber's typology of rationality, the affirmation of a value and the rejection of others is the domain of value rationality that is characteristic of religion. Some might think that Karl Löwith is overstating the case when he says that Weber lays bare the fact that science is more than just the expression of formal rationality because "value-judgments of a moral and semi-religious type"[12] are an irreducible part of the practice of science. But this is not an over-statement on Löwith's part, it is a restatement of Weber's position. In the last public lecture he gave before his death, Weber explicitly states that the presupposition "scientific truth exists and is valid" is "essentially a religious and philosophical presupposition".[13] Consequently, the integrity and legitimacy (actually the very possibility) of science as a human activity is dependant on the affirmation of "a religious and philosophical presupposition". This means that a rejection or even marginalization of value rationality by science (or scientists) cannot but undermine the legitimacy and vibrancy of science itself because it deprives science of the rational grounds on which its underlying presuppositions can be affirmed. Along the same lines, for science to marginalize or deny the legitimacy of theoretical rationality jeopardizes the well-being of science because the grammar of scientific language is rooted in abstract concepts. Additionally, science cannot marginalize or deny the legitimacy of practical rationality because the questions and issues that make up the subject matter of scientific study are almost always the result of the need to solve particular practical/mundane problems.

While the discussion on the contradiction in rationalism on vertical plane has focused on science, it must be kept in mind that science was selected for illustrative purposes. Everything that has been said about the contradiction on the vertical plane applies to the human activities called religion, philosophy and mundane pursuits. For example, while value rationality is the defining character of religion, formal, theoretical and practical rationality types are always and inevitably present in the actual practice of religion. This means that any human activity—be it science, religion, philosophy or mundane pursuits—depends on acknowledging the reality and affirming the legitimacy of rationality types that are not only different from but usually in tension with (to the point of contradiction) the defining/dominant rationality type in the particular activity. For a practicing scientist, religionist, philosopher, etc. to reject or even question the reality of rationality types that are implicit in his/her particular activity amounts to undermining the reality and legitimacy of the activity. This is another way of saying that since every single human activity is the outcome of an interaction between facts, values, needs and concepts it is not logically possible for either science, religion, worldly interests, or philosophy to give a comprehensive and exhaustive account of any particular human activity—to say nothing of giving a comprehensive account of all of reality. In addition to the two contradictions discussed above, there is a third contradiction in the concept of rationalism at the intersection of the horizontal and vertical planes. While this suggests that the problematic is becoming more acute, this is also the point where Weber's oeuvre contains pointers for meaningfully redressing the contradictions.[14]

Redressing the Contradictions—A Weberian Possibility

The third contradiction comes in the form of the limitations of science and the needs of cultural beings. In conversation (and agreement) with Tolstoy, Weber identifies the limitations of science: "Science is meaningless because it gives no answer to our question, the only question important for us: 'What shall we do and how shall we live?' ".[15] We must keep in mind that "science", as Weber uses it here, refers to the practice of using universal laws, rules, and regulations derived from the experimental manipulation of reality to conceptually and practically master reality. The meaninglessness of science is accentuated by the fact that it is equally unqualified to answer a related but different question: "What shall we value and how shall we believe?" Science is not qualified to either construct world-images (*Weltbild* or *Weltanschauung*) in which human beings can put their faith or pass judgment on the validity of value-ideas (*Wertideen*) on which human being could base their actions. In short science is incapable of answering *the most* pressing questions of cultural beings.

Weber was openly contemptuous of those individuals who turned to science for the answer to the question "What shall we do and how shall we live?" and offered the allegedly "scientific" answers as a way for human beings to achieve happiness in the world. He notes:

> After Nietzsche's devastating criticism of those "last men" who "invented happiness," I may leave aside altogether the naïve optimism in which science—that is, the technique of mastering life which rests on science—has been celebrated as the way to happiness. Who believes in this?—aside from a few big children in university chairs and editorial offices?[16]

Weber is no less contemptuous of those who turn to science to definitively answer the question "What shall we value and how shall we believe?" to provide allegedly "scientific" meaning (*Sinn*) for human existence in the world:

> Who—aside from big children who are indeed found in the natural sciences—still believes that the findings of astronomy, biology, physics, or chemistry could teach us anything about the meaning [*Sinn*] of the world? ... If these natural sciences lead to anything in this way, they are apt to make the belief that there is any such thing as "meaning" of the universe die out at its very roots.[17]

In sum, science is equally incapable of definitively answering any questions having to do with the happiness of human beings in the world and the meaning of human life in the world. In short, science is as unqualified to pass judgments on matters of ultimate value as religion is unqualified to pass judgments on matters of empirical fact. Given Weber's position on the inability of science to answer the really important questions, the point of interest for us is: on what grounds does he affirm his own faith in science and justify living his life in pursuit of scientific knowledge, while rejecting the pursuit of philosophical or religious ideals?

Weber chooses science because it offers him cultural goods that he finds to be more valuable than those offered by religion, philosophy, or practical interests. The goods provided by science come in the form of "the provision of concepts and judgments which are neither empirical reality nor reproductions of it but which facilitate its analytical ordering in a valid manner".[18] Weber posits that science is unique among all perspectives because the scientific method offers objective criteria against which the validity of science's truth claims can be checked. Sating Weber's position in philosophical terms, we can say that in contrast to religion, philosophy and practical interests science eschews the a-priori attitude in its method of inquiry and in the contents of its truth claims. For Weber, science is self-critical and self-conscious in a qualitatively different way than religion, philosophy, etc. It is worth noting that Weber's claim regarding the unique character of science is not an a-priori claim, it is the result of the praxis of science. Consequently, Weber's faith in the presupposition that scientific truth is "worth being known" is not blind faith—he has scientific reasons (in the sense of being amenable to analytical and experimental criticism) for affirming this faith claim. In sum, while science cannot answer "the only question important for us", science can be of uniquely valuable service "to the one who puts the questions correctly"[19] —the one who is willing to forgo all a-priori commitments for the sake of following the truth wherever it may lead.

Weber's descent into the postmodern abyss is prevented not only by an affirmation of science, but also by a conditional affirmation of religion. It is widely known that Weber described himself as being "unmusical in matters religious", but this is hardly a complete picture of Weber's position. The context in which he made the remark presents us with the irony of a religiously unmusical but scientifically rational affirmation of religion. In a letter to his friend Ferdinand Tönnies, Weber first observes that modern theologians have made impressive strides in "digesting" the findings of the modern natural and physical sciences by bringing them into conversation with religious teachings. This amounts to an implicit (though cautious and not completely worked out) affirmation of modern science by the theologians. In stark contrast, most members of the scientific community have linked the affirmation of modern science with the rejection of religion. Weber notes that there are many scientists constructing "scientific" metaphysics on the back of physics, biology, etc. with the hope/goal of replacing traditional religious metaphysics. After this comparison, Weber becomes self-reflective.

It is true that I am absolutely unmusical in matters religious and that I have neither the need nor the ability to erect any religious edifices within me—this is simply impossible for me, and I reject it. But after examining myself carefully I must say that I am neither anti-religious nor irreligious.[20]

Weber does not shy away from explicitly stating the implications of being unmusical in religious matters: "I am like a tree stump from which new shoots can sometimes grow, but I must not pretend to be a grown tree." Weber finds that his scientific scholarship is incapable of making him a "grown tree", a complete human being. He is very conscious of the fact that many of his contemporaries are also struggling with the same issues—the issue of being fully human in the modern, disenchanted cultural condition. While he has resigned himself to the fate of not becoming a fully grown tree, he does offer an evaluation of those making this attempt, i.e. the liberal theologian who seeks to bridge the divide between modern science and traditional religion and the secular modernist/scientist committed to fashioning a naturalistic metaphysics on the back of modern science with the hope of replacing religion. Addressing Tönnies, Weber notes:

> For you a theologian of liberal persuasion (whether Catholic or Protestant) is necessarily most abhorrent as the typical representative of a halfway position; for me he is in human terms infinitely more valuable and interesting . . . than the intellectual (and basically cheap) pharisaism of naturalism, which is intolerably fashionable and in which there is much less life than in the religious position.[21]

Weber explicitly states that the theologian attempting to reconcile the teachings of religion with the findings of science is "infinitely more valuable and interesting" as a human being than the scientist seeking to displace religion with science. He also finds the religious position to hold a more hopeful prospect in nurturing life than the anti-religious position. Especially in light of the fact that Weber recognizes the "essentially religious and philosophical presupposition" that makes the practice of science possible, his reflections in the letter to Tönnies can be considered a conditional affirmation of religion.[22] Weber's affirmation of science and conditional affirmation of religion is no less a resource for Scriptural Reasoning's interaction with the modern social sciences than Weber's exposition of the world of contradictions in the concept of rationalism. As a matter of fact, these two aspects of Weber's thought are intimately related to each other.

Religious Musicality and Bridging the Divide

The foregoing discussion provides the grounds for some second order reflections on the relevance of Weber's ideas for bridging the divide between religion and science. These reflections center on the possibility of establishing a relationship between science and religion by bringing formal rationality into relation with value rationality. As already noted, the distinguishing feature of science is the fact that it alone offers an objective method that is free of a-priori claims for checking the validity of truth claims about empirical reality. Similarly, the distinguishing feature of religion is the fact that it alone offers an objective claim that the cosmos and human existence in the cosmos is meaningful. This means that articulating an objectively valid claim of the meaningfulness of empirical reality requires bringing formal rationality into relationship with value rationality. This relationship would mean that both science and religion modify their self-understanding as a result of the encounter with the other. For religion this means that it consciously chooses to identify and redress the a-priori attitude/claims within itself. And it can do so most efficiently by adopting the scientific attitude. Charles Sanders Peirce has called such a religion a "religion of science"[23] because,

> it is a religion, so true to itself, that it becomes animated by the scientific spirit, confident that all the conquests of science will be triumphs of its own, and accepting all the results of science, as scientific men would accept them, as steps towards the truth, which may appear for a time to be in conflict with other truths, but which in such cases merely await adjustments which time is sure to effect. This attitude, be it observed, is one which religion will assume not at the dictate of science, still less by way of compromise, but simply and solely out of a bolder confidence in herself and her own destiny (6.433).[24]

At the same time the encounter between religion and science also means that science consciously acknowledges the meaningfulness of empirical reality even though the meaning (*Sinn*) cannot be learned from scientific analysis of the cosmos:

> The fate of an epoch which has eaten of the tree of knowledge is that it must know that we cannot learn the *meaning* of the world from the results of its analysis, be it ever so perfect; it must rather be in a position to create this meaning itself. It must recognize that general views of life and the universe can never be the products of increasing empirical knowledge . . .[25]

In light of what Weber has said about the inability of science to judge *Wertideen* or construct a *Weltanschauung*, the only way it can be "in a position to create this meaning itself" is by taking the religious attitude seriously. We can call the science that adopts such a stance towards religion a "science of religion". Such a science would approach the study of the religious attitude with the same humble attitude that it approaches the study of the natural world (i.e. considering all of its hypotheses about the object of study to be rational but fallible and acknowledging the right of the object of study to effect a modification in the hypotheses.) Peirce describes this "science of religion" right after his description of a religion of science:

> Meantime, science goes unswervingly its own gait. What is to be its goal is precisely what it must not seek to determine for itself, but let

itself be guided by nature's strong hand. Teleological considerations, that is to say ideals, must be left to religion; science can allow itself to be swayed only by efficient causes; and philosophy, in her character of the queen of the sciences, must not care, or must not seem to care, whether the conclusions be wholesome or dangerous (6.434)

Given what Weber has said about the contradictions in rationalism on the horizontal and vertical planes it is obvious that a rationally coherent case for self-legitimacy on the part of science and religion requires two things. Firstly it requires an affirmation of the alien other—an affirmation of value rationality that is characteristic of religion on the part of science and an affirmation of formal rationality that is characteristic of science on the part of religion. Secondly, it requires recognition of the limitations of the self—religion must acknowledge and state that it is incapable of judging the validity of truth claims about empirical reality, and science must acknowledge and state that it is incapable of judging the validity of ultimate ends/values. In sum, the affirmation of the alien other and recognition of the limits of the self on the part of religion and science is possible only if the world of contradictions within the concept of rationalism is recognized and accepted by both. The possibility of a religion of science and a science of religion is implicit in Weber's critique of the modernist understanding of rationalism that does not see (or does not want to see) the contradictions in the concept of rationalism. But the explicit formulation of such a possibility has to go beyond Weber because the formulation presupposes a religiously musical perspective. Scriptural Reasoning can be seen as one attempt at such an articulation.

Bridging the Divide: The Qur'anic Affirmation of Material Reality

Weber's explication of the contradictions within the concept of rationalism, augmented by Peirce's pragmaticist insights, provides the (social) scientific warrant for moving towards bridging the science vs. religion divide. Now the discussion turns to the Qur'anic warrant. The fact that such a warrant is real can be demonstrated by looking at the way the Qur'an employs the word *"ayah"* (pl. *ayaat*). This word is often translated as "verse"—thus the Qur'an is composed of more than 6000 *ayaat* (verses). But the translation of *ayah* as "verse" is insufficient. In addition to meaning "verse", *ayah* also means "sign, token, mark; miracle; wonder, marvel, prodigy; model, exemplar, paragon, masterpiece".[26] Consequently each "verse" of the Qur'an is simultaneously a "sign", "token", and/or "exemplar" pointing towards something beyond itself. The "something beyond itself" is the reality towards which the Revealed Word draws the individual's attention. It is obvious that the Qur'an draws the individual's attention towards "spiritual" realities such as God, prophets, life here-after, angels, etc. But in addition to drawing attention to these "spiritual" realities, the "verses" of the Qur'an draw attention to the material, mundane, profane reality because this "non-spiritual" reality also contains the *ayaat* of Allah. Extending Muhammad Iqbal's observations on the way that the Qur'an employs the word *ayah*[27] we can summarize that the Qur'an states that, in addition to the Qur'an, the *ayaat* of Allah are also contained in: a) the world of nature, b) the unfolding of the historical process and c) the individual and collective human self. In other words the natural cosmos, the evolution of history and the human individual/society are as much modes and loci of Divine Self-Disclosure as the Revealed Word.

The fact that the exact same word is used to describe the contents of the Qur'an and the different components of material reality suggests that there is a direct relationship between the (religious) understanding of the Revealed Word and (scientific) knowledge of the material world. Before exploring this point further it would be useful to identify explicitly some of the Qur'anic the passages that use the term *ayah/ayaat* to refer to both the Revealed Word and material world. The fact that Qur'an itself is composed of *ayaat* is made clear in the following passages:

- *Ta. Sin. These are the ayaat of the Qur'an—a divine writ clear in itself and clearly showing the truth: a guidance and a glad tiding to the believers ...* (26:1–2)
- *Alif. Lam. Mim. Ra. These are the* ayaat *of the Book: and what has been revealed to thee [O, Muhammad] from your Lord is (indeed) the truth—yet most people will not believe.* (13:1)

One does not have to look far for examples of passages that locate the *ayaat* of Allah in the world of nature. After stating that the Qur'an is composed of *ayaat* sent for the guidance of humanity (Surah 13:1) Allah says:

> *It is Allah who has raised the heavens without supports that you can see, and is established on the throne of almightiness; and He has made the sun and the moon subservient [to His laws,] each running its course for a term set [by Him.] He governs all that exists. Clearly does He spell out these* ayaat *for you so that you might become certain that you destined to meet your Lord. And it is He who has spread the earth wide and placed on it firm mountains and running waters, and created thereon two genders of every plant; [and it is He Who] causes the night to cover the day. Verily, in all this are* ayaat *for people who think.* (Surah 13:2–3)

The next *ayah* explicates in some detail the wonders in the plant world, where all the plants are watered by the same water from the sky but each plant has its own distinctive taste, characteristic and use. The *ayah* concludes: "*Verily in all this there are* ayaat *for people who use their reason!*" (Surah 13:4) As if to draw our attention to the fact that human identity cannot be considered in isolation from the world of nature and the passage of time, while at the same time instructing us that the world of nature, human identity and the passage of time are symbols of the sacred, Allah says in the Qur'an:

And among His ayaat is this: He creates you out of dust—and then, lo! you become human beings ranging far and wide! And among His ayaat is this: He creates for you mates out of your own selves, so that you might incline towards them, and He engenders love and tenderness between you: in this, behold, there are ayaat for people who think! And among His ayaat is the creation of the heavens and the earth, and the diversity of your tongues and colors: for in this, behold, there are ayaat for all who have knowledge. And among His ayaat is your sleep, at night or in daytime, as well as your [ability to go about in] quest of some of His bounties: in this, behold, there are ayaat for people who [are willing to] listen! (Surah 30:20–23)

Imagine for a moment that this passage is specifically addressing you as an individual—the following is a partial summary of a plain sense reading: "My wife/husband, the love and tenderness that bind us, the language that I speak, the color of my skin (my ethno-linguistic heritage), my routine of sleeping in order to refresh myself, my quest to earn a living for my family—all of these are the *ayaat* of Allah (or modes and loci of Divine Self-Disclosure)." Iqbal's words sum up what has been said above, succinctly:

The Qur'an sees signs [*ayaat*] of the Ultimate Reality in the "sun", the "moon", the lengthening out of shadows', "the alternation of day and night", "the variety of human colors and tongues", the alternation of the days of success and reverse among peoples'—in fact in the whole of nature as revealed to the sense-perception of man. And the Muslim's duty is to reflect on these signs and not to pass them by "as if he is dead and blind", for he who does not see these signs in this life will remain blind to the realities of the life to come.[28]

If it is indeed the case that material reality is no less a mode/locus of Divine Self-Disclosure than the Revealed Word, then it must be the case that critical investigation of and rational reflection on the workings of material reality is akin to prayerful contemplation of the Divine Word. In the conclusion of a chapter titled "The Conception of God and the Meaning of Prayer," Iqbal argues that this is indeed the case:

The truth is that all search for knowledge is essentially a form of prayer. The scientific observer of Nature is a kind of mystic seeker in the act of prayer. Although at present he follows only the footprints of the musk-deer, and thus modestly limits the method of his quest, his thirst for knowledge is eventually sure to lead him to the point where the scent of the musk-gland is a better guide than the footprints of the deer. This alone will add to his power over Nature and give him that vision of the total-infinite which philosophy seeks but cannot find.[29]

Given the manner in which the Qur'an employs the term *ayah* and Iqbal's interpretation of the meaning of prayer, it is difficult to see how religious reflection on the words of the Qur'an can be divorced from scientific inquiry into the workings of material reality. In other words, the Qur'an appears not only to anticipate but almost to require the emergence of a religion of science (as described by Peirce above.)

Furthermore, there is reason to assert that in addition to anticipating a religion of science, the Qur'an also anticipates a science of religion. The Qur'an records a number of debates between the Blessed Prophet and his detractors. One of the recurring themes in these debates is the demand on the part of the detractors that the Blessed Prophet produce some type of super-natural miracle as evidence to support his claim of being God's Prophet. After stating that it is indeed within Allah's power to grant a super-natural sign (or miracle) that would demonstrate the veracity of the Blessed Prophet's claim, the Qur'an goes on to reject the detractors' demand. The reasons for the rejection are especially relevant in the context of the present discussion:

> And they [the pagans] say: "Why has no miraculous sign [ayah] been bestowed on him from on high by his Lord?" Say: "Behold, Allah has the power to bestow any sign [ayah] from on high." Yet most human beings are unaware of this—all the creatures that crawl on the earth or those that fly with their wings are communities like yourselves—We have left nothing out of the Book—and in the end they will be gathered to their Lord. Those who reject Our signs are deaf, dumb, and in total darkness. (Surah 6:37–9)

Instead of producing a super-natural miracle (or super-natural *ayah*) demanded by the detractors, the Qur'an asks them to rationally reflect on natural phenomena (the *ayaat* in the material world.) In other words the Qur'an rejects the pagans demand for a super-natural *ayah* and directs their attention not to the *ayaat* of the Revealed Word, but to the natural/material *ayaat* in the created world. From the Qur'an's perspective the sensual and cognitive encounter with the material world reveals characteristics, relationships, habits, and values of living creatures that validate the verity of the Prophet's claims no less authoritatively than any super-natural miracle would/could. Commenting on this passage, Muhammad Asad notes:

> ... The meaning of the above passage is this: Man can detect God's "signs" or "miracles" in all the life-phenomena surrounding him, and should, therefore, try to observe them with a view to better understanding "God's way" (*sunnat Allah*)—which is the Qur'anic term for what we call "laws of nature".[30]

This observation is further supported by the fact that all things in the natural world (animate and inanimate) speak a language that, in the final analysis, is nothing other than the glorification of the Creator:

> *Say, "If there were other gods along with Him, as they say there are, then they would have tried to find a way to the Lord of the Throne. Glory to Him! He is far above what they say! The seven heavens and the earth and everyone in them glorify Him. There is not a single thing that does not celebrate His praise, though you do not understand their praise: He is Most Forbearing, Most Forgiving.* (Surah 17: 42–44)

In very concrete terms, understanding the "speech" of the natural world is equivalent to recognizing the fact that God is the Creator, Sustainer and Lord of the universe—because "there is not a single thing that does not celebrate His praise". In Peirce's words, the universe is "a great symbol of God's purpose, working out its conclusions in living realities" (5.119). If it is indeed the case that the universe is a "great symbol of God's purpose" or God's "great poem" (5.119), then the ultimate purpose of science, cannot be anything other than "simply and solely knowledge of God's truth" (1.239). Whereas the manner in which the Qur'an employs the term *ayah* suggests that the Qur'an anticipates a religion of science, the manner in which Qur'an privileges natural phenomena over super-natural miracles in its response to pagan polemics suggests that the Qur'an anticipates a science of religion. As sound as this conclusion appears, we must push the investigation further because there is a possibility that the depiction of the Qur'anic anticipations is being forced from the outside (by the author) rather than emerging from within the Qur'an (with the author playing the role of facilitator).

The hypothesis that this conclusion is internally emergent and not externally imposed is best supported by the fact that the Qur'an recognizes the possibility as well as the validity of following the "imperative of consistency" in thought and action from a non-Qur'anic perspective. In other words the Qur'an recognizes not only the reality but also the legitimacy of rationalizing human thought and action from a variety of perspectives—including non-Qur'anic perspectives. The Qur'anic perspective (understood as a value-judgment) on how one should live one's life in this world is that there should be a balance between this-worldly and other-worldly concerns. The Qur'an has the righteous among the Israelites giving council to Korah in the following words:

"Seek by means of what Allah has granted you, [the good of] the life to come, without forgetting, withal, your own [rightful] share in this world." (Surah 28:77) In other words, the Qur'an sees a mutually enriching relationship between practical rationality (i.e. the pursuit of this-worldly goods) and value rationality (i.e. the pursuit of next-worldly ideals) and suggests that a balance be maintained between the two. At the same time the

Qur'an is conscious of the fact that there are those would depart from the value-position advocated by the Qur'an and adopt an alternative value-position, i.e. favoring the pursuits of worldly goods without any regard for next-worldly ideals (Surah 2:200). It goes on to contrast their attitude with those who hope for the goods of this life as well as the next life (Surah 2:201).

The interesting point to note is that beyond being conscious of the possibility of the non-Qur'anic attitude, the Qur'an accepts the "rationality" and "validity" of a life shaped exclusively by the pursuit of this-worldly goods:

> *If anyone desires the harvest in the life to come, We shall increase it for him; if anyone desires a harvest of this world, We shall give him a share of it, but in the Hereafter he will have no share.* (Surah 42:20)

While the Qur'an repeatedly states that human beings should rationalize their thoughts and actions by keeping this-worldly and next-worldly values in balance, nowhere does it state that individuals cannot rationalize their lives according to purely this-worldly needs and interests. On the contrary (Surah 42:20) explicitly states that those who rationalize their lives exclusively in this-worldly terms will get some of what they desire. While the Qur'an describes the final outcome of a life lived purely in pursuit of this-worldly goods in vivid detail, in the final analysis it leaves the human being free to choose this perspective. In Weberian terms (and in line with Weber's stance on the acceptance or rejection of science), the Qur'an does not label a life lived entirely in pursuit of worldly goods as "irrational" in some absolutely objective sense, it simply identifies the benefits the individual will be foregoing as a result of the decision—no "harvest" to reap in the next-worldly life—as well as the costs that the individual will incur as a result of the decision.

The Qur'anic treatment of material reality evidences a consciousness of the contradictions within the concepts of rationalism. Its refusal to entertain the request of the pagans to produce a super-rational miracle in favor of rational reflection on the natural phenomena contains an implicit recognition of the contradiction in rationalism at the vertical level. Rational reflection on facts in "profane" or "natural" reality should lead to the recognition of "religious" or "spiritual" values. Similarly, the Qur'anic recognition of the validity of the rationalization of life from a purely this-worldly perspective contains an implicit recognition of the contradiction in rationalism at the horizontal level. An individual can lead a meaningful life from a variety of different perspectives, not all of them being in accord with the particular perspective that the Qur'an favors. If it is indeed the case that the Qur'an is conscious of the contradictions in rationalism at the horizontal and vertical planes, then the hypothesis that the Qur'an anticipates a religion of science and a science of religion would be emergent from within the Qur'anic narrative rather than being a conclusion being imposed from the outside.

A Final Word

The goal of the present discussion, as noted in the introduction, was to illustrate the fruitfulness of the exchange between Scriptural Reasoning and the social sciences in one particular case. Assuming that the essay made satisfactory progress in this regard, the issue of the relationship between my particular presentation and SR in general remains outstanding. Because there is no necessary link between the particularity of my argument and the practice of SR more generally, I would like to conclude with some remarks on this topic. David Ford describes SR as a way of forming a "mutual ground" between Islam, Christianity and Judaism in the secular university. This allows each of the three religious traditions to bring its own unique resources to the table in discussions about the common good and public responsibility in a multi-cultural and inter-religious social setting. We can call this "mutual ground" an "inter-religious mutual ground". To the degree that my presentation of the relationship between Weber, Peirce and the Qur'an is sound, I think that the inter-religious mutual ground formed by SR is an indexical sign that similar grounds can also be formed amongst the religious traditions and non-religious (or "secular") academic disciplines in the modern university—let's call the latter "extra-religious mutual grounds". The extra-religious mutual grounds would be a place where a group of religious traditions (or one religious tradition) establishes a relationship of collegiality with "secular" disciplines in the university with the goal of addressing/redressing issues of common concern. This means that SR offers a novel perspective not only for inter-religious interaction in the secular academy, but also a novel perspective for the interaction between disciplines that have been traditionally labeled as "religious" and the "secular" academic disciplines.

Furthermore, because SR is a practice before it is a theory, there is no a-priori "orthodox" position regarding the defining characteristics of Scriptural Reasoning. This allows each practitioner to identify the characteristics that appeals to him/her the most. I will use the latitude afforded thereby to offer some remarks on what I see as the most tantalizing fruit offered by the exchange between Scriptural Reasoning and the social sciences. Peter Ochs notes: "Our knowing is a relationship, only partly cognitive, that leads us into further circles of relationship as we seek to pursue knowledge further." Explicitly identifying "knowledge" with "relationship" is the characteristic of SR that appeals to me the most. It gives me objective criteria by which to judge whether or not the knowledge offered by a particular practice, methodology, etc. is valid and meaningful (and thereby worth affirming). The knowledge is valid and meaningful insofar as it nurtures existing relationships and gives birth to new relationships. If the knowledge produced in/on the inter-religious mutual ground is worth affirming, it must contribute to the actual creation (or realization) of new and mutually enriching relationships that were only latently potential before. Looking for such possibilities across the religious vs. non-religious (or "secular") divide (with the religion vs. science divide as a well-known example) is as good a place as any to begin. The explicit goal of the essay was to demonstrate the fruitfulness of the exchange between Scriptural Reasoning and the philosophy of social science by showing how such an exchange can contribute to bridging the religion vs. science divide. To the degree that progress was made towards this goal, it can be seen as a sign pointing towards a different but related reality—SR making a real contribution to creating a mutual ground (or building relationships) between the traditional religion and the modern, "secular" academy.

NOTES

1   Robert Bellah, "Between Religion and Social Science" in *Beyond Belief: Essays on Religion in a Post-Traditionalist World* (Berkeley, CA: University of California Press, 1991), pp. 237–259; p. 245.
2   *Ibid.*, p. 237.
3   Max Weber, "Religious Rejections of the World and Their Directions" in *From Max Weber: Essays in Sociology*, edited by Hans Heinrich Gerth and C. Wright Mills (New York, NY: Oxford University Press, 1946), pp. 323–359; p. 324.
4   Max Weber, "The Meaning of 'Ethical Neutrality' " in *Max Weber on the Methodology of the Social Sciences*, edited by Edward A. Shils and Henry A. Finch, (Glencoe, IL: The Free Press, 1949), pp. 1–47; p. 34.
5   Max Weber, *The Protestant Ethic and the Spirit of Capitalism*, trans. by Stephen Kalberg, (Los Angeles, CA: Roxbury Press, 2002), p. 170, fn. 10.
6   *Ibid.*, p. 37.
7   Stephen Kalberg, "Max Weber's Types of Rationality: Cornerstones for the Analysis of Rationalization Process in History", *The American Journal of Sociology* Vol. 85 (March, 1980), pp. 1145–1179; pp. 1151–1159 passim.
8   This is an extremely abridged summary of Weber's position on the relationship between particular types of rationality and particular types of human activities. Weber's analysis of the relationship is far more sophisticated and nuanced than my summary suggests.
9   Max Weber, "Science as a Vocation" in *From Max Weber*, pp. 129–156; p. 143.
10   Max Weber, " 'Objectivity' in Social Science and Social Policy" in *Max Weber on the Methodology of the Social Sciences*, pp. 49–112; p. 110.
11   *Ibid.*, p, 55.
12   Karl Löwith, "Max Weber's Position on Science" in *Max Weber's "Science as a Vocation"*, edited by Peter Lassman, Irving Velody, with Heminio Martins, (London: Unwin Hyman, 1989), pp. 138–156; p. 146.
13   Max Weber, op. cit. "Science as a Vocation", p. 154.
14   For an excellent summary of Weber's oeuvre see Fritz Ringer, *Max Weber: An Intellectual Biography* (Chicago, IL: The University of Chicago Press, 2004).
15   *Ibid.*, p. 143.
16   *Ibid.*
17   *Ibid.*, p. 142.
18   Max Weber, op. cit., " 'Objectivity' in Social Science and Social Policy", p. 111.
19   Max Weber, op. cit., "Science as a Vocation", p. 143.

20 Wolfgang Schluchter, "The Paradox of Rationalization: On the Relation of Ethics and the World" and "Value Neutrality and the Ethic of Responsibility" in *Max Weber's Vision of History: Ethics and Methods*, edited by Guenther Roth and Wolfgang Schluchter, (Berkeley, CA: University of California Press, 1979), pp. 11–116; p. 82 fn.

21 *Ibid.*

22 For a detailed treatment of a Weberian possibility for bridging the religion vs. science divide with reference to Weber's writings on the sociology of culture/religion and the methodology of the social sciences see my *The Postmodern Significance of Max Weber's Legacy: Disenchanting Disenchantment* (New York, NY: Palgrave Macmillan, 2005).

23 Given the limitations of space, it is difficult to discuss in detail the relationship between Peirce's valuation of religion and his pragmaticist philosophy. Michael Raposa has treated this topic in detail and has made a convincing argument that Peirce's philosophy of religion cannot be separated from his philosophy at large: *Peirce's Philosophy of Religion*, (Bloomington, IN: Indiana University Press, 1989). I hope the following observations by Michael Raposa are (at least partially) sufficient for the present purposes. In the introduction to his exploration of Peirce's philosophy of religion, Raposa posits that Peirce's ideas on religion

> are less adequately conceived as constituting a part of his thought than as supplying an illuminating perspective on the whole of it. Indeed, they are among those guiding principles by means of which "the whole calls out its parts" (p. 6).

After looking at Peirce's metaphysics, phenomenology, semiotics, logic, and philosophy of science (among other topics) from this perspective, Raposa comes to the following conclusion: "Peirce's own ideas about religion, no matter how incomplete they may appear to be, are continuous with what he thought and wrote about in detail on other topics" (p. 154).

24 The reference is to the volume and paragraph number of C. S. Peirce *Collected Papers of Charles Sanders Peirce*, edited by Charles Hartshorne and Paul Weiss (Cambridge, MA: Belknap Press of Harvard University, 1934/35). Hereafter citations from this work appear in the main body of the essay as *CP*.

25 Max Weber, op. cit., " 'Objectivity' in Social Science and Social Policy", p. 57.

26 Hans Wehr, *The Hans Wehr Dictionary of Modern Written Arabic*, edited by J. Milton Cowan, (Ithaca, NY: Spoken Language Services Inc., 1976), p. 36.

27 Muhammad Iqbal, *The Reconstruction of Religious Thought in Islam* (Lahore, Pakistan: Institute of Islamic Culture, 1996), p. 102.

28 *Ibid.*

29 *Ibid.*, p. 73.

30 Muhammad Asad, *The Message of the Qur'an* (Gibraltar, Spain: Dar Al-Andalus, 1997), p. 177, fn. 30.

10

THE PHENOMENOLOGY OF SCRIPTURE: PATTERNS OF RECEPTION AND DISCOVERY BEHIND SCRIPTURAL REASONING

GAVIN D. FLOOD

A phenomenology of scripture as a descriptive enterprise would, of course, be a vast project, especially one that crosses diverse traditions, and a project that would fall under deep (and justified) suspicion in late modernity. But while there are fundamental problems concerning the scientific or objective aspirations of a descriptive phenomenology of religion,[1] problems linked to the claim that any comparative phenomenology of religion is a form of colonialism,[2] a second level phenomenology sensitive to the contexts of its performance that seeks to look behind appearance raises theologically and philosophically interesting questions. Such a phenomenology is necessarily hermeneutical. While I do not intend to strongly defend a comparative phenomenology of scripture and justify the category in the light of its critique, I do wish to claim that a hermeneutical phenomenology raises profoundly interesting questions about the nature of scripture across traditions and contributes to a semiotically informed understanding that takes seriously both external, text-historical scholarship and internal theological concerns. I wish therefore to raise second level phenomenological questions or questions within a hermeneutical phenomenology and to move from there to a semiotics of scripture; a move necessitated by those very questions. Indeed, one route to Scriptural Reasoning (SR) is by way of a phenomenological questioning that requires a non-teleological, textual engagement of the kind performed in SR. But first a note of terminological clarification of my title: what I understand firstly by phenomenology and secondly by scripture.

Gavin D. Flood
Department of Religious Studies, University of Stirling, Stirling FK9 4LA, Scotland, UK

Husserl spoke of phenomenology as description[3] in the first instance, the mapping of the general structures of consciousness in a static mode. More recent studies of Husserl have shown that the descriptive enterprise, so often associated with phenomenology *tout ensemble*, was only one side of his understanding and that a descriptive or static phenomenology (*beschreibende Phänomenologie*) he contrasts with genetic or explanatory phenomenology (*erklärende Phänomenologie*), which inquires beyond description into origins and the ways in which appearances arise.[4] While not wishing to operate exclusively within Husserl's boundaries, I think it important to think of phenomenology both in terms of description which entails the bracketing of the being or truth behind appearances and in terms of a deeper inquiry that allows for questions about being and source to be raised. We clearly need a descriptive phenomenology in order to clarify the relationship of scripture to community but we also need a second level phenomenology or hermeneutical phenomenology that is open to deeper questions of being and truth and the answers presented within scriptural traditions. Such a hermeneutical phenomenology is not coterminous with Husserl's genetic project but because its aspiration is general (if not universal), it necessitates comparison in some form and dialogue across boundaries. I therefore take phenomenology firstly to mean description that entails the suspension of judgement about the being behind appearances (the *epoché*) and, secondly, as an inquiry into questions of source beyond description. Both of these are predicated upon a fundamental assumption of intentionality (see below).

The second term of my title, "scripture", is a category whose contents have been widely contested in the history of Abrahamic religions but a category that at a simple level I take to refer to the texts, oral and written, of historical traditions that set them aside from other texts because of the claims they make on human communities. Usually it is claimed that these texts bear witness to a revelation: in the case of the Qur'an the text is the revelation of God mediated through the Prophet, in the case of the New Testament the text bears witness to the revelation of Christ. Other scriptures are understood in other ways. For the atheistic Mīmāṃsakas the Veda is revelation (*śruti*, that which has been heard by the sages) which is authorless while the Tāntrikas have a hierarchy of revelation from a hierarchy of cosmic levels, their own texts transcending the restricted revelation of the Veda. While, of course, the Hindu texts are very different from the Jewish, Christian or Moslem texts, the category "scripture" meaningfully applies across traditions although accounts of what scripture is will vary greatly. We might say that scriptures comprise primarily injunctions to act along with accompanying prohibitions and narratives. Some traditions have emphasised the injunctive nature of their scriptures (such as the Mīmāṃsakas claim that the Veda is primarily concerned with injunction (*vidhi*)) while others have emphasised the narrative dimensions (such as more recent narrative theology). It is important that common questions can be asked across the divides of tradition about the nature of scripture, questions which will be answered in different ways.

Assuming the text-historical mapping of the scriptures of traditions, perhaps the most important questions that arise at the level of a hermeneutical phenomenology inspired by Ricoeur are: of what is scripture an index, for whom is scripture an index, and how is scripture an index?[5] Scripture is in some sense a sign that points to an object and I take "index" to be the phenomenological relationship between sign and object. It is to these intimately related questions that I shall address this essay.

Of What is Scripture an Index?

"Of what is scripture an index?" is a primary theological question the response to which will depend upon the context of its occurrence. There can be no truly general answer to such a question but we can examine more closely what is involved in any particular answer. It is a question of the relation between scripture as a sign and an object to which it points or to which it is in some relation. Although the language of sign and object is somewhat impersonal, a phenomenological inquiry necessitates *in the first instance* the avoidance of any particular theological language, such as the claim that scripture (sign) is an index (causal relationship) of God (object), if it is to offer some kind of account across traditions. A theological reformulation of this statement could be explicit about the sign-object relationship through saying that scripture is an index *from* God. Any phenomenological account is both a weakness and a strength; a weakness in that from tradition-internal perspectives scripture is not simply an index of a transcendent source as its "object" but is a living presence brought to fulfilment in the life of a community. Yet a phenomenological account is also a strength in opening out an analysis that provides a framework that goes beyond particular traditions and so is inherently comparative. Such a phenomenology is more a mode of reception than a method. While a closed theological position would see comparison as pointless, I would argue that in principle comparison in the mode of phenomenological reception allows development in the human sciences and refinement in theology through the clarification of difference. While the question "of what is scripture an index?" will be filled out with varied theological content from Islam to the Mīmāṃsakas, I would wish to identify the question of the index, namely the relationship between the scripture as a sign and its object, perhaps a transcendent source, firstly as a question of intentionality and secondly as a question of narration.

Any phenomenology of scripture must take intentionality as one of its primary categories, as this is the starting point of Husserlian phenomenology. By intentionality Husserl simply means that consciousness has an object—we are always conscious of something, the *cogito* bears witness to a stream of *cogitationes*.[6] By extension, and in accordance with the term's everyday use, we might say that intentionality means a subject's direction towards an object which entails the idea of positive or negative desire: desire for a situation to come into being or desire that a situation should cease. "I am drinking a cup of tea" is intentional in that the cup of tea is the object of my consciousness and the object of desire.[7] In Husserl's fundamental phenomenological language, cognitive activity or *noesis* has content, a sense of meaning or *noema*. The cognitive act is directed towards its intentional object. With regard to scripture this relationship is highly complex and we need to identify the *noesis-noema* relationship within scripture, which leads to the question of the *noesis-noema* relationship between scripture and community of readers. This last question is actually our question "for whom is scripture an index?"

If we assume, as I think we must, that scripture/s has/have an intentionality, then we might say that the *noesis* of the texts is the scribal process whereby the meaning or object is arrived at. The *noesis* is intimately bound up in the question "who speaks?", which refers to the narrator of the text (who may or may not be coterminous with the author). If the *noema* of scripture is the object of the *noesis* or processes of narration by the narrator, then we have two senses of the term. *Noema* points in two directions away from the text, firstly to an extra-textual source to which it bears witness (the voice in the burning bush, the source of the light in the niche) and, secondly, to the reader or community of readers who become the object of the text's *noesis* or noetic process. The first sense, the trans-textual *noema* to which the text bears witness and to which the narrator wishes to draw attention, is always deferred and always approached tangentially or indirectly (through the burning bush, through the lamp in the niche). The second sense of *noema* is, in fact, the implied reader of the text to whom the narrator addresses his injunctions and narration. *Noema* in the sense of deferred transcendent referent is the "about" of the text in contrast to the second sense of *noema* as the "to whom". To illustrate this complexity let us take a concrete example, endlessly rich, from the Hebrew Bible, commented on by others here, especially by Oliver Davies.

> There the angel of the Lord appeared to him in a flame of fire out of a bush; he looked, and the bush was blazing, yet it was not consumed. Then Moses said "I must turn aside and look at this great sight, and see why the bush is not burned up." When the Lord saw that he had turned aside to see, God called to him out of the bush, "Moses, Moses!" And he said, "Here I am." Then he said, "Come no closer! Remove the sandals from your feet, for the place on which you are standing is holy ground." He said further "I am the God of your father, the God of Abraham, the God of Isaac, and the God of Jacob." And Moses hid his face, for he was afraid to look at God.[8]

Here there are different levels of narration. The implied narrator of the text is not, of course, a conscious agent coterminous with the author, but the narrative voice is always present whenever the text is read. The narrator uses the processes of narration to indicate a content (*noema*), which is indicated through that which is set aside as sacred. The voice from out of the burning bush speaks in the first person yet is nevertheless the object of the narrator's narration. This "object", whose extra-textual existence is presumed, is nevertheless only encountered within the text. Any extra-textual encounter with the *noema* of scripture is phenomenologically distinct from an intra-textual intentionality. Similarly, Moses as an index of the reader (as Oliver Davies shows), perhaps an image of the implied reader, is likewise the intentional content of the narrator. Thus the *noema* of the text points in two directions, to an extra-textual source of the narrated voice and to the narratee to whom the text is addressed. It is this question of "to whom" that we must now take up.

But are not all texts like this? Do not all texts contain an intentionality that points to an extra-textual referent and to the narratees implied within it? From a haiku to a science fiction novel or even an advertisement, all texts contain intentionality and an implied narrator addressing an implied narratee about an extra textual referent. What is it, then, that distinguishes the intentionality of the burning bush passage from that of other texts? This is a difficult question. On the one hand, one could create a first level or descriptive phenomenology that would be able to distinguish a scripture from a magazine advertisement—perhaps with reference to semantic density, to degree of openness, or the way the text is received by a community. Yet one cannot so easily distinguish scripture, which refers to an extra-textual transcendent source from, say, a science fiction novel which refers to an extra-terrestrial source, simply by an appeal to a distinction between history and fiction (as perhaps some communities of reception would wish to do). Ricoeur can, once again, be of help here. For Ricoeur history is a kind of narrative in so far as it explains events by making causal links between them. Thus testimony becomes archive which can then be turned into history. But similarly a fiction draws causal connections between events created in the narrative. Both share emplotment (*mythos*) or the ordering of events but what distinguishes the ordering is that in fiction events are internal to the narrative whereas for history events were lived. Fiction opens up the kingdom of "as if"[9] whereas with history we have the emplotment of stories that were lived. A novel, Ricoeur observes, is different from a history book and the distinction lies in the nature of the implicit contract between the writer and the reader, a contract which entails distinct expectations. In fiction "the reader is disposed to carry out what Coleridge called a 'wilful suspension of disbelief' with the reservation that the story told is an interesting one. . . . In opening a history book, the reader expects, under the guidance of mass of archives, to reenter a world of events that actually occurred."[10]

History and fiction both share emplotment but one is real, the events linked by the narrative happened, the other is false existing only in the realm of imagination. Where, then, does the story of the burning bush stand between these two poles? Clearly many scriptures are narratives characterised by emplotment and many followers of scripture would wish to place their texts closer to the realm of history and to distance them from fiction in contrast to secularist or historicist readings which would wish to place scripture closer to fiction than to history.

It seems to me that scripture occupies a place between history and fiction. To claim either that scripture is coterminous with history or that it is only fiction is in the former case to reject scholarship in the space of rational discourse and in the latter case is to reject the force of scriptural claims about human life. The binary truth/falsity distinction mapped on to the history/fiction distinction does not do justice to the complexity of the scripture-community relationship. Clearly questions regarding the origins and composition of texts must be interrogated— there can be no "no-go" areas in text-historical scholarship, even (or especially) in the case of the Qu'ran and Veda—but clearly questions regarding the meaning of scriptures for communities need to be explored by religious communities themselves as well as by the secular academy. Scripture cannot be reduced to either fiction or history. Like history, scripture is emplotment that makes a claim to truth and, like fiction, it is emplotment in so far as scripture's narrative as a living force is not deeply accessible outside of the religious imagination. The claims of scripture are not fictional claims for the traditions but nor are they historical claims in the sense of history understood by Ricoeur. We can explore this further by examining the relationship between the narratees or community of reception and the narrator, the voice of the text, which is not identical with the author. It is this relationship that clearly separates scripture from both fiction and history and it is this relationship that comes into view through the question "for whom is scripture and index?"

For Whom is Scripture an Index?

This question is not simply one of first level phenomenology, a historical question about communities who revere a particular text, but is a second level phenomenological question about the nature of sacred text itself seen in the relationship between *noesis* and *noema* or, in other words, between narrator and implied reader or receiver of the text. From the perspective of the community of readers, the narratees, we can take *noesis* to be the process of reception of the text or more accurately the reception of the text's implicit intentionality.

As we all know, the role of the author and the authorial voice in texts is a contentious one ever since Roland Barthes declared the death of the author. The problem of authorial voice in sacred texts is, of course, problematic for many sacred texts were composed over long periods of time and for some the authorial voice is regarded as transcendent by the community of reception. But we can say that a general feature of reading texts, as Wolfgang Iser and others remind us, is an interaction between the structure of the work and its recipient. As we have learned from German literary theory, *Rezeptionsgeschichte* or *Rezeptionsästhetik* of Hans Robert Jauss, that every act of reading evokes a horizon of expectations (*Erwarungshorizont*) or set or cultural, ethical and literary expectations on the part of readers "in the historical moment".[11] The text is not simply passively received by the reader but actively constructed from within the reader's horizon of expectation and the relationship between reader and text is quite dissimilar to that between perceiver and object. This is so with sacred texts as much as with literature. The text is brought to life and its meanings opened out only in the present moment of its reception. In this reception, the truth of the text is constructed by the imagination of the reader or the shared imagination of the community of readers, often acted out in a liturgical setting.

The analysis of this relationship is of key importance in understanding the relationship between sacred text and community where the "fulfilment" of the text comes in the reader. Wolfgang Iser refers us to Husserl's seminal essay on time to understand this relationship. Iser quotes Husserl, who writes: "Every originally constituent process is inspired by protentions, which construct and collect the seed of what is to come, as such, and bring it to fruition."[12] These protentions, Iser explains, are expectations implied at sentence level, a structure inherent in all intentional sentence correlates. The sentence correlate or intentional correlate is that to which the sentence points and, for Iser, the literary object is built up by these intentional correlates, the totality of these sentence correlates constituting the "portrayed world" of the work.[13] In the process of reading, each sentence prefigures a horizon which becomes the background of the next sentence correlate which modifies it, and so on. The reader has expectations as to how indeterminacies in the text are to be concluded with some expectations being resolved and new expectations being evoked. In literary texts these expectations are often disrupted and the text reassessed and modified. Memory here undergoes a transformation and "that which is remembered becomes open to new connections, and these in turn influence the expectations aroused by the individual correlates the sequence of sentences". The act of reading therefore consists of "a continual interplay between modified expectations and transformed memories".[14]

While Iser's formulation is an important point for understanding the process of reading, it needs to be modified in the context of religious reading where transformed memories are not only connected with the individual's life-path but with the tradition and the nature of the intentional correlates within the text are of a different order to that of the literary text. This is not to claim privilege for sacred texts on the grounds of some identifiable, inherent quality that separates them from fiction, but it is to claim that the sentence correlates are distinguished by the horizon of expectations of the reader or community of readers. Complementing this with Jauss' emphasis on history, we might say that these horizons of expectation must be understood within the history of a text's reception. The act of religious reading in different temporal and social locations, in variable senses with variable degrees of intensity, brings with it the memory of tradition. Religious reading invokes the memory of tradition in solitary, devotional reading and in communal, liturgical reading and recitation. The protentions of the sacred text are configured within the reader's imagination, which entails a kind of attentiveness, a bringing to mind the memory of tradition.

There are, then, two poles in the reception of the text; the pole of the author or more specifically the authorial intention or voice within the text and the pole of the reader (Iser calls these the artistic and the aesthetic). While we must recognise the highly contested claims about authorial intention (especially as regards sacred text where, in many cases, the "author" is believed to be God), we can distinguish between the extra-textual author and the author's voice or authors' voices within the text.[15] The narrator of the text is the intentionality of the text, which is distinct from its author or authors. This distinction between author(s) and narrator allows us to claim that the act of reading is guided by the narrator and received within the horizon of expectations of the reader or community of readers. Tzetvan Todorov is helpful here in mapping out this relationship. No two accounts of the same text will be identical, he claims. This diversity is explained by "the fact that these accounts describe, not the universe of the book itself, but this universe as it is transformed by the psyche of each individual reader."[16] The vision or *imaginaire* of a sacred text, perhaps produced over several hundred years, constantly interacts with the readers' imagination where it is reconfigured and brought to life in the present moment, under contemporary circumstances. The protentions of the text from the past are configured in the imagination of the reader or community of readers afresh in each reading. Emplotment is refigured as action in the world; the narrative of a life is made to conform to the narrative of tradition. This chain of readings is a chain of memory that functions to inform the present and offer a model of thought and behaviour re-confirmed by the community in its repeated acts of reading, which are simultaneously its repeated acts of re-constructing tradition. "For whom is scripture an index?" is therefore a question about the nature of reception, inseparable from the question "how is scripture an index?"

How is Scripture an Index?

The text is made present for a reader or community of readers in the act of "reading". I put inverted commas around the word "reading" because while reading is an important model of the reception of sacred text, there are other modes of reception that are intimately linked to it. To the question "how is scripture an index?" we might answer "through acts of reception". Scripture is made present through not only religious reading, but through liturgy and the development of certain kinds of interiority in asceticism.[17] Scriptures are enacted through liturgical performance and even solitary prayer is not private for it participates in the memory of tradition in looking back to a past origin which is simultaneously the anticipation of a telos. All this is brought to life in the present through the enactment of the text or what might be called the entextualisation of the body.[18] But this is not the place to develop a description of ritual, reading and scribal practices of the traditions, but rather to present a hermeneutical phenomenology of the process of scriptural reception. I shall therefore simply assume that acts of reception of scriptures can be adequately described (as I have tried to do elsewhere with a range of Sanskrit textual material).[19] Here we need to inquire more deeply into the process of reception and the formation of readers by showing some of the limitations of the phenomenological project I have so far proposed, and then suggesting a complementary approach that ends up as SR.

A phenomenology of scripture is constrained by a number of intimately related problems, firstly descriptive phenomenology on its own is bound by Husserlian assumptions about the self as the detached agent viewing appearances to consciousness as though from a distance, even outside of the world. Secondly this notion of subjectivity entails the idea of a universal rationality; and, thirdly, it entails the separation of meaning from existence through the act of bracketing. I have developed these critiques elsewhere,[20] but we can encapsulate the heart of the problem by saying that a phenomenological philosophy of consciousness is brought into question by what V. N. Voloshinov called the philosophy of the sign; that consciousness itself becomes "a viable fact only in the material embodiment of signs".[21] The implications for us are that any phenomenology of scripture needs to take account of the embodied nature of scripture seen in its modes of reception (reading, ritual, asceticism). This is where a hermeneutical phenomenology is an improvement on a purely descriptive phenomenology in that it recognizes the temporality of scripture and the need to relate the description of first level phenomenology to an account of narrative and history.

Scripture must be understood in the context of historical reception by human beings bound within the constraints of their time and place, including the phenomenological inquiry itself.

While the questions "of what is scripture an index?" and "for whom is scripture an index?" can be addressed in terms of *noesis* and *noema*, narrator and narratee, as I have attempted above, to address the question of "for whom?" we need to extend our analysis beyond that of subject and object. Hermeneutical phenomenology can take account of the material nature of signs and the historical context of inquiry. Indeed, we might ask not only "for whom is scripture an index?", but "for whom is phenomenological inquiry?" At one level the answer is for "the academy" outside of scriptural traditions, but this is not necessarily the case and a phenomenology of scripture is revealing for practitioners of scriptural hermeneutics within traditions. But certainly the question "for whom?" entails us going further and developing a semiotics of reception which flows naturally from phenomenology. The questions "for whom is scripture an index?" and "for whom is phenomenological inquiry?" both entail not only a subject and an object, a *noesis* and a *noema*, but an interaction through time that creates a third entity in the space of rational discourse. Scripture is a sign for a community or person. This is true of scriptural traditions themselves but also true of the scholar inquiring into scriptural traditions in the mode of detachment. This is where the practice of scriptural reasoning becomes interesting. The practice of SR involves a hermeneutical phenomenology in so far as those engaged in the practice must implicitly suspend judgement about the being behind the appearance of others' scriptures. This might not be recognized by practitioners of SR but it seems to me that it must be a part of the process in which there is resistance to reducing a plurality of scriptural claims to a shared vision at the cost of the particularity of tradition. To maintain the particularity of scriptural tradition we must suspend judgement about the being behind the scripture. Scripture is an index of something, but that something is implicitly bracketed in the act of scriptural reasoning with others. This is not a restriction but a liberating process. Secondly SR entails a semiotics of scripture in that it creates a discourse outside of particular scriptural traditions. This discourse is hospitable to others and is fundamentally text-based, but the emergent readings of the practice are not those of any one tradition. The third space of scriptural reasoning is semiotically rich and might be seen as a consequence of a phenomenological process in which the dynamics of scripture and scriptural reception, described in a phenomenological account, come into play across different traditions of reception.

By way of conclusion we might say that a phenomenology of scripture can address the three questions "of what is scripture and index?", "for whom is scripture an index?" and "how is scripture an index?" in a process that begins with a description of the *noesis-noema* structure, moves on to a deeper engagement in a hermeneutical phenomenology that can provide an account of textual reception, and from which follows a semiotics that recognizes the emergent discourse and discovery of new worlds characteristic of Scriptural Reasoning. Traditional communities of textual reception change through history and new communities of reception emerge. Scriptural Reasoning might be seen as one such new community, true to the spirit of dialogue but grounded in text and hermeneutically sensitive.

NOTES

1   E.g. Timothy Fitzgerald, *The Ideology of Religious Studies* (Oxford and New York: Oxford University Press, 1999), pp. 6, 54–71, 237; Gavin Flood, *Beyond Phenomenology: Rethinking the Study of Religion* (London and New York: Cassell, 1999), pp. 91–116; Russell T. McCutcheon, *Manufacturing Religion: the Discourse on Sui Generis Religion and the Politics of Nostalgia* (New York: Oxford University Press, 1997), pp. 118–119.

2   E.g. David Chidester, *Savage Systems: Colonialism and Comparative Religion in Southern Africa* (Charlottesville and London: University of Virginia Press, 1996), pp, 5–29. For a critique of textual bias see Richard King, *Orientalism and Religion: Postcolonial Theory, India, and the "Mystic East"* (London and New York: Routledge, 1999), pp. 62–81.

3   Edmund Husserl, *Cartesian Meditations: An Introduction to Phenomenology,* trans. Dorion Cairns, (Dordrecht, Boston and London: Kluwer Academic Publishers, 1991), pp. 39–46.

4   Donn Welton, *The Other Husserl: The Horizons of Transcendental Phenomenology* (Bloomington, IN: Indiana University Press, 2000), chapters 8 and 9.

5   These questions echo Ricoeur's question in the context of memory "from 'What?' to 'Who?' passing by way of 'How?' " See Paul Ricoeur, *Memory, History, Forgetting,* trans. Kathleen Blamey and David Pellauer, (Chicago, IL: The University of Chicago Press, 2004), p. 4.

6   Husserl, *Cartesian Mediations,* pp. 31–33.

7   But we must not forget that Heidegger rejected Husserl's understanding of intentionality providing an analysis of phenomena within the field of *Dasein's* operation, such as this example, as "present to hand".

8   Exodus, 3:2–6 (*Holy Bible: New Revised Standard Version*).

9   Paul Ricoeur *Time and Narrative,* Vol. 1, trans. Kathleen McLaughlin and David Pellauer, (Chicago, IL: The University of Chicago Press, 1984), p. 64.

10   Ricoeur, *Memory, History, Forgetting,* p. 261.

11   Hans-Robert Jauss, "Literary History as Challenge to Literary Theory", *New Literary History* Vol. 2 (1970), pp. 7–37; p. 14; Hans-Robert Jauss "The Idealist Embarrassment: Observations of Marxist Aesthetics", *New Literary History* Vol. 7 (1975), pp. 191–207.

12   Edmund Husserl, *Zur Phänomenologie des inneren Zeitbewusstseins* (*Gesammelte Weke X*) (The Hague: Martinus Nijhof, 1966), p. 52. Quoted in Wolfgang Iser, *The Act of Reading: A Theory of Aesthetic Response* (Baltimore, MD: John Hopkins University Press, 1978), pp. 110–111.

13   Wolfgang Iser, *The Act of Reading,* p. 110, quoting Roman Ingarden.

14   *Ibid.,* p. 111.

15   For Genette the author is outside the text and the narrator is within it. Only the narrator is the concern of narratology. Gérard Genette, *Narrative Discourse: An Essay in Method* (Oxford: Blackwell, 1980), pp. 25–27.

16   Tzetvan Todorov, "Reading as Construction", p. 72 in Susan R. Suleiman and Inge Crosman (eds.), *The Reader in the Text* (Princeton, NJ: Princeton University Press, 1980), pp. 67–82.

17   I have developed this idea in *The Ascetic Self: Subjectivity, Memory and Tradition* (Cambridge: Cambridge University Press, 2004).

18   *Ibid.*, pp. 166, 181.
19   Gavin Flood, *The Tantric Body: The Secret Tradition of Hindu Religion* (London: I. B. Tauris Press, 2006).
20   Gavin D. Flood, *Beyond Phenomenology: Rethinking the Study of Religion* (London: Cassell, 1999), pp. 91–116.
21   V. N. Voloshinov, *Marxism and the Philosophy of Language*, trans. Ladislav Matejka and I. R. Titunik (Cambridge, MA: Harvard University Press, 1986), p. 11.

11

READING WITH OTHERS: LEVINAS' ETHICS AND SCRIPTURAL REASONING

ROBERT GIBBS

I propose to make what we do in Scriptural Reasoning less obvious and so more questionable. I will look at the practices of learning here as both questionable, and therefore, as something for which we could give a reason. This questioning points at how odd it is for Jewish, Christian and Muslim scholars to read scriptures with each other. Why should we do such a thing? What might we learn about each other's traditions doing so? What might we learn about our own traditions? And thus what might we learn about ourselves? And finally, what might we learn about reasoning itself from this unusual kind of reasoning?

This essay is quite complex[1]. It is a musical kind of presentation. It is like a sonata of sorts. There is a chart as an appendix. I will set out eight frameworks—each of which sketches a view of what education is. The college or university is a place of learning and inquiry, but when we study religions we also need to think about how the university compares with institutions of religious instruction (the madrassa, the yeshiva, the seminary, and so forth)—or maybe we should contrast the university with a kind of job training that might be a kind of education on how machinery works or some intake process to learn how to do the office culture practices. It may well seem odd to read religious traditional texts in the academic context—since it cannot simply contribute to the formation of a religious identity, nor is it likely to teach us some sort of know-how. Even in a more humanistic view of the university, there is a preference for a scholarly/scientific methodological and objective mode of reading texts. Each framework then offers some view of how we would interpret the reading of

Robert Gibbs
Department of Philosophy, University of Toronto, University College, Room 320, 15 King's College Circle, Toronto, Ontario, CANADA M5S 3H7

religious texts in the university. Each framework requires a different kind of analysis, a science of inquiry. Each also is represented by a particular paradigmatic instance of the framework. And, finally each has a relation to an economic practice.

So let me begin in the first framework with a theory of knowledge that is not uncommon in the universities. This will serve as an introduction before the statement of the first theme. We have a theory that there is information which is stable, and that the goal of education is to help each person gain knowledge of that information. Universities change us by augmenting our awareness, teaching us to think new things. The change in us is that we know *more* than we did before. Curiosity is a desire to acquire new information—which is most of all about objects, or fields of study. When we think, we represent in our mind that which we are trying to know. Like an object, knowledge is something to purchase, to acquire, to store, even to use, but it is unchanged by being known, and it does not change the knower. Perhaps we can represent this framework by the name Locke. Maybe we are still at that moment when we should try to distinguish a technical institute from a college or university.

Of course, in so far as some matters in the sciences are settled, there really is some*thing* to learn. And one might also object that a religious education might also try to impart knowledge of dogma: "this (and not that) is what we believe." But it seems that gaining control over fixed information is a rather minimal description of our learning, and indeed, seems to miss the nature of our reasoning. The modern theory of an autonomous subject grants to my own self authority to certify what is true, but while a learning self, an ego that acquires and then hoards knowledge, might be necessary; under this description it seems hardly worth listening to another person as such. One should research and gain information, perhaps by reading, but only to get more stuff into your head. The knowledge belongs to the self (much like everything else in a certain modern vision). But the self is brutally alone. And reason is itself a solitary accounting, keeping the various bits of knowledge in the proper columns to allow the self to keep a good tally of what it knows and at what expense. A theory of consciousness here obtrudes, and also begins to lead beyond itself.

Let me then move to a second framework, and the presentation of the A theme. For the realm of acquisition is not simply a question of consciousness, but requires a currency. That is, the way we learn and know the world is through a medium of exchange—in the exchange of things: money, in the process of knowing: language. Despite the long journey in this essay, the early frameworks are not abandoned. Hence if there were an allegory about acquisition, hoarding, and reasoning as accounting in that first framework, it is not that we will end up later on with a framework where learning produces no resources, finishing in a world with neither things nor property.

But this shift to a linguistified model of learning occurs when we realize that we can have a bank account only because there is a money system. Or perhaps less allegorically, that our consciousness of the world is through language. Our awareness appears in the medium of language. Consider the slogan: the limits of our language are the limits of our experience. Language names things, and there is a specific reciprocity between things and words. Learning is a project of description or semantics (for which I will call to mind the proper name Russell). In its own way it continues our original image of a self getting knowledge. The primordial act of acquisition, then, is a naming of something. To name is to mark a thing as my own, and we cannot have experience without affixing a name to something. The difference achieved by our first step is that knowledge is held through a medium: language. And so the self is able to assimilate the world to itself through language. Anything can be deposited in me as in a bank if it is determined as monetary value, because a bank exists only for exchange and accumulation of money. The world is created by words, and so we have a deep resonance in our knowing it, if the "I" is not only a word, it is also a word. Reasoning here is an effort to specify with clarity just what our words mean, exchanging more vague terms for more clear and determinate ones.

But this relation of self and thing, mediated by language, prepares for a more radical meaning of language, represented best by Heidegger. The third framework focuses on how language itself is a coming into presence and not merely a matter of the names of things (theme B). Here the verbality of language, as opposed to the nominality of it, comes into focus. Language thus displays not only the named thing, but it also displays the speaking of language, the way that words work. That is, language speaks about speaking (in an interesting parallel with the way that thinking can think about thinking). When language speaks about speaking it shows us that speaking is not simply affixing labels on things that are already there. Rather the things appear in language—as does the self. Using language allows the self to appear as speaker. So language is the coming into presence, or a first gathering of our world. In this framework, consciousness is itself a development from language speaking. Because both "I" and the things appear through the speaking of language, even the "I" belongs to language as much as either language or a thing *belongs* to me. The subject of language is the one that comes to be within language and more importantly by the action of language. The self is not the source of itself, does not govern language. And language operates to show not only a world, but also a speaking, a way of letting things come to my awareness. The most fundamental kind of speaking has no content, but shows merely the emergence of a place, of a topic, in which things may appear. Hence language shows both the coming into presence and the shadows, the hiddenness. Language, before revealing either myself or anything, reveals revealing and at the same time a hiding. In a move familiar from transcendental reflection, if language making present is a condition for things appearing to us, then *as* condition, language also points for us to what is not becoming present, what is hidden in the linguistic presence.

Because the poet is the one whose task is to reveal this play of darkness and light, poetics more than semantics governs our understanding of what we do in knowing the world, in this third framework. Reason here would be both the gathering together of things into presence, collecting so that the world might appear, but also there is a further thinking or reasoning—not simply poetical, but rather poetics, a reasoning about how poetry reveals and discloses things in speaking. How learning about the world is also dogged by an ignorance. Revelation is veiled. And such a reasoning cannot strip off the veil. Here learning requires that we read poetic texts, and learn to see the darkness as well as the light, the darkness in the very light. And to speak not only the light and the darkness, not only the lightening and the darkening (for poetry does speak about poetry), but also *about* that light and darkness—in the reasoning of poetics.

I will not ignore that the frames of accumulation and of banking seem very far from this poetics in which the subject no longer is sovereign. We seemed, for a time in the first frame, to have a clear modern subject, a student who learned what she could by acquiring knowledge. But now we don't seem to have such a student, but rather to have a poet (perhaps), and a philosopher. For the student in this framework will have to learn through poetry, to think like that philosopher who reasons about poetics. We might read poetry in class, but best of all would be to hear it read, and then to read (or hear) a commentary upon it, but in such a way that it was like a lecture, evoking the reality that was the poem itself, calling in and from language.

Heidegger's seminars were not (at least to read them now) experiences of give and take, just the distance we might expect from the currency and acquisition of the first two frameworks. Indeed, if there is an economic image here, it might be coining, as the poets coin the words: they engrave or stamp upon inchoate reality the symbol which will allow us then to exchange the words without having recourse to the original experience of finding a word to bring both light and shadow. While we might treat knowledge like coins, looking only at their exchange value, the minter is aware of just the interaction of the image and the matter. Hence the seminars were an opportunity to watch, to listen, to see the words being struck. Heidegger did teach students to listen to the poem, to read with an eye to the darkness and the light, indeed the darkening and the lightening. The poem became poetry, became poetics, in Heidegger's reading. If we began with a direct appropriation of the object by the subject, we now have a complex mediation of learning: the student listens to the reasoning of poetics, in order to hear the poetics of dark and light in the poem, which itself opens (and shadows) the place where a thing can appear. The self is veiled, as is the thing, and the unveiling which is the poem, the generation of the topic—the place—displaces language as a code that marks and fixes the things. And in this sense, the orality of the lecture plays in alternation with the writing of the poem, which itself requires an oral performance. But here we may be ahead of ourselves.

The move to a fourth framework, however, is much more radical, and introduces a truly different theme, C. For instead of treating what is not known as something yet to be known (a new acquisition, a new coin) or as bound up in the shadows of light, we now encounter the unknowable as the other person—the one to whom I listen. For there is a breakdown of the first, the second and third frameworks when I am face-to-face with another person. Levinas calls this moment of disruption, the face, where my own efforts to know and so to assimilate the other person are called into question. In his main texts this moment of the face first appears as a moment of being addressed in language by the other person: solicited (both for money or help, or also in the sense of challenged). Here the relation of appropriation turns backwards as I am called to give to the other from my resources. In his later texts, the moment is more attenuated, and the encounter does not "happen" in a present moment at all, and the solicitation is more a matter of finding myself called when I myself speak it. I leave this latter sense aside for now and define this fourth framework as one where my own position is asymmetrically constituted. I am called to respond in a way that I cannot resolve into a general condition (where we might say that everyone is so called,) nor perhaps the more "obvious" way, where the other person is called by me just as much as I am called by her. The irony here is that the "I" of the first framework is not dissolved into a general case of anyone, but retains a certain stubborn distinctiveness, but now that "I" becomes a "me", someone who is in the accusative and is addressed.

That being questioned, addressed, solicited, now constitutes me. I cannot dodge that role. I am called to give of my own resources, to make a donation. Of course, I might respond by not being responsive. I can shout or turn away, I can lash out, or even kill the one who calls to me. But that passivity of being called I cannot expunge or escape. It is not simply that I am an object for another subject. I become me, a person who can speak (and not a sheer thing) in this moment of address. Questioned, I now can answer. And the other person is no longer an object of inquiry. She becomes an interlocutor, and that means, most of all, that she speaks and interprets what she or I will say. And that ability, or really authority to speak, means that I cannot know her. I do not and can never know what she will say. In this framework, I listen because I can never know what is coming next. I listen, in part, to learn again and again, that I don't know the other person. She is not an object to me, nor is she my equal. She is rather my teacher. One on one, the other is always my teacher.

Rosenzweig had noticed that not knowing what the other will say also makes me unknown to myself: that I don't know what I will say either. Dialogue is about taking time, experiencing interruption, at each turn being challenged and so learning that I don't know. Learning, in this sense, is profoundly interpersonal, depending on other people to whom I listen.

Here is a double move by Levinas that is contested. First, we have an asymmetry. The index of "me" cannot be shaken or overcome by noticing that others also are addressed, because I still am elected, chosen, singled out. And second, this is a moment of conversion from epistemology to ethics—what I cannot know (the other person) becomes the fulcrum for a need to respond to and for this other person. In some works, it is to produce just this shift that Levinas dawdles for pages over the modern epistemological project, to show that knowledge arises in responsibility. Our need to accumulate is now grounded in our prior responsibility to give. Again, we are not discarding the earlier framework, but are engaged in a complex reconfiguration of it.

Election is traditionally a theological concept. It always seems exclusive, and the Jewish solution has often been to say that we were chosen to bear more responsibility for each other and for the world. Election is not extra treats and pleasures, but extra commandments and duties. But also deep within this discussion of election lies a very different sense of uniqueness, one not purchased directly through an epistemology, but rather within the intensity of love. Election is a mode of being loved—singled out as love must. The beloved is irreplaceable, at least in the instant of love, or perhaps, as in the Song of Songs, in the instant before she responds. What does it matter to me that others have loved before? What does it matter to me that I want my lover? In my eyes we are not equals, and the miracle of being loved elicits love from me, commands it, but is not simply a fair exchange.

But is there, in the speaking to another, a sense of this being called, of needing to answer with an urgency and exigency akin to the beloved's? What happens in the bedroom is not what happens in the street, and certainly not what happens in the college lecture hall. So what is the warrant for this extreme interpretation of interlocution? Can Levinas simply turn aside the objection that most of the time people don't (and maybe shouldn't) discover themselves to be infinitely responsible? Or, more pointedly, that I am not and ought not to be responsible without measure to the person in front of me?

Here we must briefly indicate a gap between my own way of addressing these questions and Levinas'. Levinas makes his way with phenomenology, albeit the key moment of the face breaks with the phenomenality of the phenomena—that is, phenomenology breaks apart with the other person. Levinas discovers in the face of the other person a breaking up of the horizon, the inclusive context for what appears in my consciousness. The interruption of which I just spoke is not so much a matter of our talking to each other, but rather of the project of knowing my world by assimilating it. Such an interruption finds this hole in the project of consciousness, and generates a spiral that can have no end. I represent an other person, and then that other's face is a break-up and away from each representation, and again I represent and again have my efforts interrupted. There is a check upon my efforts to know, and at the same time, a recovery of the self as trying to know. Thus each rule or boundary for my own duty to the other is vulnerable to another question from the other. As a phenomenology, this is an insight into a dimension of responsibility and not a rule for behaviour or a principle of ethical reasoning. It is not meant either as a practical guide or as an empirical description. The infinition is not a blank cheque for another person; rather, it is produced in the spiraling of trying to know and encountering what cannot be known.

My interpretation of this scene, however, focuses on the pragmatics of being addressed. By pragmatics I mean the relation between signs and their users. Here I wish to argue that speaking itself is bound up with a responsibility to listen. For my account, too, this is not an empirical description (although we might imagine a genetic account that would focus on the child being addressed prior to be speaking). Rather it is a norm of the practice, and as such may also be ignored or even violated. So much for its status—what is its justification? The justification lies in the heart of the question of justification. For justification presumes not that I owe a reason for a claim *to* myself, or *to* the nature of things, but precisely *to* another person. A reason why is an answer to a questioning that comes from another. Thus the justification of this claim is itself that which makes *justification* needed—that I am called to answer to the other. And if the other is unreasonable? In this moment of a face-to-face, reasonableness is not prior to answering and being called. On the contrary reason emerges in responding. Again, this is not the articulation and justification of a principle of ethical reasoning. Here we are addressing an ethics of responsibility. Here is a new kind of reasoning: reasoning as responding to a question.

The translation from epistemology to ethics, then, is articulated either as the collapse of the knowing subject, even a phenomenologically reduced one, before the questioning of another person, or as the switch from justification as an independent task of reason itself, to one that understands justification as precisely the situation we find ourselves in, listening and responding to another person. Not that we always persuade the other that our view or even our existence is justified, nor that we always seek to do so, but that we can grasp that we are always called to do so in the face of the other. This is the pragmatics sense of saying, as Levinas likes to say, that Ethics is First Philosophy.

But we move to the fifth framework, by adding a person, a third person. This person also makes a claim upon me, and before the third I now negotiate conflicting infinite responsibilities. The introduction of the third is a step closer to a description of empirical experience, but it also has a phenomenological dimension. For Levinas, we are never simply alone with one other person, and the infinite responsibility I discern for the other, as we spiral through knowing and not-knowing, requires a limitation, a measure, a rule because of the conflicting claim by another on both me and upon my other. It is, he says, the claim of justice that requires that we measure the immeasurable. Justice requires that we thematise, that we ascribe properties to the others in front of us. It allows for all of the stuff of ethics: principles, rules, a calculus, and so on. We regain the cognitive order that we have just displaced. Representation, and even assimilation, the reinstallation of a fixed horizon, and indeed, currency and a stable semantics are all required for justice. For the sake of justice, I must also make a claim for myself. While the asymmetry in the fourth framework has often invited people mistakenly to see it as masochistic or self-destructive, this step to a claim for justice is not simply the abandonment of infinite responsibility. It is, rather, the multiplication of responsibilities.

This is the A^1 theme, and the alteration here involves a composite of the A theme from the second framework with the C theme: that is, this is still other-centered, but it opens a need for words to have stable semantic meanings. Those meanings are not simply referential (from the word to the thing), but are rather inflected over other speakers, so that the relations to others animate our use of words to name things. On the contrary, the meanings arise because of our needs to coordinate our responsibilities between people. A word has a dimension of responsibility as a response to a call, but it has a second dimension because it is addressed not to just one person but also to a third (and in that sense to anyone). This latter dimension allows words to be general, where generality is the capacity of each word to allow something to appear to any hearer or reader. The range of possible interpreters accounts for the generality of a word (or more generally of a sign). Again, we find that a relation to other people determines how words work (in contrast with a relation to beings or things or the world or . . .). And so the idea of syntax is not merely the relation of words or signs but really the relations of people as interpreters of signs.

What is most important here, however, is that when we learn we are not confined to a relation of teacher and student in isolation. We are called to judge for the sake of others, even others who are not present. This might be teachers of the teachers, or students of our students, but our language disperses from our classroom, from our notebooks, and lays open some themes for untold others. While we must teach (or learn) from each other who confronts us, the need for some *what* to be learned does not revert to the pure dignity of knowing the world, but rather revolves around the ethical need to give to each, to adjust our understanding of the world in order to make it public.

Justice requires a discipline of the donation we should give to the other. If the bank stored currency, then in the fourth framework we gave charity. But in the fifth there is commerce and circulation. The opposite to acquisition is donation; the opposite of hoarding is circulation. Justice enters us into systemic relations, "represented" by the linguistic network, but better understood as the circulation between people of that which we value. Justice is not an after thought in this ethics, and it cannot resolve the problems of asymmetry and infinity. On the contrary, justice is always vulnerable to a critique, an infinite demand from the one before me. Thus the demands of justice (with rationality as balancing and counting) and the demands of ethics (with reasoning born from the need to respond) are simultaneous or perhaps utterly divergent. For there is no empirical moment of pure response to the single other; and there is no justice so just that it is free from critique from the single other. Two and three are unresolved, and generate a dialectic of reasoning that is neither pure dialogue nor stable principle.

The sixth framework takes us to the need for reading and writing texts in order to learn. This is a socialized revision of the poetics of the originary speaking in the third framework (a B^1 of the B theme, due to the relation to the C theme). In the fourth framework we saw that there was an asymmetry of responsibilities. So in this sixth framework the writer and the reader are not simple inversions of each other. Reading is not just acquiring information through a doubly-coded process. We are not simply exchanging secondary code (written code) in place of primary code (oral code) of our thoughts. The reader is constituted through the reading—what I can "do", can think, can feel all arises in the practices of reading. The subject is a reader, not a thinking self who then reads (anymore than the subject is a thinking self who happens to speak). We can expand reading to a practice of interpreting signs that linger, but we must here take a deeper look at what it is we read. What is writing?

The thematics of this sixth framework draw heavily on Derrida (although they are largely consistent with several of Levinas' works). And we now engage in a study he called Grammatology (or even more awkwardly, Pragrammatology). What makes writing work is the way that a written sign does not mean in a present moment but defers meaning to the future. There is a tempo, a hesitation on the first beat (when it is written), that awaits a second beat (when it is read). But the meaning is unstable precisely because we don't know what someone will make of our writings. (There is a close parallel to the fourth framework of a dialogue, where we don't know what someone else will say). But the written word is committed to paper with just that deferral "in mind". I might try to "make" someone read this page the way I had thought, but if I do write, I must recognize that I cannot control the uptake. The readers will make of it what they will. They may cite it, parody it, and worst of all for a writer, ignore it. Hence the subject is also a writer, someone who is vulnerable to the next reader. The absence of the writer when the reader reads, the sense that control, authority, and so forth are all suspended by the medium of the written—these shape a challenging asymmetry around books and texts. What is written is consigned to others, redeemable ultimately only by the reader.

Thus the task of writing is to hold open (or to narrow) the access of the reader. And the task of reading is not so much to return the text to its author, but to find as much meaning as we can in the text. Derrida writes that he has tried to have no "intending to say" in his writings, that he has tried to withdraw the claim to determine his reader, in part through a series of cancellations, and by a seriality of crossing out the previous terms. He finds, indeed, just this seriature as the key to Levinas' own writing. But as readers, we read for this string of terms, we look for what can teach us, not by restoring original intention, nor by returning to the poetic origin of meaning. Instead, our reading is a construction and discovery of ever richer meanings. (In my work, reading itself produces the commentary—a writing of a reading, one that reopens a text that seems closed, holding open, again, an opening that was generated in the text. I cannot linger over the task of the commentator, but it points out the rich alternation of reading and writing). The reasoning of writer and reader is a kind of engendering of responsibility, of seeking out not so much knowledge but ethical practices in the texts I read.

But if we now move one more step to the seventh framework, we invoke all of those other people: the ones with whom we read. Now we are reading in the context of the classroom, the seminar—that is, we are reading texts with others. Let us call this C^1 as we repeat the move to the fifth framework, the move to a third, to another, but this time they are not only our contemporaries. A dialogue construed around a text is now a complex drama: there is the text, the reader, the writer, the matter about which the text speaks, and also other readers. We find a social dimension to reading and writing that exceeds this asymmetry of differential meaning. For the discipline of this depositing and seeking for truth comes from the other people with whom we read. Here we discover not a subject alone, but rather a people of the book. Our commentaries are not simply what we can unearth from the texts, but are created for other readers, readers with whom we share a semantics (a language), and also with whom we share principles and rules of interpretation and indeed, of behaviour. The demands of justice constitute our work as readers. And so there is a textual recasting of the dynamics between the responsibility for the single other and the claims of the third for justice in terms of the vulnerability and creative reading of the sixth framework with the communal norms of reading and commenting in this seventh framework. But we also have a very different notion of the community here: for here it is a community framed by reading practices.

And reading depends on a deferral of meaning. But that means that the people who wrote are not present with the people who read. And the people who read are not present with the ones for whom they read and write commentaries. In short, we begin to get a tradition, a set of readings that stretch out over time. But they stretch in jumps of discontinuities. History emerges in this seventh framework as the gap between two different sets of readings of the "same" text. Reading in a tradition is not merely to have a reading partner, but also to re-read earlier readings. We can read in our tradition to challenge the dominant reading of our times, as well as to challenge a long line of normative readings. A written tradition provides the very divestment of authority that writing provides in general—depending on how we as a community of readers approach the text now. Thus a community can struggle to insist on continuity, smoothing over the disagreements between strata of tradition, and can seek consistency and uniformity in its tradition; but a community also can learn the voices of dissent and the ways that readings have shifted and broken against earlier traditions of reading. Often the continuity claim is used to legitimate the current authorities—as a disguise for the real struggle and conflict within a tradition and between generations.

In both of those cases and several other possibilities, one insight remains: there is something to be learned by exploring the tradition. But the something to be learned implies that our present understanding of the world and of our tradition is not perfected. Whether it is gauged as a falling away from a previous truth, or is rather the attempt to discern new truth and insight in the older layers of the tradition, reading with others opens up the present moment and displays its insufficiency in itself. An historical sense (but now under this view of a tradition of readers) is key to our practices of learning from traditional texts. To recognize that we think and have our ethical responsibility standing in our traditions of reading is a profound hermeneutic insight. Even the New Age spirituality arises through a tradition of religious traditions; just as the modern secular world emerged in a Protestant context. But our traditions of reading also include English Common Law, and American Constitutional law, the history of the novel, the phenomenological tradition, and Marxist-Leninist traditions, and so on. The claim that a community of readings has upon us cannot be escaped by ignoring our traditions, nor can the tradition be assimilated and appropriated under the guise of a bookshelf of information. We are too deeply formed, our moral intuitions and patterns of reasoning, all framed by these communal claims and sedimentations of readings over generations. Our self-consciousness of these traditions will give us purchase upon the chance to criticize and re-evaluate them. But such an activity recognizes that we never read and write alone—we are haunted by past and future, and we are called for the future to re-engage the past of our traditions.

For my work, and a small community of Jewish scholars, the way was paved by a series of Jewish thinkers in the last hundred years starting with Hermann Cohen, and including Martin Buber, Franz Rosenzweig, and Emmanuel Levinas who each re-read Jewish traditional texts in order both to participate in the work of re-reading and to articulate a hermeneutic theory as primary to the task of their thought. We more recently formed a group called Textual Reasoning to re-read traditional Jewish texts with this hermeneutic sensibility. We turned to a dimension of the traditional texts that philosophers had largely ignored: the complex multivocal texture of talmud and midrash. Not every activity in the university is so critically engaged with history—but in many disciplines the history of the discipline is studied intently, with just this critical hermeneutic perspective. To read and to write in a community of readers, is to learn in responding to the past for the sake of the future.

Finally, the eighth framework consists of the practices that we can call Scriptural Reasoning. That is a practice of reading across traditions, in a dialogue or better still with three traditions. We meet and read each other's Scriptures together, and so far it has been Jews, Christians, and Muslims. There are good reasons for these three to read together, but there is not an a priori exclusion of other religious traditions, say Confucian or Hindu or Buddhist. It is not hard to anticipate how each of the previous themes will re-emerge in this last framework, yielding the core justification for this practice. But I will try to explain, at least a little of our practice and its ethical implications.

We do not meet as a religious institution. We are not founding a new religion, but each person retains affiliation in his or her own tradition (however fraught those affiliations may be). We meet twice or more a year in a few different groups. We are not seeking the common ground—the moral or theological or even methodological claims we can all agree to. We select texts by committee on a theme approved by the whole. So far, some of our themes have included wisdom and signs, Moses and Pharaoh, forgiving debts and problems of usury and interest, and prophecy. But as we read the texts, we are constantly surprised by the ways that the texts overlap and diverge. Each tradition negotiates with a complex problem in its own style. Indeed, one of the key discoveries is what we found in the seventh framework: that traditions are internally diverse and conflictual. But we are called upon by each other to explain a position to another person, one who is not part of my tradition, who is not hostile to it, but who also is not being wooed to convert. Indeed, perhaps the strongest aspect of this practice is a deep respect for the differences between the three traditions and how communication is not only not prohibited because of these differences but is actually enhanced by it. We learn more studying with each other: more about another tradition, but also more about our own. Justifying our own texts to each other, we learn about the internal dynamics of our own traditions.

Others might focus on the theory of truth and the relation to a messianic promise for truth, but perhaps now all the pieces and I have taken can begin to assemble. The step to listening to the other sets a fundamental tone of ethical responsibility. We listen to each others' reading of each others' texts because we don't know what each tradition has to teach, and we certainly cannot know what reading the other person will give (of our texts or of hers). The otherness is a permanent fixture of the situation. We work with that, and in some ways accentuate it, within an environment of real trust and patience. We would not read with each other if we were not prepared to learn about our own traditions and about the others. To institute that otherness is to honour a responsibility we have in knowing others. It is humbling, and so it should be, because whatever truth my own tradition may have, at any moment what I know is not sufficient. Because other people are formed in parallel ways by their own traditions, my own (however good and right it is) lacks something that only others can provide.

We read, however, because each reader of a text is given some authority to read. When we invite people from other traditions to read our texts *with us* we are obliged to listen to them. It is not that people do not bring along their internal libraries—their expertise in their own traditions and in their theoretical formation—but rather, that there is a kind of equality of authority, or even, if I may dare say so, an asymmetry here. The others, although less learned, seem to occupy a role of arbiter of the interpretations offered. Their otherness allows them a privilege that we perceive as calling upon us to justify our own texts and traditions. Not to form a syncretism, but to offer a best reading, to make sense of the text to an other person from another tradition. Were we merely presenting a conceptual account of different rules or theological doctrines or whatever, we would not need to yield the authority of interpretation the same way. Moreover, the explicit encounter with a diachronic tradition of disparate readings provides a specific kind of opening in our conversation with each other. It makes us more porous in relation to our traditions as we go back and forth with others. Precisely because of the hermeneutic challenges within any single tradition, the call to re-read and innovate in each tradition is accentuated by the reading of another parallel tradition, and even more so by reading with the other person. The separate traditions of texts make claims for justice and attention to their own distinctiveness and their own claims of truth, but reading with others underscores how truth is dynamic even within a single tradition.

This dynamic arises because of the profound claim that we make upon each other. If this sonata of modes of learning and frameworks and sciences of reasoning must draw to a resolution at its end, then that final chord surely is the chord of harmony of different people. I have claimed that individuals are indeed the nexus of responsibilities, or readings and traditions of readings, of listening to others and of adjudicating multiple responsibilities—that as such we arise and live as individuals. The harmony we pursue is thus in those complex practices and not simply an agreement on a theological principle or a political agenda. Such harmony requires difference. It is delicate and can be performed only in person, but it offers the true hope of learning—a learning that represents the highest goals of the academy.

Appendix

	Framework	Science	Paradigm	Economics
1	information acquisition	representations	Locke	accounting
2 A	linguistic "turn"	semantics	Russell	banking
3 B	language speaking	poetics	Heidegger	minting
4 C	listening and asymmetry	pragmatics	Levinas	donation
5 A^1	justice (and the third)	syntax	Levinas	circulation
6 B^1	reading and writing	grammatology	Derrida	consignment
7 C^1	commentary in tradition	hermeneutics	Textual Reasoning	redeeming
8	reading with other traditions		Scriptural Reasoning	

NOTE

1 An oral version of this was delivered at Pomona College as part of the Clark-Horowitz Lectures in November 2005, where I was joined by Vincent Cornell. In addition to the hospitality and support of Pomona, the Social Sciences and Humanities Research Council of Canada provided support for this essay.

12

THE PROMISE OF SCRIPTURAL REASONING

DANIEL W. HARDY

Preliminaries: Elemental Matters

If—at least in my view—we stop to think carefully about *what* the Scriptures of the Abrahamic traditions are, and *why* they are so important to these traditions, we are driven to conclude that they are the *public form* of *primary discourse of God*; they are *that* discourse made public in these texts. In that sense, they embody elemental speech by—and of—God, although this does not imply that all of the Scriptures have equal standing as such. That, presumably, is what is realized in the reading and interpretation of them, and comes to light again in interactive reading and interpretation in which the three traditions share. How do we know that? This discourse is established as primary discourse of God when we *find* how it leads us deeply into the infinity of the identity of the Divine, as this in turn enriches and integrates the traditions, and fructifies their interaction. Furthermore, we find that it has the capacity to repair ruptures in discourse of God within and between the traditions and in the ways in which these have begotten—whether directly or indirectly—the troubles of the world.

That gives some notion of why the three Abrahamic traditions consider that their Scriptures are of central significance for them. It is not simply a matter of popular consensus; their agreement as to the importance of the Scriptures is more like a second-order agreement based on the discovery there of primary discourse of God. And all who wish to take these traditions fully seriously will know that, with regard to each, *their* study of *their* Scripture must occupy a primary place in any attempt to understand them, because their interpretation *realizes* this primary discourse of God; and the interaction of Scriptural interpretation between the traditions will do the same insofar as this primary discourse reappears there.

Daniel W. Hardy
Faculty of Divinity, University of Cambridge, West Road, Cambridge, CB3 9BS, UK

In my view, the determination to bring about such a finding of primary discourse of God in the engagement *between* the Abrahamic traditions' interpretation of their Scriptures, without attempting to stand outside of them or to generalize from what is found in them, constitutes the very simple *raison d'etre* of Scriptural Reasoning. For a member of one Abrahamic tradition to participate with members of others in the study of his/her and their Scriptures, respectfully and interactively, is the *fons et origo*—the "source and origin"—of Scriptural Reasoning (SR).

By this determination to find primary discourse of God with members of other Abrahamic traditions in our/their interpretation of our/their Scriptures, SR challenges what is frequently the everyday view of religions in the West, that they are primarily general systems of beliefs, ideas and practices that can be "held" alongside each other in some overarching frame of reference, for example as instances of a category called "religion", or "religions" within a secular public sphere, thereby enabling them to be treated "equally" (as a "plurality") or encouraging them to engage with each other ("pluralism"). Instead, SR concerns itself with the primary discourse of God in the particularities of the Abrahamic traditions, as seen through their particular interpretation of their particular Scriptures, not in order to compare them and derive what is thought to be common to them, but in order to allow them to disagree or agree and by doing so illuminate the others. That is why I was shocked recently to hear one person say of SR, "participants only need to agree that they worship the same God", as if there were some prior commitment by which they come together. There is no such prior agreement: on what they agree or disagree emerges only within ongoing interactive Scriptural discussion; and it is not presumed to be generally applicable to all of that Abrahamic tradition.

Always as attentive as they can be to each other's Scriptures, those who engage with each other in SR always do so as "reasoners". The unexpressed assumption is that by some means they have acquired a capacity for reasoning which carries them and their colleagues deeply into the meaning of the texts, not by avoiding the "plain sense" but by probing the "logic" and "dynamics" which appear in the texts, and their implications for the tradition whose texts these are. The sources which are drawn upon in this "capacity for reasoning" vary widely amongst those involved, but in the *practice* of Scriptural Reasoning their differences are usually muted because of the primacy given to texts and interpretations and—as we will see—the fact that they release sources of reason and compassion.

Introduction

Although it is demonstrably the case that SR can be practiced successfully under widely varying circumstances, from amongst trained Western-style

academics to those expert in historical inter-traditional religious engage-
ments to students in higher education to groups of Jews, Christians and
Muslims concerned with reconciliation, from Virginia to Cambridge, from
Capetown to London, the focus in this issue is primarily on the first group.

The essays in this volume are preliminary offerings addressed—in the
terminology found in David Ford's essay—from "tent" to "campus". Here
are voices from amongst those of all the Abrahamic traditions who by their
twice-yearly meetings for some years have created a space constituted by
their very particular interactions. Call that a "tent of meeting" or even (in
a still more open image) a space of hospitality made by a "flier" tarpaulin
suspended between tents: what is primary is that there is space in which
to be hospitable to each other without predefined ownership of the place.
There, like Abraham and Sarah, we find ourselves visited by the Divine. In
practice, however, there is an understandable reticence in declaring *that* this
is so, and concern with *how* it is so.

What happens in this "SR place" is mostly interactive study of Scriptural texts, which proceeds in definite ways. In this case, the space is
populated by people whose usual form of discourse is academic, and
who are accustomed to "think" what happens in the space by reference
to histories of practices, disciplines, and concepts usually found in universities. After David Ford's essay "Framing" SR practice in Part 1, there
are three others by Steven Kepnes, Nicholas Adams and Ben Quash in
Part 2 ("Describing") which outline the procedures and explore some of
what actually happens. SR is informed by the kinds of academic reasoning to which the participants are accustomed, as well as by the
sources by which they are informed (their "internal libraries"). And some
examples of the use of academic reasoning *within* scriptural interpretation
to attend to what is there and to meet the reasoning found within the
Scriptures are seen in the essays by Susannah Ticciati, Oliver Davies and
Tim Winter in Part 3 ("Reading"). Academic reasoning is also used in
different ways to reflect on the inner logic or dynamics of Scripture and
its interpretation; the essays by Peter Ochs, Basit Koshul, Gavin Flood
and Robert Gibbs in Part 4 ("Reasoning") show different possibilities for
this.

The aim throughout has been to help to show an academic audience
where SR *does connect* with established academic pursuits, while also
showing the ways in which it may "repair" the problems of a world
which—inexplicably—is now a profound mixture of religious and secular
life, not any longer a secular one in which religions "appear". Indeed,
from this viewpoint, it now seems that the problems which beset the
world *cannot be* resolved except by drawing deeply from the religious
traditions which for centuries have been excluded from the public
domain *while also* engaging with the world seen in everyday ways. In
that, the "tent" in each of—and between—the participants in Scriptural

Reasoning, "thinking" the Scriptures with academically-trained reasoning, is peculiarly important.

The kinds of reasoning employed in SR, and the purpose envisaged for them, are matters of great importance. With respect to the different forms of academic "reasoning" brought to the "SR place", do they carry us more deeply into what is found in the Scriptures, and what more is to be found there, enabling us to place it within the full range of meaning and implications for life which those Scriptures carry, or is their reasoning too "thin"? Even if their declared intention is to let the Scriptures speak in their own terms, do they in effect encapsulate and modify the Scriptures and scriptural interpretation by placing them within another determinative context—perhaps within some account of philosophy, theology or social science—which is thought to be necessary to preserve the truth and continuing value of the Scriptures?

During its history, SR has not always escaped difficulties of this kind, where the very thing which helps an academic audience understand where SR does fit into their categories also fails to help people practice SR more deeply. Two examples may help to see the problem. For years, the meetings of the Society for Scriptural Reasoning (held during the American Academy of Religion as "additional meetings") attempted to combine thematic Jewish-Christian-Muslim historical-critical, philosophical or theological-style presentations with sessions for group study of the Scriptures. In these "hybrid" occasions, as I would call them, the conceptual discourse of the presentations—themselves often more like bravura solo performances than interactive between the Abrahamic traditions—almost always overcame the practice of Scriptural Reasoning. No doubt that partly reflected the metier of AAR audiences, but it also demonstrated that—given the two "styles"—conventional academic reasoning too easily dominated reasoning and reasoners whose ideals were to be attentive to the meaning and reasoning of the Scriptures and to probe their logic and dynamics.

The same problem also sometimes happens in reverse. The twice-yearly sessions of the Scriptural Reasoning Theory Group—a main focus of insight and energy for SR—give intense attention to texts and, more often than not, display extraordinary insight, vitality and excitement, as if to testify to the indefinitely rich content of the Scriptures. But the Group has also found it very difficult to "debrief" afterward, or to discuss how to identify, "hold", "agree" or "transfer" the insights generated. It is clear enough that *for those present* the "interactive particularity" of Jews, Christians and Muslims interpreting their Scriptures together *is* highly generative of probing insight into both texts and their constitutive importance for the Abrahamic traditions and their contribution to today's world, both severally and together. But *how* are the results to be communicated? It is clearly illuminating, even transformative, for *these* Jews, Christians and Muslims, and that is no small achievement. The impact of the practice of SR on the Abrahamic traditions is very great, and may continue to grow exponentially, but the impact will be confined to those who directly participate—and even in them remain fragile—unless *ways are found to identify, hold and transfer what is found, ways which promise to carry us further and not limit us from doing so.*

This is an issue from which none of those whose essays are presented in this volume would want to retreat. At their best, they provide deep insight into how the Scriptures do show primary discourse of God and how human logic may meet divine. Even at the risk of summarizing them too crudely, it will be worthwhile to examine them with such issues in mind and to link them by some common threads.

As we do so, we need to remember that for the most part the essays are not examples of *interactive* Scriptural Reasoning. They are necessarily "single voices" speaking from within a particular Abrahamic tradition, although sometimes very differently, yet with the benefit of having engaged with others and clarified what they consider "true" to their tradition, and contributing that to future tradition-interactive discussions.

That points to two important characteristics of this special issue on Scriptural Reasoning: the fact that these "single voices" already meet—not blend—in "virtual" interaction, and will carry that on in future Scriptural Reasoning. They may also be heard interactively by the readers of this issue, in a developing awareness of what interactive Scriptural Reasoning may be. The best way in which this "Response" may help with both will be to identify as clearly as possible what are the positions taken, how they connect with each other, and where there are issues still to be addressed. These essays are themselves important and different kinds of contribution in the "space" of Scriptural Reasoning. While they may be different, they are not divisive, because they are held together by the responsible dialogue which constitutes the space of SR. The only question is how to continue the dialogue most effectively.

This "Response" may also help to push the learning of Scriptural Reasoning forward a little. After we have tried to find some of the ways in which the essays "virtually" interact, therefore, we will identify some further questions for SR:

1. What are the most central seminal characteristics of the Abrahamic traditions, between them, and between them and the world? Implicitly, most of the essays here contribute in various ways to answering, but a more focused attempt to identify them would help SR.
2. How can we target the deepest suppositions of the Abrahamic traditions: the patterns of the activity of the Divine, the highest reaches of humanity (reason, passion, compassionate care, love, justice, social well-being, etc.) to which we are abductively attracted by the Divine?
3. Finally, we need to *audit* our success in moving toward these targets.

Answers to such questions as these might carry us significantly forward with the contribution Scriptural Reasoning may make to Abrahamic mutual understanding and to Abrahamic contribution to today's world.

Connecting the Essays

The opening essay by David Ford ("An Interfaith Wisdom") traces the genesis of Scriptural Reasoning, sets the terms used, gives an initial description, and places it in the context of the history of universities, suggesting the important contribution a "plurality of wisdom traditions" sharing institutional space might make. He focuses especially on some of its key characteristics: openness to the sacredness of others' scriptures and questions which may be raised about them, willingness to live with deep differences, honest intellectual argument, sharing of academic resources, patience in reading and considering many questions and possibilities, interpreting for the sake of peace, moving from hospitality to friendship, etc., all as ways of coping with the three unfathomable oceans of meaning—the "superabundance" of their meaning which appears in SR. As he points out, for Jews, Christians and Muslims together to go deeper into their own scriptures and into "wisdom-seeking conversation" with each other and with all who have a stake in the public good, may form those "who might be exemplary citizens of the twenty-first century, seeking the public good for the sake of God and God's peaceful purposes". We will need to return to some of these key characteristics—such as those listed above—later.

In Part 2, the way SR practice is maintained is set out as conditions and attitudes ("rules") necessary for the practice of SR in Steven Kepnes' "Handbook of Scriptural Reasoning". One of the most interesting features of SR it brings to light—which he puts differently from David Ford—is that group reading of Jewish, Christian and Muslim scriptures *releases sources of reason, compassion and divine spirit* for healing the separate communities and for repair of the world. It seems to me that this gets it right: as mentioned earlier, this account acknowledges the highly potent matters at stake in SR, that it realizes the primary speech of God, and what is inherent in this primary speech: reason, compassion and divine spirit for healing the separate communities and for repair of the world. Although this too can be contentious—as we will see later—Kepnes also gets the priority right: it is the study of the Scriptures that is prior in renewing reason and energy and wisdom for Abrahamic "houses" of worship, and in showing the brokenness and suffering of the world, not the capacity of human reading or academic analysis of problems in the world. It makes an equally strong claim for the way SR engages with "academic" forms of reasoning, by resisting the assimilation of SR to these others: Scriptural Reasoning is "the reasoning that is 'disclosed' as members engage in dialogue about Scripture."

In a fashion we will meet many times, Kepnes privileges the use of semiotics in SR, as meaning arises out of the relationship between "the sign, referent and community of interpreters" (who bring with them their prior knowledge of Scripture, their tradition's interpretations, and other academic disciplines). And the result, when interpreters reflect on what they have done, will not be systematic philosophy or theology but "summary, commentary and rules", and the attempt to enact SR as peace-making. This is a striking view of the way SR operates, not via academic discourse as an intermediary, but as a focusing of what has been found by attentive reading and a distillation of the "logic" operative in Scripture, both of them recapturing the values, traditions and devotion to God as they arise in reading. It is a liturgical activity, as if to say that—like the liturgies of the traditions—"the scriptures thus read carry the 'DNA' of the Abrahamic traditions", and their "DNA" is the better seen when they are read together. It is also eschatological: when they are read interactively, they are seen to be contingent in the sense that together they anticipate "an end time in which all the children of Abraham will live together in peace". Despite the modesty with which this "Handbook" is expressed, it sees Scriptural Reasoning as the embodiment of a hermeneutic which not only takes the Scriptures as living sources of divine interaction with humanity but also brings the "healing of the nations" amongst and beyond the Abrahamic traditions. SR yields a "reasoning of the heart" which transforms readers and their practice.

In "Making Deep Reasonings Public", Nick Adams traces some of the implications of SR practices still further. He distinguishes it as a practical "unity of reason" which happens between members of different traditions and can be used without specifying or "grounding" it. SR has identified general conditions for its own best practice, but many of its sessions are generative in ways that could not have been engineered in advance: informal processes are used (in the selection and study of texts, for example), but actual practice is more likely to be patient, hopeful and—for unaccountable reasons—surprising. SR operates by no narrow conception of causality, preferring rather to give a future prepared-for by the past room to occur unanticipated. In this respect, Adams finds, the traditions are quite similar, even if in their eschatologies are quite different. As it practices, furthermore, it places a premium on learning the "languages" as the "houses of wisdom" they are—especially "patterns of usage, shapes of thinking, ways of describing and judging" of other traditions—as preparatory to forming friendships. So we see that SR is less about expertise and intellectual authority and more about the establishment of relations between persons with respect to texts than about the informative value of the texts alone: this is a practice of persons with texts in relation. In that sense, it acknowledges the relational character of information, and thus the importance of communities of persons as the embodiment of traditions.

192 Daniel W. Hardy

Likewise, the premium is not on consensus so much as friendship, and trust built through in-house or inter-traditional disagreements. All of these come together in offering forums for high-quality public debate between members of different traditions which might themselves model the ways in which public differences can be handled, which is itself a hopeful reparative activity. In that way, SR may itself model the traditions' convictions about divine providence.

In "Heavenly Semantics", Ben Quash helps still more to find what is implicit in SR practice, but also to enlarge conceptions of what it does by the use of a different set of categories. He shows how the full extent of reading together—co-reading, raising questions and suggesting answers—is unexpectedly creative, even making one's own tradition "strange" and promoting deeper relationship with it. The very mobility and provisionality of SR space, with participants expected to take responsibility for it, in such a way as to be generative of relations deeper than "tolerance", is very important. Interestingly, what stimulates this is the appearance of differences, which in turn bring arguments and a "community of argument and collaborative reasoning", where high quality argument is preferred over propositional conclusions. (The task is more like "improving the quality of disagreement": "to be given a debate might be as enriching as to be given a doctrine".) Three factors emerge as especially important: provisionality, sociality and readiness for surprise. Unlike doctrinal attempts to minimize their revisability, the Abrahamic Scriptures unsettle and bring discussion: promoting interrogative, argumentative and collaborative patterns of study amongst particular gatherings of people. Ben Quash explores these through various kinds of literary approach, where poetry—not monological prose best suited to conclusions—is the "language of reality". It has possibilities for encountering the whole, allowing sympathy a role in knowing and integrating all in the shared public world of experience and action. Multiple, polyphonic meanings in everyday communicative activity cannot be fully mapped, and resist finalization; there is perpetual surplus here, as in history itself. The wide range of these genres is valuable to SR as it encourages the dialogization and conflictual interaction of Abrahamic texts, whose dramatic heart for the Christian is "the creative, redeeming and sanctifying activity of God in relation to his creatures".

In Part 3 (Reading), we move into three examples of how the Scriptures are actually interpreted or "reasoned" in different ways, by Susannah Ticciati, Oliver Davies and Tim Winter. Susannah Ticciati traces the inherent and permanent "strangeness of the biblical world"—seen in its "resistance to interpretation"—which radically dispossesses the interpreter from claims to the universality of his/her interpretation. The very "resistance to interpretation" found in the Scriptures undermines the temptation by Christians to substitute their "religion" for the biblical world, and thereby to follow the totalising logic of the secular world. How instead the Scriptures bring the kind of conversion undergone by Moses, or the way of dispossession—the loss of one's life in order to save it—found in Christianity, is the question. Her view of the reasoning which is best brought into play is semiotic. She views Scripture as symbol, treating it by analogy with Moses' approach to the burning bush, a sign of the "excessive nature of reality", and draws on Umberto Eco's view of semiotics as an "inferential labour . . . at work in every semiotic event" whereby the interpreter must posit a context within which something is understood as a sign of something else. As Steven Kepnes argued, the relation between sign and referent happens in a community of interpreters; Ticciati emphasizes this "inferential labour": "a sign only ever signifies within a humanly posited context . . . for someone". When she considers this in relation to Moses and the burning bush, it leads her to the inexplicability of the burning bush as a sign of the "ultimate inexplicability of God"—"to which no expression or manifestation can be given". And the only legitimate response is where this frees creaturely reality to be itself. While abduction for Eco brings a reconfiguration of one's conceptual furniture, she insists that abduction in the Bible brings about a "transformation of one's whole life": "it changes everything". "To receive an excessive identity . . . involves being dispossessed of one's humanly constructed identities . . . The more fully I inhabit the biblical world, therefore, the stranger it becomes, leading me to more and more fundamental dispossession, or more positively, to the deeper and deeper reception of myself from beyond myself." "The only form 'abduction' can take here is the transformation of life: conversion". There are major questions here as to how semiotics operates within SR, and—as we will see—to the varying use of abduction made in other (and in the present) essays.

As distinct from Susannah Ticciati's use of semiotics in the interpretation of Scripture, Oliver Davies' essay uses metaphysics in interpretation, because—he suggests—metaphysics is the kind of foundational thinking which engages with the world as a totality and articulates its ordering principles or structure. With Aquinas's insight that "being" is "in fact more a verb, an act", something that inheres within anything we perceive through the senses and can lead us to think in certain ways about God as Creator, he reads the text of the burning bush "on its own terms", finding there two "intensities of seeing", indeterminate and determinate. Only when Moses engages in determinate (focused) seeing does God speak from the burning bush and he responds "here I am". God calls Moses into relation by triggering his curiosity about something out of the ordinary, suggesting a divine presence there, as distinct from places without such presence. Replying to Moses' doubts, God names himself "I am who I am", "the Lord, the God of your ancestors" whose name is this "for all generations". (Davies claims that we can know the voice only in its effects.) Yet this text-world is one which we—in our own real world—can inhabit vicariously, though differently from a non-believer. Already cast in metaphysical terms, through which indeterminate seeing is contrasted with determinate, and God "calls" through triggering an extra-ordinary curiosity, the reading becomes more explicitly metaphysical, when the text is seen as reminding us of the "intense experience of the immediacy of the real", showing us that it is at "the centre of the here and now that we shall hear the divine voice": the text draws us vicariously into an indexical awareness of encounter with God. Thereafter our relation to the everyday real is redefined by this text. Understood in Christian terms, this is how God enters the world, and is incarnate in history: God is incarnated into the here and now, and the incarnation is "the self-communication of God from the heart of the real, from the unfathomable depths of the present moment." "God is already at the centre of the world, at the place of its emergence". This "metaphysical reading" yields important cognitive and doctrinal results.

Where Ticciati saw the text in terms of semiotics, and Davies saw it in terms of metaphysics, Tim Winter's "Qur'anic Reasoning as an Academic Practice" sees the Qur'anic text through the Islamic tradition-history of interpretation and measures such activities as Scriptural Reasoning thereby. He approaches the Qur'an as a *pleroma* (a term he does not use) with which the faithful reader needs to be "aligned" if he/she is to find its distinctive truth. That can happen in different ways: the "outward" aspect of the scripture available to ordinary Muslims gives way to "inward" rationally deduced theological insights which reach their limit in abstract philosophical texts, beyond which is the knowledge triggered by contemplation of the divine speech unveiling direct self-disclosure of God. In the past, academic learning has tended to challenge these ways, but the defence has been to see the Qur'an as an "apologetic miracle", in its literal force an aesthetic marvel which testifies to its divine provenance, by which errors can be corrected.

The comparable problem for Muslim theology today, academic practices of criticism, are not therefore necessarily incompatible, but—as with Scriptural Reasoning, "by no means an intrinsically liberal method"—interacting with them may allow "a mutual fecundity". While SR has a "promiscuous openness to methods" unfamiliar to Islamic ways of reading, conventional Enlightenment-based (for Muslims) techniques of Biblical studies may be more of a problem. The problem for Muslims is not the liberal abandonment of Scripture so much as fundamentalist misappropriations. And to correct such problems, they must interpret Scripture from traditional masters in an unbroken succession reaching back to the Prophet. The historicity of the Qur'an is axiomatic, and Muslims are para-witnesses to the scripture and to "exegetic cumulation". That is not to suppose that the tradition is univocal: there is an "immense and ambiguous body of

Hadith". Yet exegesis "has the right to be true, rather than merely illuminating", and is to be expressed in "powerfully pure and consistent language"; neither iconic associations of signifier and signified (the basis of logocentric theology) nor vagueness and fallibilism are the point, and may "tar" SR with the brush of liberalist progressivism. In a latent universalism, Muslims "affirm the need to act in fidelity with the kerygmatic Qur'anic address to Christians and Jews, who are called to love and affirm the Ishmaelite prophet". Non-Muslim scriptures are to be disputed courteously, but "the diversity of 'human tongues and colours' [is] a sign of God". There are some ways in which Muslims are closer to Jews, their nomocentrism and less teleological view of history, than to Christians. In principle, the access of both to the divine was always already complete, even if wounded, and therefore "monotheism itself does not advance".

The three readings in Part 3 are remarkably different, in both interpretation and conclusion. Clearly, they are already held together in the practice of Scriptural Reasoning; and this is what has brought the clarity of their respective arguments. SR is also corrigible by inner- and inter-traditional discussion. But what mediates between such readings? Are there kinds of mediation that operate between them which are rooted in each? The essays in Part 4 ("Reasoning") may help us face these issues. A common feature of them all is that they seek to *place* Scriptural Reasoning amongst other approaches to religious traditions while also showing how they believe it operates.

Peter Ochs' "Philosophical Warrants for Scriptural Reasoning" places SR as "pragmatic" (identifying problems of everyday and institutional approaches to repair), "postliberal" as a response to problems both in modern liberal theology (especially its tendency to stop short of problems in everyday practice) and also in the modern anti-liberal self-grounding of reasoning in confessional approaches. The means by which it reaches beyond these is Jewish-Christian-Muslim reading of scripture as formational. Ochs' essay is intended as a "logic" to warrant the work of SR and other postmodern criticisms of modernist projects, and show their deepest thrust. It focuses on the issue of binary logics and their surpassing through triadic logics. Binary logics appear where there is a collision of ways of life which brings suffering and oppression, and may also be used as if they are a logic of repair, where—let us say—one "moral conviction" set against another both expresses a sense of oppression and begets the idea that renewed conviction is the best method of repair. Triadic logics, on the other hand, are more appropriate for recognizing and recommending repair and redemption. Abbreviating the subtleties of Peter Ochs' exposition, let us say only that it renders all "universal", "necessary" "impossible" or binary claims suspect, treating them prima facie as non-claims which nonetheless are disruptive both in ourselves and in society. Two "reasonable hypotheses" about what is amiss are suffering and oppression, and they are identified as such by reference to the possibility of repair or redemption; this arises through a form of reasoning which is beyond them, abductions warranted either in the long run of history or by a community that shares them. One such abduction Scriptural Reasoners as a community find is that their scriptural traditions converge on the command to care for those who suffer by means different from the logic of suffering and oppression.

This brings Ochs to consider more generally how SR operates. Read in terms of—and with the help of—philosophical pragmatism, the Scriptures also require Scriptural Reasoners to read Scripture abductively because all knowledge in the created world—including knowledge of God—is abductive, and to reason only for the sake of repairing institutions that otherwise fail in repairing the broken practices of everyday life. To make this clear, Peter Ochs uses C. S. Peirce's studies of the elemental categories of our experience of the world—in terms of "firstness", "secondness" and "thirdness"—to interpret scripture's account of creation, division and relationship/mediation/love in the world:

(1) The "firstness" of creation is the prototype of freedom and spontaneity, which contradicts mechanistic and deterministic views. This is seen in the asking of very specific questions whether by scientific procedures or by rabbinic reading of the Scriptures, both abductive and both displaying chance (recall Nicholas Adams' emphasis on "luck"!), newness and spontaneity. The conclusion to be drawn is that Scripture needs to be read as abductive because all knowledge in this created world—including our knowledge of God—is abductive: God known only in his actions, creating worlds and speaking Scripture, but thereby "knowing that He is there as certainly as we know anything, but knowing of Him only in relation to how and where we know and always subject to further refinement and correction".

(2) This creation gives way to "secondness", being thrust out of the Garden of Eden into struggle (as well as gift): this is a negation of what had preceded it, a non-relational "two-ness" marked by sheer difference, which evokes pain and the cry of pain (recalling David Ford's discussion of the "cry").

(3) To hear and approach the cry of pain—as something that has meaning—is to make a further move, to "thirdness", the irreducible presence of relationship/mediation/love as that to which we are called. This too assists in the interpretation of Scripture, showing that in the world created by God, a cry means that someone is in pain, and there is both a need and imperative to act here and now, not only "in general": "there is also somewhere a redeemer". By attentive reading of Genesis and Exodus, Ochs then shows how this "logic of caring" is distinct from the binary logic of suffering and oppression, and how it manifests God's redemptive activity as actual, as indefinitely expanding circles of relationship and action in which the defining features of God's redemptive work are seen. This,

indeed, is what he finds in Scriptural Reasoning, where reading each word and text of Scripture together "participates in a potentially infinite process of semiosis", where readers can find and witness how they suffer and the reading community can practice "the prototypical work of SR: reparative reading that, at once, opens the text of Scripture and the life of the sufferer, one to the other, until, between them, a third something arises that we call 'scriptural reasoning' per se".

In "Scriptural Reasoning and the Philosophy of Social Science" Basit Koshul seeks to show how the work of Max Weber, one of the founding fathers of modern social science, on rationalism and rationality can be bought into conversation with the treatment of material reality in the Qur'an. Weber, it appears, can be seen as a mediating figure between religiously-reductionist science and religion, for he shows the limitations of conceptual frameworks derived from natural and physical sciences in the study of religion and other aspects of reality, and how the split between them can be resolved. For Weber "rationalization" is an expression of the "imperative of consistency" necessary to master the chaos of experienced reality, but historically he also recognizes that the "rationalizing" of life is carried out in many different and contradicting ways (for which he develops a typology). Yet the presupposition on which science rests is that what it finds is worth being known. This cannot be proved scientifically; it "can only be *interpreted* with reference to its ultimate meaning, whose acceptance depends on "our ultimate position towards life", itself the product of certain cultures. The judgment between the validity of such positions, however, is a matter of faith; indeed, "the affirmation of a value and the rejection of others is the domain of value rationality that is characteristic of religion". For all its value as objective and self-critical, science is precluded from constructing world-views in which human beings might put their faith, but it itself relies on essentially religious presuppositions.

How then, Koshul asks, can the gap between the formal, objective and a posteriori rationality of science and the "value rationality" of religion, its objective claim that the cosmos and human existence are meaningful, be bridged? Interestingly, this requires that both will modify their self-understanding as a result of their encounter, science by acknowledging the meaningfulness of empirical reality and religion by addressing its aprioristic claims, and science by recognizing that it is incapable of judging the validity of teleological ends, religion by recognizing that it cannot judge empirical truth claims. Basit Koshul carries this discussion into one about the *ayaat* of the Qur'an, each *ayah* of which is also a sign pointing beyond itself, both to mundane reality and to the Revealed Word of Allah. In other words, for the Qur'an there is a direct relationship between knowledge of the material world and understanding of the Revealed Word (seen in a different way in Oliver Davies' essay). In effect, the material is thereby ordered as signs, and critical investigation of the material is "akin to prayerful contemplation of the Divine Word". To understand the "speech" of the natural world is equivalent to recognizing God as Creator, Sustainer and Lord of this world, and to use the one rightly is equivalent to responding rightly to the other. Hence, the Qur'an "anticipates a religion of science and a science of religion".

In "The Phenomenology of Scripture", Gavin Flood explores the possibility of a hermeneutic phenomenology for scripture which might open up mediation between traditions, and allow for external text-historical scholarship and internal theological concerns. On the one hand, for him this requires the use of phenomenology as a mediating philosophy, a form of inquiry which brackets the truth behind appearances while also addressing sources beyond description; and on the other, it requires a full inter-traditional awareness of what scriptures are in the different traditions, for which they have normative importance: they "comprise primarily injunctions to act along with accompanying prohibitions and narratives". Hence, the Qur'an is the revelation of God mediated through the Prophet, the New Testament is witness to the revelation of Christ, and in non-Abrahamic traditions their importance is different.

Of what then is Scripture an index, for whom, and how? These are Gavin Flood's three questions. He takes the phenomenological question, which needs to avoid particular and theological language, as helpful for clarifying and refining. This leads us to say: "this sign is an index of (causally related to) that object", even if for a particular tradition the more appropriate way to speak would be to say that "this Scripture is a living presence brought to fulfilment in the life of a community". These are also matters of intentionality, however, incorporating a subject's cognitive direction to—desire for—an object, for its sense of meaning (*noema*). If Scripture has an intentionality, it lies in the scribal process whereby the meaning or object is arrived at, which is bound up with the question of "who speaks, which points away from the text toward an extra-textual source to which it bears witness and also to the reader(s) who become the object". The former is "always deferred and always approached tangentially or indirectly", while the latter is addressed through injunctions and narrations. Flood illustrates by the same example used before by Oliver Davies and others, but soon finds how—phenomenologically—these are similar to other kinds of literature. Scripture, he finds, occupies a place between history and fiction, and the truth/falsity distinction mapped directly onto the history/fiction demarcation fails to do justice to the relationship between scripture and community: the meaning needs to be explored. That in turn raises the question of "for whom" the Scriptures are an index, which requires extending the analysis beyond that of subject and object, and considering the material nature of signs and the historical context of inquiry (not only for whom scripture is an index, but for whom it is a phenomenological inquiry). It will involve the complex questions of how they are actively constructed—in the present—within the horizons of expectation of those who read, and how these are constantly being modified by the texts while still operating either within the memory of tradition or from a position of detachment. Flood draws some important conclusions: (1) The practice of SR involves the kind of hermeneutical phenomenology he has outlined insofar as those involved must suspect judgment about "the being behind the appearance of others' scriptures", lest they reduce the particularity of that tradition, and that this is liberating, not restrictive. (2) In creating a discourse—and a "third space"—outside of particular scriptural traditions, and arriving at readings that are not those of any one tradition, SR entails a semiotics of scripture that is hospitable to others and richly text based. It seems that this "third space" of discourse, and a phenomenological semiotics, is necessary for what happens in SR.

With such a remarkable range of rich possibilities as appear in the sections on "Describing", "Reading" and "Reasoning", it helps then to have an essay by Robert Gibbs placing Scriptural Reasoning within a history of recent philosophical frameworks, "Reading with the Others: Levinas' Ethics and Scriptural Reasoning". Like so many others in this special issue, Gibbs recognizes the seeming oddity of reading religious texts in a primarily academic environment, and shows the many issues that intersect in the juxtaposition of the two, issues differently handled in the eight philosophical frameworks he identifies for the practice of learning, which we can only recount now in simplified form:

(1) A very widespread notion of the academy is that it focuses on the acquisition of information, which implies that there has to be something to learn, over which the "learning self" is to gain control and for which he gives account.

(2) Consciousness of the world, however, requires a currency through which, as a medium of exchange, we learn the world. This medium is language, and through its use we describe things by words; reasoning here serves the "linguistification" of thought by providing greater clarity. I recall what Bertrand Russell is purported to have said to A. N. Whitehead: "you see the world as on a misty English morning; I see it with the clarity of the noon-day sun".

(3) With Heidegger, there arrives a more radical view of language, as itself a coming into presence; language displays how things appear, and even the subject of language comes to be within the action of language. In this case, much as Ben Quash suggested in his essay, poetics (as a code that marks and fixes things) governs our understanding of knowing, there is a very complex mediation of learning, and we cannot reach beyond the veil to the self, to things, or to Revelation.

(4) With Levinas, language is reconceived in terms of being addressed by another person, reversing its domination by the self as I am called to give to the other. This is an "asymmetrical" constitution of the position of a

human being which interrupts consciousness, "checking" any efforts to know or be a knowing self: "being questioned, addressed, solicited, now constitutes me", and I must give, not accumulate; the other person is no longer an object of inquiry but one to whom I must ethically respond. Stressing the challenging dynamics of dialogue, Rosenzweig offers a challenge to this view: is it a full enough view of inter-personality? (The views of both are in line with Jewish conceptions of the infinite responsibility that arises in being elected in love.) Focusing this view on the pragmatics of being addressed suggests that speaking is always bound up with an ethical responsibility to listen; reasoning is responding to a question.

(5) Where there is *a third person* also making a claim upon me, justice is required. A third person introduces "conflicting infinite possibilities"; and this requires all the principles, rules, calculus, etc. of justice by which we consider others and coordinate our responsibilities. In this case, Gibbs suggests, our responsibilities become systemic, and we are required to circulate what we value between people.

(6) It is also possible, however, that a reader is constituted—in what he/she can do, think or feel—in the practices of reading. The absence of the writer only consigns responsibility to the medium of what is written, which is redeemed only by the reader. Hence, the task of reading is to find as much meaning as possible in the text; and reading is a construction of ever richer meanings.

(7) Reading texts with others invokes all the foregoing frameworks: it brings a dialogue which is a complex drama; in which we become "a people of the book", a community framed by reading practices, principles and rules of interpretation, behavioural practices arising from the demands of justice, and commentaries which recall people who wrote but are no longer present (a tradition). All this provides the hermeneutical sensibility with which Jews re-read traditional texts in Textual Reasoning, concentrating on the "complex multivocal texture" of talmud and midrash and forming a new community responsible for the past for the sake of the future.

(8) As a reading with other traditions, Scriptural Reasoning is a different kind of listening to others through which we learn more of their traditions, but also more about the internal dynamics of our own; and communication is not prohibited, but rather enhanced, by our differences. The listening to the other within an environment of trust and patience sets a fundamental tone of ethical responsibility, by which we honour a responsibility we have in knowing others. We learn that our own tradition, however good and right, lacks something that only others can provide; this is an asymmetry of authority which constantly shifts. And encountering diachronic traditions of disparate readings always reopens both our awareness of the dynamic of truth within each tradition and renews our conversation with each other. In that all the elements reviewed in the other seven frames of

reference reappear, but in the pursuit of a harmony built on complex practices, not theological or political agreement. That represents the highest goals of the academy.

In this "cumulative" account of eight frameworks for learning, Gibbs shows how—in important respects—they invoke each other; and religious reading—as with Textual and Scriptural Reasoning—offers true hope of the learning for which the academy also stands. We might call this an inter-philosophical interpretation of the movements which appear in Scriptural Reasoning.

Pushing Forward

In one sense, it is no surprise that the positions found in these essays are so diverse, for they incorporate both different religious views drawn from the Abrahamic traditions and also widely varying views of the disciplines most appropriate in a discussion which is both academic and religious. What Tim Winter said of Muslims—"They are not required to be custodians of a univocal tradition"—applies doubly here. Those from each Abrahamic tradition do not take themselves to be custodians of a univocal tradition. And there is no uniformity in the present-day academic environment: it has no master-discipline, but many partly integrated ones. And the two inter-sect: there is evidence in these essays to suggest that what people find it possible to *say religiously* is strongly affected by what they find it possible to *think*; and that is often due to the tradition of religion and its correlative reasoning or reasonings in which they stand. For example, one thing that appears repeatedly among the essays is a preference for phenomenologi-cally derived notions, yet these are used differently, sometimes to illumi-nate and sometimes to mute, but they often mute explicitly religious claims. Few say "God speaks"; and the few who do look for this primarily—if not exclusively—in "the effects".

It is time, however, to distil some of the main issues under discussion so that we can then ask how Scriptural Reasoning can move forward.

The presumption under which SR operates is the sacredness of the Abrahamic traditions as centred in their scriptures. Whether expressed as "elemental speech of God", the density, depth and intensity of the scrip-tures, the "unfathomable oceans of meaning" found there, or their "resis-tance to totalizing interpretation", there seems little question of the sacredness evident in the Scriptures for their traditions. This is not dimin-ished, but rather enlarged, by the practice of group reading which is a primary feature of Scriptural Reasoning. In that group reading, the Scrip-tures are found to be sources of "reasoning, compassion and spirit", apparently lifting reasoning to a new level by what several people call "abduction". Perhaps that is what explains the capacity of Scriptural Reasoners to live with, and patiently pursue, the deep differences which appear between them, for the sake of the "good" and "peace" which is the goal of SR both in itself and for wider society. This is what some call the "wisdom-seeking" which is inherent in SR.

If sources of reasoning emerge from the Scriptures in group reading, it is clear also that the different traditions of interpretation, both in and between the Abrahamic traditions, *enlarge* reasoning; and other independent traditions in and beyond the academy do so also. The capacity of Scriptural Reasoners patiently to engage with these enlargements, and with the insights which they nourish in each other, is a matter of great importance; indeed, the "listening" necessary to this probably needs to become more explicit in the agenda of SR. This may be the way in which, out of its expansions, reasonings may be *re-gathered* and *referred back* to the Reason implicit in the Scriptures themselves, even to the "elemental discourse of God'. In other words, the re-gathering and redirection of reasonings may itself be an abduction which uncovers the Reason of Scripture.

Some would express this in terms of a "practical unity of reason" already found in Scriptural Reasoning, or a "wisdom" found through learning the "languages of wisdom", or the "peace" that is found in the intensely social process of inter-traditional readings, as *persons* are *related* through *texts*. These, I take it, are different ways of expressing what happens through the gathering of people—with their different embodiments of wisdom, of reasoning, as different persons—in peace. It is more than such words usually convey: it recovers the Reason of the Scriptures themselves.

Nonetheless, it is inadvisable to be too quick to specify what does happen, lest the "enlargements" of reason are prematurely collapsed into a standard pattern which is, in fact, difficult to find in the Scriptures. After all, both traditional metaphysics and doctrine have tended to move away from the Scriptures exactly where they have supposed that the Scriptures conform to a monolithic form of reasoning; and it is right to shy away from that. There is good reason, therefore, for emphasizing the poetic and polyphonic character of reality, the provisionality and anticipatory character of judgments, the disagreements characteristic of scriptural interpretation, the surprise—or "luck"—of new interpretations that emerge, and the unusual logic which is necessary to understand the Scriptures! Far from doing damage to the process of inter-traditional Scriptural Reasoning, all of these only indicate the seeds which are gathered in group reading! There is another side to it, too: what kind of sociality is needed in SR if these seeds are to germinate and flower? There would need to be an ease with each other, and a high level of personal relationship, even in the presence of difference and disagreement. These are often spoken of as "friendship" and "trust", but are those enough?

How are texts handled in SR, then? Bringing Part 3 ("Readings") together with Part 4 ("Reasoning"), we can ask, furthermore, what kinds of reasoning are used for them?

In the ways suggested in Part 3 by three of our number there are interestingly different possibilities—semiotic, metaphysical and traditional—but all very decisive in their conclusions. They exemplify strong positions taken by individuals in the group reading, which are held within the more "explorative" possibilities for group reading emphasized above. And respectively they draw on—without altogether agreeing with—some of the forms of reasoning outlined in Part 4.

The semiotic argument in the first piece—Susannah Ticciati's in Part 3—insists that the scriptural world is so persistently strange as to resist interpretation, and to disqualify any universal claims for an interpretation, since the interpreter can only interpret within a context he/she has posited by abduction. This "negative theological reading" of Scripture serves, however, to call him/her to conversion, like Moses, in the presence of an inexplicable God. While "resistance to interpretation", at least interpretation of such a kind to authorize universal claims from any one tradition, may be one important facet of what is found in SR practice, a question remains whether this entails the supposition that all interpretations are based on humanly-generated abductions. Is all abduction an "inferential labour", or is it a meeting of human labour with the impartation of the Divine? In this view, the Divine arrives only to reverse what is "human": he who saves his life loses it. It is a strongly scriptural reading: the reading of Scripture is necessary for the (dialectical) process of conversion.

By way of comparison, Peter Ochs in Part 4 argues for the pragmatically (positively) formative position of Scripture. That is not to say that there are not problems both in reading the Scriptures and the world, but they arise from the prevalence of binary logic, which—by making distinctions into divisions—bring about oppression and suffering, or seek to remedy them by reasserting the divisions which brought them in the first place. Reading the Scriptures abductively gives rise to a new triadic possibility through which we can recognize the true awfulness of oppression and suffering, and of binary "healings", and move to *caring*. Where does this "third" come from, which can surpass the (binary) "second" of "twoness"—Adam and Eve thrust out of the Garden of Eden—which befell the "first" of createdness? He does not, I think, mean a humanly-generated context for reading à la Umberto Eco, but a "third" found through the communal reading of Scripture. Even this opens the question of whether we are not together *attracted* to read Scripture by the possibility offered there from the Divine, and *pressed* toward wider and wider reparative activity.

The second, neo-metaphysical, way of handling Scripture offered by Oliver Davies in Part 3 is also, but very differently, definitive. It is a realist view which sets out to develop "foundational thinking" for the world and its structure, but by reference to Scripture taken in its own terms, the two "thought together" as it were. Hence it is in the natural "out-of-the-ordinary" that God appears to Moses; and the text of the Burning Bush reminds us of the "intense experience of the immediacy of the real" which thereafter redefines our relation to the everyday real as an indexical awareness of encounter with God, who is already at the "heart of the real" communicating himself, as in the incarnation of Christ. This is a full-blown and philosophically-scripturally-theologically exciting reading of God's position in relation to the world, whose purpose is to discern and declare the truth of God. For all that, it would be worth exploring two things. (1) Does the argument not underrate the complexity of the Scriptural account of God's self-declaration to Moses; the "I am that I am" can be taken as much more than a straightforward self-naming by God, as the Lord's *self-reservation* in *calling* the people of Israel, an "infinitely intense identity" which is evident in the loving self-communication by which this people is elected. (2) Does this metaphysical reading not produce too general a set of categories *from* Scripture *for* the interpretation of Scripture, which both illuminate and also "thin" the texture of the Scriptural account, making it serve the argument too simply?

In some ways, and strangely, this way of handling Scripture resembles the position for reasoning developed by Gavin Flood in Part 4. There he develops a hermeneutic phenomenology as a philosophy to mediate between the Scriptures found in and beyond the Abrahamic traditions. While allowing the normative value of their scriptures for the traditions (they are "injunctions and narratives" for them), he finds it necessary to make a "third space of discourse" if the particularity of the Scriptures and traditions is to be defended in comparing them; and this "space" brackets the truth behind appearances, "deferring" the truth of the Scriptures. While, like Davies, this provides a remarkably perceptive account of the position of the Scriptures for the traditions, it is inevitably a generalization for the purposes of comparing their use in the traditions; it subjects them to a standard set of external categories. So he too develops categories *from* the traditions' use of Scriptures *for* the comparison of their uses. By doing so, he looks beyond the internal variations in their Scriptures and their use of them, and the sheer density of what is found there.

The third reading of Scripture, in this case the Qur'an, in Part 3 is by Tim Winter. This too is definitive, but distinctive by comparison with the others. Here it is argued that the Qur'an is to be viewed and interpreted entirely within an unbroken tradition of interpretation that reaches back to the Prophet himself, which guarantees the historicity of the Qur'an and the integrity of interpretations within the tradition. This is not to suggest that there is a narrow lineage of "truths" there, for the Qur'an is a complex text and there is multiplicity and ambiguity in the sequence of interpretations; but it is controlled by the truth of the Qur'an, the fidelity of interpreters, and the need in exegesis to express truth purely and consistently. If I judge by some of the Scriptural Reasoning group studies in which I have participated, this conception of the proper task of Muslims in respecting and communicating their sacred Scripture is often difficult for Western postliberals, with (according to Tim Winter) their "promiscuous openness to methods", to appreciate. With their inclination to the use of Scripture for "illumination", they have difficulty recognizing the legitimacy of what appears as an ontological (or at least scientific) approach to the interpretation of Scripture and the strong moral imperatives which can emerge from it. Yet it is obvious in the inter-traditional discussion of SR that this "scientific" approach illuminates other conceptions of Scriptural interpretation, as they in turn open up what is potentially a very restricted use of the Scriptures by Muslims.

Corresponding to these two sides of an important issue for SR, whether it aims to be *illuminative* or more sharply *principled*, whether in knowledge or ethics, are the two other essays in Part 4.

Basit Koshul sustains the second of these two possibilities, by considering western social science. Through careful consideration of one of the founders of the social sciences, he traces one attempt to reunite science and religion, and concludes that it is possible for them to coexist, with some mutual modification in their claims. Nonetheless, within their own spheres, there are rich possibilities. The natural sciences can make judgments about empirical reality. But the *ayaat* of the Qur'an are signs pointing beyond themselves to worldly reality and the Revealed Word of Allah, showing that natural speech can point to God as Creator, Sustainer and Lord. What is implicit in this account is that science and religion are mutually implicated, at least in general. What still needs to be explored is how they are mutually implicated in what they actually say.

The other side, that SR aims to be more illuminative, is represented by the rich history of academic and religious philosophy provided by Robert Gibbs. Although much more concerned with the continental philosophical traditions than with (say) the analytic tradition of Anglo-American philosophy, it opens a stunning range of intersecting philosophies of language, poetics, consciousness-interrupting interpersonal/ethical and reading-constituted views, each with its own ideas about how to proceed and to what purpose. The history culminates with their combination in the hermeneutical sensibility with which Scriptural texts are read, which aims for a harmony built on complex practices enhanced by the differences between traditions. Fittingly, the piece is highly illuminating about the inner dynamics of truth in each of these philosophies, and the inter-dependence of Scriptures and traditions of interpretation. It is far from being unconcerned with truth and clarity, but finds these enhanced by the shifting asymmetries between philosophies and traditions. As someone once said of Schubert's Ninth Symphony, it has a "look, Ma, no hands!" quality about it, a preparedness to allow that many philosophical reasonings can meet in mediating the truth of the Scriptures. It contrasts interestingly with the inner-traditional controls found necessary in more "principled" accounts of the Abrahamic traditions.

Now, after we have seen some of the ways in which the essays are related, and identified some of the differences and lacunae which appear between them, we have uncovered some of the challenges which face Scriptural Reasoning. The essays, and their counterparts in SR practice, show that the inter-traditional readings of Scripture and the uses of academic reasonings are so complex and multileveled that they may slow the effort of mutual understanding and the contribution SR might make to the world today. Are there any ways by which SR can work even more effectively?

This Response has matched contributions from participants in SR in two ways, by "connecting" them as they appear in each part of the volume, and by "crossing" between the parts. In doing so, a number of major common (or at least contiguous) ideas have appeared, which have not been pursued far; and amongst them are some of the most seminal factors found in and between the Abrahamic traditions and between them and the world. It seems to me that there is much to be said for trying carefully to *identify and attend to* these in further reading and reasoned interpretation of the Scriptures. They include:

- matters related to the interpretation of all the Scriptures, the meaning of their "resistance to interpretation" and its implications for recognizing the "primary discourse of God" there;
- the kinds of discourse most appropriate to interpreting the Scriptures (e.g. "scientific" or illuminative);
- the patterns of the activity of the Divine in the world abductively attracting humanity and human sociality to their fullest stature; and
- the highest ideals for human life present in the traditions (e.g. reason, passion, compassionate care, love, justice, the common weal), which are not quite the same as the insight, understanding and friendship which figure more prominently in the essays.

Careful attention to such matters, and their appearance in the Scriptures, traditions of interpretation and forms of reasoning might refine SR by providing an *agenda* for further consideration of fundamental issues, and offer the possibility of concentrating the work of Scriptural Reasoning—and its contribution to worldly affairs—more intensively. This set of essays invites such an agenda-setting conversation.

Above All

This Response has set out to reintroduce Scriptural Reasoning as it has been portrayed in foregoing set of essays, to show the varieties of readings and reasonings found here, to show how they may shed light on each other, and to identify some unrecognized lacunae in and between them. All this has, however, to be set in the context of the highly dynamic and sustaining practice of actually reading and reasoning our Scriptures together. It is an indication of the strength of SR that its participants can bring strong views to the table. But reading and reasoning our Scriptures together is what "holds" these diverse views in a "space" where we take responsibility not only for our own views, but also for others'. Our mutual hospitality is a *responsible* one, which itself anticipates peace between the Abrahamic traditions and also begins to make a contribution to repairing a world filled with oppression and suffering. *"Above all"*, then, is the ongoing practice of reading and reasoning our Scriptures together, in which we learn from a variety of strong presentations like those found in these essays, and learn the possibilities of complex harmony between us. There is indefinitely more still to learn from our Scriptures, our readings and our reasonings.

Index